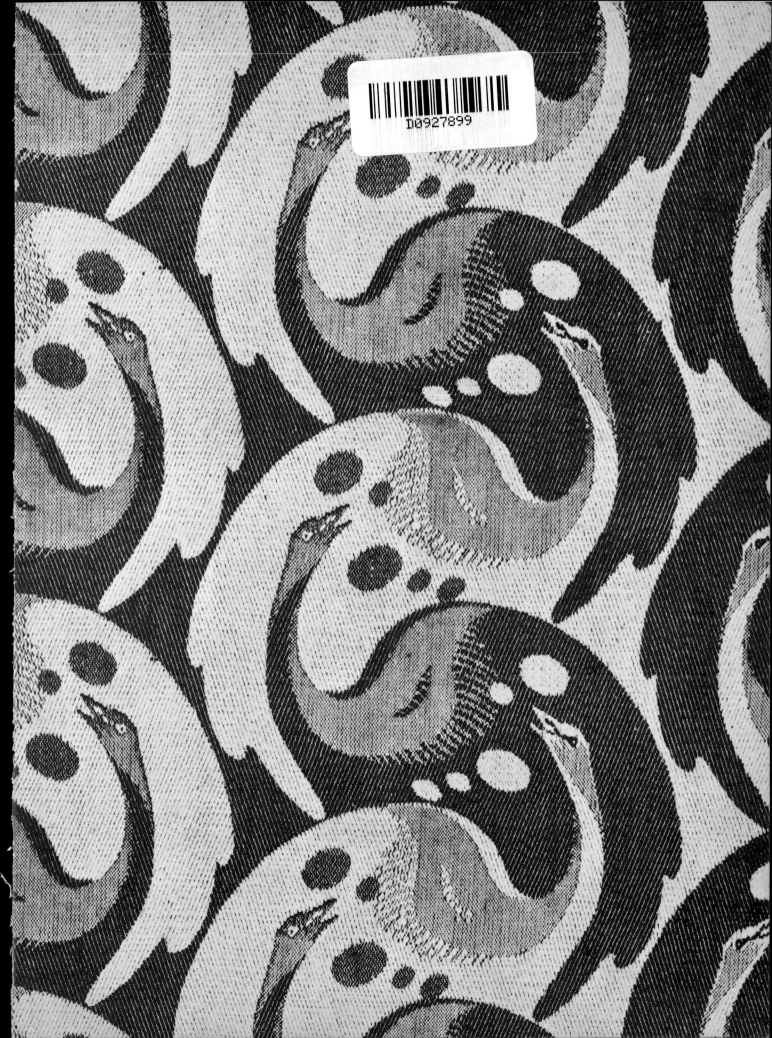

for Aunt Mary —
with great affection
Janet

THE SACRED SPRING

Endpapers:
Kolo Moser
Cotton textile 1902
Design for Johann Backhausen und
Söhne, pale yellow Naples to
buttercup and steel grey
Österreichisches Museum für
Angewandte Kunst

THE SACRED SPRING
THE ARTS IN VIENNA 1898-1918

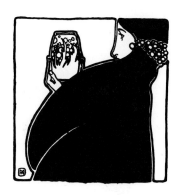

by

NICOLAS POWELL

with an introduction to the
cultural background
by Adolf Opel

New York Graphic Society

To remind my nephews Mick and Nicky of Vienna,
and for all my friends there

International Standard Book Number 0–8212–0619–2
Libary of Congress Catalog Card Number 74–78460

Copyright © Nicolas Powell (pp. 1–14 and 43–224); Adolf Opel (pp. 15–42) 1974
The illustrations on pages 170, 171, 172 and 194 (top left) are
© 1974, Copyright by Cosmopress, Geneva.

First published in Great Britain 1974 by Studio Vista, London.
Published in the United States of America 1974 by
New York Graphic Society, Greenwich, Connecticut 06830.

Printed in Great Britain.

Contents

Historical Table

1866	Battles of Custozza and Lissa
	Battle of Königgrätz
	Loss of Venice
1867	The *Ausgleich* with Hungary
	Execution of Emperor Maximilian of Mexico
1869	Opening of the Vienna Opera House
1872	Death of Grillparzer
1873	World Exhibition in Vienna
	125 banks crash
1874	Johann Strauss's *Die Fledermaus*
1875	Death of Ferdinand I in Prague
1878	Congress of Berlin. Austria gets her last territorial gains
	Bosnia and Herzegovina are occupied
1882	The Triple Alliance: Austria, Germany and Italy
1884	Opening of the Arlberg railway
1888	Founding of the Socialist Party
	Opening of the Vienna Burgtheater
1889	Suicide of Crown Prince Rudolf at Mayerling: Franz Ferdinand, the Emperor's nephew, becomes heir to the throne
1891	Opening of Semper and Hasenauer's Kunsthistorisches Museum building
1896	Death of Anton Bruckner
	Chicago World Exhibition visited by Adolf Loos
	Theodor Herzl: *Der Judenstaat*
1897	Death of Johannes Brahms
	Secession founded
1897-1907	Gustav Mahler director of the Opera House
1898	*Kaiserjubiläumsausstellung* (Jubilee for fifty years reign of Emperor Franz Joseph)
	Assassination of the Empress Elisabeth in Geneva
1899	Death of Johann Strauss
	Karl Kraus founds *Die Fackel*
1900	Sigmund Freud: *Traumdeutung*
	Arthur Schnitzler: *Der Reigen* (first played in Vienna in 1921) and *Leutnant Gustl*
1902	Secession Beethoven Exhibition

1903 Death of Hugo Wolf
Secession Impressionist and Klimt
  Exhibitions
Otto Weininger: *Geschlecht und Charakter*
Suicide of Weininger
1905 Klimt group leaves Secession
Bertha von Suttner awarded the Nobel
  Prize
Franz Lehar: *Die lustige Witwe*
Ernst Mach: *Erkenntnis and Irrtum*
1906 Robert Musil: *Die Verwirrungen des
  Zöglings Törless* (written 1902)
1907 Universal suffrage in Austria
1908 Annexation of Bosnia and Herzegovina
1908-9 Kunstschau
1909 Alfred Kubin: *Die andere Seite*
1910 Rainer Maria Rilke: *Die Aufzeichnungen des
  Malte Laurids Brigge*
1911 Richard Strauss and Hugo von
  Hofmannsthal: *Der Rosenkavalier*
Death of Gustav Mahler
Arnold Schönberg propounds his twelve-
  tone system
1912 Alfred Adler: *Über den nervösen Charakter*
1914 28 June: murder of Franz Ferdinand at
  Sarajevo
25 July: Austria-Hungary declares war on
  Serbia
Graf Sascha Kolowrat founds the Austrian
  film industry
Suicide of Georg Trakl
Franz Kafka begins to write *Der Prozess*
  (published 1925)
1915 Italy declares war on Austria-Hungary
1916 Dr Friedrich Adler shoots the Prime
  Minister, Graf Stürgkh
21 November: death of Franz Joseph I
1916-18 Karl Emperor of Austria-Hungary
1917 Hugo von Hofmannsthal: *Der Schwierige*
  (performed 1921)
1918 Deaths of Klimt, Schiele, Moser, Otto
  Wagner, Girardi, Viktor Adler
1919 Titles of nobility abolished in Austria

1920 Richard Strauss director of the Vienna
  Opera House
Death of Peter Altenberg
1922 Kraus: *Die letzen Tage der Menschheit*
Rilke: *Duineser Elegien, Sonette an Orpheus*
Stroheim: *Merry-go-round*
Eliot: *The Waste Land*
Joyce: *Ulysses*

KEY TO MAP
(anti-clockwise round the Ringstrasse)

Buildings

1 Kaiserbad dam on the Danube Canal
2 Rossauer Kaserne
3 Börse
4 Votiv Kirche
5 University
6 Rathaus
7 Burgtheater
8 Parliament
9 Museums
10 Burggarten and Neue Hofburg
11 Akademie der Bildenden Künste
12 Secession building
13 Opera house
14 Künstlerhaus
15 Musikverein
16 Konzerthaus
17 Stadtpark and Wien Fluss tunnel
18 Museum für Angewandte Kunst
19 Former Ministry of War
20 Postsparkassenamt
21 Urania

Monuments

A Deutschmeister Regiment
B Waldmüller
C Strauss-Lanner
D Empress Elisabeth
E Grillparzer
F Archduke Karl
G Prince Eugene
H Mozart
I Marc Antony
J Beethoven
K Canon
L Johann Strauss
M Makart
N Bruckner

Map of Vienna: the inner city and
Ring (reproduced by permission of
Freytag-Berndt und Artaria, Vienna)

8

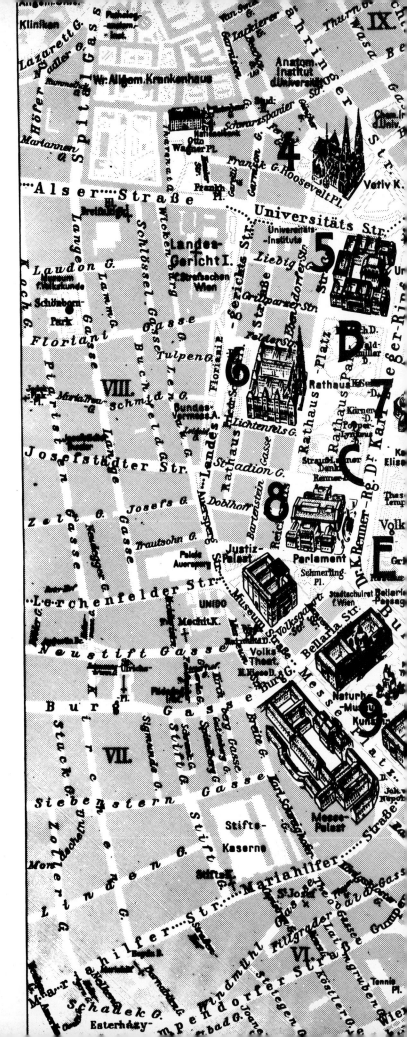

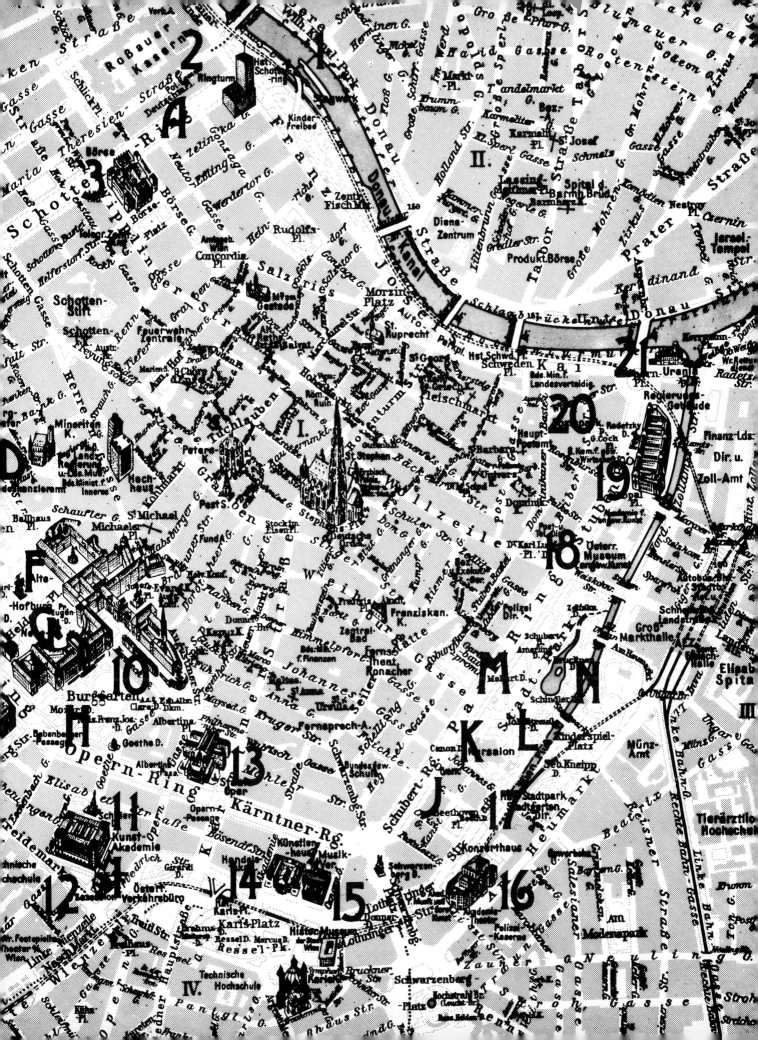

Preface

Dies Österreich ist eine kleine Welt, in der die grosse ihre Probe hält. ('This Austria is a little world, in which the large one is tried out.')

Friedrich Hebbel

The twenty years from 1898 to 1918 are not even a generation, but they affected the whole of Europe. The Austro-Hungarian Empire still covered a huge area round the Danube. Besides German, more than seven main languages, including Italian, Polish, Hungarian, Czech, Serbo-Croat, Rumanian and Slovenian, were spoken. In the ten years before 1900 the population of its capital, Vienna, rose by a hundred thousand to 1,764,957 (which is about the present figure). By 1910, it had reached over two million, falling sharply after the end of the First World War. The almost Byzantine bureaucracy, especially the ministries of foreign affairs, war and finance, was centred on Vienna. After the battles of Magenta and Solferino Austria had lost Lombardy and Milan. 1866 was a year of disaster: although Archduke Albrecht won a resounding victory at Custozza, and Admiral Tegetthoff rammed the Italian flagship at the naval battle of Lissa, yet Venice was lost. (Strangely, Filet Tegetthoff is still served in Harry's Bar in Venice.) The battle of Königgrätz in Bohemia was even more far-reaching. The Austrian artillery behaved heroically, but several regiments refused to obey the orders of their German speaking officers, and the Prussian breech loading rifles won the day against the Austrian and Saxon Infantry, and Bismarck, having broken Austria's power in the German lands could afford to be generous, and was.

These were years of disillusionment, with the bank crashes of 1873 and yet of increasing wealth and growing industrialization, with yet more peasants seeking their fortune in Vienna. This last flowering of an empire, if not of Austria itself, has a feeling of a St Martin's summer, a *fin-de-siècle* bravura. It must not be forgotten that Austria, as we know it, was an invention of the punitive Treaty of St Germain. Vienna, as we know it–a capital of a tiny German speaking country, but still a city with the apparatus of empire, theatres and museums, institutions and roughly one third of the entire population within its boundaries–was a concept that the Austrian themselves found difficult to comprehend, so that between the wars it was completely unviable economically.

Vienna has always been a magnet. It attracted Gluck, Beethoven and Brahms from Germany as well as Haydn and Mozart from nearby. Writers and thinkers came here, like Friedrich Hebbel from North Germany, the Swiss Gottfried Keller, as well as the novelist, Adalbert Stifter and for a short time Kafka from Bohemia, not forgetting Leon Trotsky, who came to the only country willing to accept him. It suffers from a hot July and August, and some liability to a southerly wind (*Föhn*), with the attendant malaise in spring and autumn. It has cold snowy winters, and to the Romans Vindobona was the *urbs ventosa*–'windy'. It is extremely relaxing; and there can be little doubt that an enormous amount of coffee is drunk, and the waltz was invented to keep the Viennese going.

In this political and climatic turbulence, Vienna changed physically. The first breaches in the wall had been made under Napoleon. After the revolution of 1848, when it was felt necessary to rethink the conception of Vienna as a fortress, Franz Joseph, in the year 1857, signed the decrees for the improvement of the city – the creation of the Ringstrasse by pulling down the fortifications and allowing building on the *Glacis*, the green space outside the walls. By 1898 it was all but complete, except for the Post Office Savings Bank building of 1905, the Neue Hofburg which was never completed as planned, and the Ministry of War which was finished significantly enough in 1913.

1898 to 1918 were probably the most creative years in Austrian history, and one of the most active periods of artistic and imaginative production anywhere. It is a phenomenon which merits exploration. Otto Breicha has called this period 'Finale and Introduction'. 1898 was the year of the Imperial Jubilee Exhibition that celebrated the fifty-year reign of the Emperor, but it was also the year of the assassination of the Empress Elisabeth on a landing-stage in Geneva. This was the last point in the personal tragedy of the Emperor Franz Joseph. It was also the year of the first prefabricated steel-framed marble and stucco metropolitan railway station by Otto Wagner on the Karlsplatz, and the year of the opening of the Vienna Secession building.

In 1911, Mahler died. Colonel Redl, the Russian spy on the Austrian General Staff, was forced to shoot himself in 1913. In 1914 the heir to the throne was assassinated at Sarajevo, and in 1916 Friedrich, the son of the socialist Victor Adler, shot the Prime Minister, Graf Stürgkh; that year, the Emperor himself died. In one year, 1918, Klimt died on 6 February, Otto Wagner on 11 April, Kolo Moser on 18 and Schiele on 31 October. On 12 November the Republic was proclaimed.

This flowering cannot be explained except in terms of the feverish peak of a dying epoch, and the compensation for loss of political power that goes with such an end, and which constitutes a beginning. The exquisite, escapist, pleasure-garden, never-never-was land of Hofmannsthal and the cruel medical knife of Schnitzler are both products of the Empire's end, but they do not explain the hurtful modernity of Kafka or Musil. Otto Wagner was established enough to build decorations in front of the Burgtor for Makart's procession at the Emperor's Silver Wedding Jubilee in 1879, but his Post Office Savings Bank and Steinhof church remain modern buildings, filled with more invention than even the buildings of Loos.

The retrogressive, romantic-classicism of a Gustav Mahler is balanced by a completely new conception of music with a twelve-tone system which is still with us. There is the explosion of the later Klimt and Schiele, two painters whose standing has not even now been fully evaluated or appreciated. This mixture of malaise and the liberation of new ideas mingles inextricably in the crucible of these uneasy years.

The interest in this period outside Austria was stimulated by the exhibition *Vienna Secession: Art Nouveau to 1970*, held at the Royal Academy in London in the spring of 1971. That it was such a success was due to the imaginative initiative of its president, Georg Eisler. He was kind enough to suggest that I should undertake this book, and has encouraged this project at all stages with helpful advice and his friendship. To him and especially to Professor Oskar Matulla, the devoted friend of the graphic work of the period, to Hofrat Dr

Hans Aurenhammer, the director, and Dr Michael Krapf of the Österreichische Galerie, to Hofrat Dr Wilhelm Mrazek, director of the Museum für Angewandte Kunst and his staff I am most grateful. To Obermagistratsrat Dr Robert Waissenberger, Michael Pabst, Frau Louise Schneider MBE, Frau Dr Inge Zimmer-Lehmann of the Künstlerhaus, I am indebted in very many ways. Gert Rosenberg has been tireless in meeting my wishes and I am most grateful to him for the brilliant photographs that he has produced. My thanks are due to Herold Verlag for permission to translate a long extract by Adolf Loos, and to those private owners and galleries who have allowed the reproduction of works in their possession.

I was most particularly helped by Adolf Opel who agreed to write on the background to the artistic events, and who is himself specially interested in Egon Schiele, by Mrs Dorothy Davies who translated his text, and by Frau Gilli Schönwald and Frau Lydia Burger, without whose patience the manuscript would never have been printable. Ann Hartland-Swann and Hugh Honour very kindly read the text and made valuable suggestions. Something of James Gaehres' enthusiasm for Gustav Mahler will be found in the section on music.

Because the personalities dealt with are probably unfamiliar to the general reader there are slight repetitions from chapter to chapter so that they may be read separately if desired. Although there is still a tendency to spell the Vienna Secession with a z instead of a c, I have adopted the spelling which has always been used by the society itself.

The purpose of this short work is to introduce the artistic life of a period, and not to document it fully, which would require a longer book and more time than is available to the author, whose day to day activity is to a large extent proof that Vienna is very much the cultural capital today that it was in the ten years before and after the turn of the century. Such shortcomings as it may therefore be found to have should be judged within the intended scope and not by the ideal of a book that it was not meant to be. If I have contrived to pass on a little of the love I have for Vienna I shall be well content.

C.N.P.P.

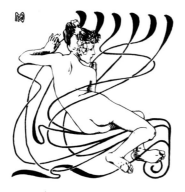

INTRODUCTION

The Legacies of Dissolution

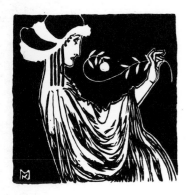

'The golden age of security'[1]* is how Stefan Zweig characterized the period before 1914, the *belle époque* of the Danube Monarchy, whose end marked also the collapse of Old Europe. Today it is tempting to think back to the Imperial and Royal political structure, 'Austria-Hungary', that unique conglomeration of peoples with its bewildering variety of faces, of conflicting forces and impulses, as an occidental 'Middle Kingdom', a pan-European confederation. Old Austria has become a myth, surviving in literary retrospect as 'Kakania' or 'Tarockania' in a form that never really existed (*v.* Musil, Herzmanowsky-Orlando and many others).[2]

In his essay, *Panorama of Kakania's Decline*, Otto Basil writes:

> 'Kakania in its last days was not just a kingdom of this world – to demonstrate this alone would be too simple – but rather a condition of latent revolution. And this condition could be adopted by a process of autosuggestion by people of another kind, foreigners, visitors, one might almost say heretics – indeed, even Prussians, and that is saying a lot. The expression 'an Austrian by training' is typical of such situations, and of strictly limited applicability. Just try to make a comparable statement about such nationally intact, historically well-defined groups as the French or the English.'[3]

Vienna, as seat of the reigning house and imperial capital, was politically and culturally the focal point of the Habsburg state, and hence the nucleus of the myths and the fascination which emanated from the Imperial and Royal *mise en scène*. Immigrants from the most remote provinces of the Empire flocked to Vienna merely to be assimilated, to absorb the way of life and the prevailing atmosphere. But they also brought rebellious, anti-monarchist ideas with them, especially people from the eastern provinces with their aspirations to nationalism and self-government. Even today for half the Balkans, for the Slav Succession States of the Monarchy, Vienna is a sort of secret metropolis, which plays a much more important rôle in their intellectual life, and indeed as a general point of orientation, than Paris or Berlin. It may be of significance that Vienna lies exactly on the vegetation frontier between east and west, which cuts right through the Vienna landscape. This was scientifically proved in the so-called 'Crown Prince's Work' (a mammoth work produced in 1886 with the aid of Crown Prince Rudolf, entitled *The Austro-Hungarian Monarchy in Words and Pictures*, a copy of which was never lacking in any salon worthy of the name). The 'East' begins then, from the purely geographical point of view, in the centre of Vienna. The way of life and the architectural styles in Old Vienna were different beyond Sankt Marx and Simmering from those in Hietzing or Döbling; the architectural dividing line can still be traced today in Erdberg. It is a well-known saying of Metternich's that 'the Orient begins in the Reisnerstrasse'.[4]

The opening towards the east meant for Vienna and the Danube Monarchy

*The footnotes will be found on page 216.

16

not only an enrichment by virtue of the intellectual contributions of Poland, Galicia, Bohemia, Moravia and Hungary (Freud, Kafka, Rilke, Werfel, Kraus – to mention only a few), it also represented permanent unrest and danger. Here the Imperial and Royal policy of expansion comes into play, and even in 1912, when the Balkan War broke out, voices were raised demanding Austro-Hungarian support in order to clear up the smouldering conflict with Russia.

The only buttress of the multi-national structure of the Monarchy was the Imperial and Royal Army. Its officers and soldiers came from all the crown lands: Germans marched alongside Slovaks, Ukrainians alongside Slovenes, Italians alongside Croats. It was the first international standing army since the time of the Romans. Less an instrument of war and of the central power of the Emperor than a single unifying force, it was in a certain sense the Empire itself. All citizens were obliged to serve once in their lives in the army which democratically offered chances of promotion to all, by contrast with the hierarchical society of the Habsburg Monarchy. Twenty years later, after it had disbanded itself and the old Empire had split up into national states, Franz Theodor Csokor in his play *3 November 1918*, which until recently was performed in the Burgtheater on every national festival, was to erect a monument to the army from the more detached viewpoint of a later date: 'Unreal as this army was in essence, the army of Wallenstein, of Prince Eugene, of the Archduke Charles, equally unreal in November 1918 was the manner of its end. The Imperial and Royal Army never came home.'[5] The Succession States of the Monarchy simply removed their countrymen from its ranks. More than anything else the military in Austria-Hungary was the butt of satire – from Roda Roda's and Arthur Roessler's farce *Der Feldherrnhügel* (The Generals' Hill) to Kraus's apocalyptic *Last Days of Mankind*, a war drama designed for a Martian theatre, in which everything one would be tempted to dismiss as satirical exaggeration was proved by documentary evidence to be the simple truth. *Der Feldherrnhügel*, despite its innocuousness, was immediately suppressed by the Imperial and Royal censorship. Nevertheless, by 1913, the advent of the Redl affair,[6] it had become clear that the Monarchy was a fragile construction and that the now somewhat dimmed myth of the widely acclaimed army was perhaps built on shaky foundations.

But at first it seemed that the forty-eight years of peace between 1866 and the outbreak of the First World War would never come to an end. The imperial city of Vienna developed into a capital city of a modern stamp, like Paris and, later, Berlin. Even a chronicler as critical as Albert Fuchs, whose *Intellectual Trends in Austria* is one of the most important works on the pre-1918 period, presents us with a tranquil evocation of his youth:

'If one would picture to oneself what middle-class existence was really like in Vienna around 1910, one should realize to what a high degree it partook of permanence, security and peacefulness. It was with good reason that my parents right up to their death used to refer to the pre-war years as "the peace" – without reservations. It was the prevailing, though tacit, assumption that world history had ended with the battle of Königgrätz, a generation and a half earlier. Changes of any dimensions were no longer to be expected. Wars and revolutions might indeed still recur, but only in some remote corner of the globe. In Europe everything would remain as it was, even in Austria, in spite of a certain instability.'[7]

Thus Kakania's middle classes had no other problem than to come to terms with existing traditions; they overlooked the fact, however, that in the Monarchy's population of many millions they represented a favoured minority. The baroque metropolis of Vienna – 'for which baroque politics were a thing of the past' (Hermann Broch) – became during these years more and more a fashionable social centre. The landed gentry kept their town palaces in Vienna: enormous sums of money, deriving from the provinces, flowed into the imperial capital, which acquired a truly international imprint. In her memoirs the '*Hofrätin*' Bertha Zuckerkandl mentions a dinner given by Johann Strauss in his palace in Auf der Wieden; the menu, culinary symbol of Austrian-ness, consisted of the following dishes:

> Risotto-Suppe auf Triestiner Art
> Fischpörkelt – Ungarisch
> Braunbraten mit Zwiebeln – Polnisch
> Serviettenknödel – Böhmisch
> Bachhendeln mit Gurkensalat – Oberösterreichisch
> Apfelstrudel – Wiener Idealgericht
> Weine: Tokayer, Donauperle; Sliwowitz.[8]

Otto Basil talks of this age, devoted as it was to gastronomic pleasures, as a sort of 'second Biedermeier', one of 'the most untragic periods of world history'.[9] A realistic emblem of the time (in place of the Habsburg eagle that adorned all imperial palaces and public buildings) would have been a double-headed capon. . . .

To the Viennese idylls of the time belonged the wine taverns in the suburbs, the legendary '*Heurigen*' (the traditional wine taverns) the coffee-houses, the Prater with the newly constructed Giant Wheel (1897) – and the Viennese operetta. A cult of Vienna arose which has lasted right up to our own day (by which time it has become thoroughly commercialized): simple ballad singers in the 'Heurigen' were glamorized; everyone knew Fiacre-Milli (since immortalized as the heroine of numerous films) who, as organizer of the fiacre-balls, was surrounded by an aura of frivolity and ambiguous charm. The most popular actor of the day was Alexander Girardi for whom Johann Strauss wrote his operettas and who became part of Viennese folk-lore. He was an autodidact, came from nowhere, and suddenly was dancing Strauss waltzes 'with an indefinable blend of cockiness and aristocratic nonchalance' (B. Zuckerkandl). His dialect was all the rage and people copied his mannerisms. Like so many others he died in the last year of the Old Monarchy.

The Viennese coffee-houses of this period have achieved world fame. In the 'Griensteidl', the oldest literary café in Vienna which Grillparzer used to frequent, in the 'Museum' and in the 'Central', political decisions were made, poems and novels written. Their main advantage was as informal meeting places; one dropped in as though by chance and yet knew whom one would find and where and when. A hitherto unknown class of writers came into being – the 'coffee-house literati', the most impressive representative of whom was Peter Altenberg, a man who could only have come to the fore in Vienna and only at this period of its history.

The younger Johann Strauss, the 'Waltz King' and the most striking representative of the 'golden era' of the Viennese operetta, died in 1899. There followed a 'silver era', the first decade of the new century, when one danced to the tunes of Oscar Strauss's *Waltz Dream* (1906) and of the millionaire composer, Lehar's *Merry Widow* (1905). Although set in an imaginary Balkan state, the latter is still regarded today as the essence of everything which was stylized by the Austro-Hungarian *belle époque* into an imagined 'golden age of security'. From Vienna *The Merry Widow* set out on her victorious campaign, spreading through the world the myth of the mercurial, flippant operetta state of Kakania. It was not until 1925 that Erich von Stroheim in his film version allowed a remorselessly satiric attitude towards pre-war Imperial and Royal society to obtrude; then, in 1963, Maurice Béjart's production in Brussels, which shocked many of his audiences by turning the *Merry Widow* into an anti-war play, effectively banished to the realm of make-believe the nostalgic halo surrounding the Monarchy and Old Austria. There is, too, an overwhelming mass of contemporary evidence to justify us in exploding the myth.

Arthur Schnitzler, a sensitive analyst of his age and milieu, says of the individual, with his accustomed scepticism and insight into human nature: 'If we lived long enough, every lie related about us would probably become true. Rumour seldom knows what we do, but it knows the direction in which we are drifting.'[10] Perhaps these words might adumbrate some synthesis of myth, anecdote and fragmentary truth that would apply in retrospect to the now irreplaceable Kakania.

For most of the people of Vienna and Old Austria, during the period 'which was beginning to feel its mortality' (P. Valéry), the much quoted 'fried chicken era' probably never existed, nor could its passing have meant much to them. Ever since the eighteenth century the Monarchy had remained economically behind Western Europe, and since the *Vormärz*, the pre-1848 period, it had remained behind Germany. In the fifty years preceding 1910 the population of Vienna had quadrupled, so that it was the third largest city in Europe. Even so, it had no industry, and small manufacturers predominated. If one could find no niche in the administration or failed to establish oneself as a small shopkeeper, one was forced to work as cheap labour in some petty business or workshop. Immigrant workers were correspondingly miserable: a fifth of a man's wages disappeared in rent, and living conditions in dismal lodging-houses baffled description. In the workers' district of Ottakring only four per cent of the inhabitants had a room to themselves; in the grand Inner City on the other hand a third of the population possessed flats with more than seven rooms. Of the 178,000 inhabitants of Ottakring in 1910, some 10,000 eked out a miserable existence as 'bed-hirers'—in return for a small sum of money they acquired the right to a sleeping berth which during their absence was let out by the family concerned to others. In her book *Vienna—Legend and Reality*, from which these details are taken, Ilse Barea describes the slums which are rather at variance with the picture we have of the legendary Imperial and Royal capital (and which still exist in Vienna, even if now given over mainly to guest-workers from Turkey and Yugoslavia):

'Most of the houses built in the decades after 1880 had three floors. On each floor, a corridor would run along the rear wall facing a small court-yard, and the doors of the individual dwellings (they could hardly be called flats) would give onto this corridor, directly from the kitchen or, as the case might be, the single room. None of the tenants had a water closet or privy of his own; ten or fourteen tenants with their families would share one, either in the passage or across the yard. If there was running water, the tap too was in the corridor. Otherwise there would be a pump in the yard.'[11]

In a working-class district like Ottakring the mortality rate was twice as high as in the Inner City: tuberculosis, diphtheria and measles ravaged the poorly nourished population who sought their salvation all too often in alcoholic indulgence. This was the setting of the contemporary pornographic novel *Josefine Mutzenbacher – or my 365 Lovers* passed around at the time by hand. (It came out anonymously but was ascribed to Felix Salten, later to achieve world fame as the author of *Bambi*.) By its brazen descriptions of the coarse sexuality to which Josefine Mutzenbacher had to submit from childhood onwards in order to make her way to the top, the book deserves a place alongside the *Merry Widow* as a revealing document of the period.

Photography was developing towards the close of the century into a serious artistic medium and has left us pictures of contemporary social conditions and constellations which we are only now beginning to interpret correctly. For example the volume of photographs, *The Good Old Days* (1967), contain expressive and revealing snapshots by the photographer, Dr Carl Meyer, who has only recently been rediscovered and properly appreciated. It is only against the setting revealed by these pictures that we become aware of the gap separating us from the 'Moderns' of the two decades preceding 1918, who may be largely equated with those we consider 'Moderns' today and who are still not fully accepted.

If we are to reconstruct 'the golden age of security' and see it as far as possible shorn of its mystique and of the anecdotes that surround it, we should take account of the intellectual and political currents of the time.[12]

Liberalism constituted the most powerful trend, effective even until 1918, and thanks to which Austria succeeded in emerging from the protracted influences of the Middle Ages and embarking upon the road to constitutionalism. The repercussions of constitutionalism were visible in the decline of absolutism no less than in the high tide of cultural achievement that occurred around 1900. From 1860 to 1895 the Liberal Party made up a solid majority in the municipal council; and the liberal era left its mark on the city of Vienna as no other period in its history had done: the ramparts around the old city were levelled and in their place was built a *via triumphalis*, the Ringstrasse. Greater Vienna came into being, the suburbs being incorporated into the town in 1890, so that the urban area increased threefold. And as the German-Austrian bourgeoisie rose to become one of the dominating classes, so liberalism developed more and more into a force of reaction. As protagonists of Austria-Hungary's imperialist policy, the representatives of liberalism with the backing of the German Reich, pressed for expansion in Eastern Europe. Although from 1890 onwards the liberal party declined in importance until finally, after decades of political struggle, it was overtaken by the Christian-Socialists, the liberal ideology continued to pervade art and science; the intellectual influence of liberalism – basically a bourgeois influence – determined Sigmund Freud's position, as well as that of Schnitzler and Zweig. Officially the liberal era came to an end in 1895, but psychoanalysis and pacifism have continued to develop as independent offshoots of liberalism right into our own day.

A survey of the political forces of the period requires an assessment, too, of the importance of the press. The two liberal newspapers, *Neue Freie Presse* and *Neues Wiener Tagblatt*, under their editors-in-chief Moritz Benedikt and Moritz Szeps, attained significance beyond the national boundaries. From the time of the world-wide sensation caused by an interview with Bismarck, 1892, in the course of which the German Chancellor openly criticized the government

20

of Wilhelm II, the *Neue Freie Presse* had the reputation of being one of the best newspapers in Europe. Through its connection with financial capital in the Empire it never fell into the financial doldrums as did so many other papers. Its columnists, the best and wittiest writers in the country, were as popular as Vienna's most famous actors and singers. Within the liberal camp it preserved the most broad-minded attitude – and set the tone when the general war hysteria got under way. The age of the modern mass media was beginning, and the *Neue Freie Presse* was already one of the most important political tribunals under the Monarchy. Wickham Steed in his book *The Habsburg Monarchy* (1913) gives point to the situation with the paradoxical remark: 'Next to Moritz Benedikt, the Emperor is the most important person in the country.'

The *Neues Wiener Tagblatt* owed its advance to a position of influence to the fact that it was the first and only newspaper to report the defeat at Königgrätz (1866). Although the news was withheld by the military authorities, Moritz Szeps, the founder of the paper, succeeded in making it public. His daughter, Bertha Zuckerkandl, wife of the famous anatomist and sister-in-law to Clemenceau (the Tiger), influenced public opinion through her attacks in the *Neues Wiener Tagblatt* on bureaucracy and chauvinism, as in the Klimt scandal of 1901 with the faculty pictures.

The liberal régime had weakened the influence of the Church but not removed it altogether. In virtue of its possessions alone the Catholic Church was an economic power of importance, while the feudal, clerical group held a key position in parliament. Around 1880 the Christian-Socialist party came into being and in the ensuing years grew in strength until it became the most powerful party in parliament. In 1894 the *Reichspost* was founded as the central organ of the party. In 1895 property owners moved over in a body to the Christian-Socialists and in the same year the party gained a majority in the Vienna Municipal Council. In a curious attempt to retain power and influence the liberal government despatched a note to the Vatican drawing attention to the 'danger' presented by the ambitions of the Christian-Socialists. However, its own decline was inevitable. Dr Karl Lueger, the leader of the victorious party, was elected burgomaster on several successive occasions but failed to obtain the Emperor's confirmation; only after the fourth election in 1897 was he able to assume office.

During the final decade of the nineteenth century Catholicism exercised a strong influence on public life, due to the activities of the Christian-Socialists and of the Catholic cultural movement. On Sundays the churches were full to overflowing as they had not been for a generation. Treated with hostility by the other expanding parties – the Social-Democrats and the German National Party – the Christian-Socialists were able to rely on the support of the masses of small tradesmen. In 1907 they were responsible for the introduction of universal suffrage in place of the limited 'curial' suffrage hitherto in force. The tendency towards increased democracy and to a broadening of the power base was, however, balanced by an opposite tendency, which aimed at the clericalization of all cultural institutions and of the entire educational system. And the Christian-Socialists, even if they aroused the economic and political covetousness of the people, continued to preach absolute loyalty to the hereditary ruling house. In their agitation, indeed, they manifested anti-democratic principles, propagating a solution to the social problem by eliminating Jews from the economic life of the country. Threatened by the spread of capitalism, the manual workers and shopkeepers—the core of the Christian-Socialist vote—came to believe that big business was a Jewish invention. Dr Karl Lueger, who united and led the Christian-Socialists to victory, was a shrewd politician and demagogue. His father was caretaker at the Technical University of Vienna, while his mother and sister continued even later to run a tobacconist's shop. His speech was coarse, vulgar and witty, and his supporters called him 'handsome Karl'. His anti-semitism and opportunism were legendary. As though there were no constitution, decreeing the equality of all citizens before the law, Lueger used to make every applicant for a teaching job swear on his honour that he was not a Social-Democrat. Lueger's much quoted assertion, 'It is for me to decide who is a Jew,'[13] is now part of Vienna's folklore. To the day of his death in 1910, Lueger remained a first-class administrator, bringing gas and electricity under municipal control, completing the underground railway, and converting the horse-drawn tramways to electricity and making them a state enterprise. Under his régime the Lainz Infirmary was built (1904) as well as the hospital for the mentally sick in Steinhof (1907).

Before long, the Christian-Socialist party became respectable and conformed to the pressures of the Habsburg state, merging its politics with that of the upper nobility and of high finance. The last twenty years of Old Austria, which coincided with the Christian-Socialist era, bear the unmistakable stamp of Christian-Socialism, even if only in a negative sense. 'Official Austria' stood for the political upholders and the ideology of Catholicism, against which the germinating intellectual and artistic forces that were ultimately to leave their mark on the twentieth century were soon to be engaged in battle.

In keeping with the sluggish development of the economy ever since Metternich's day, the workers' movement took shape later in Austria than in other European countries. Only with the birth of the Constitutional Monarchy in 1867 did it begin to impress itself upon the public. In the same year *Vorwärts*, the first labour newspaper, began publication. In 1888 followed the foundation of the Social-Democratic party, and a year later that of its press organ, the *Arbeiterzeitung*. By 1907 the socialist party group had become one of the strongest in parliament. With the death of Lueger, the people's tribune, the Christian-Socialist majority on the Municipal Council suffered a severe setback, and the parliamentary elections of 1911 resulted in a significant success for the socialists in Vienna. But the Social-Democratic party failed to exploit its success; at critical moments in history it was not equal to the occasion, for in 1910 it split up into national groups and in 1914 supported the imperialist war. The leader of the party, Dr Viktor Adler, the '*Hofrat* of the Revolution', proved himself an inconsistent Marxist. The Social-Democrats allowed themselves to be appeased with meagre reforms and threadbare concessions and finally petered out as a revolutionary party in a period of prosperity, peace and parliamentarianism. In the congresses of the Internationals there was much convincing talk about the imminence of war and about revolution; but nobody in Austria seemed to believe in the possibility. The Kakania myth proved to be stronger.

And yet there was no lack of information about what was going on abroad. In 1902 Trotsky crossed the frontier illegally into Austria and immediately made contact with the Vienna socialists, Viktor Adler assisting him in getting to London where he joined up with Lenin. Trotsky saw at once that revolution in Austria would be a long time coming. In 1907, after his escape from Siberia, he was in Vienna again where, until the outbreak of the First World War, he was editor of *Pravda*. He lived with his family in a working-class district, in a house for poor people which was more wretched than that of the average worker, being forced on occasion to pawn his possessions at the Dorotheum. While the Imperial and Royal secret police kept him under surveillance without otherwise taking him seriously, Trotsky acquired for himself a versatile education, frequented all the museums and wrote brilliant art criticism. Sometimes he would play chess in the Café Central—which gives point to the sally of the Austro-Hungarian Foreign Minister, Count Berchtold, when asked who in Russia was capable of starting a revolution; he replied ironically, 'Perhaps Herr Bronstein [Trotsky's real name] from the Café Central.'[14]

When the war finally broke out, even the *Arbeiterzeitung* joined in the warmongering chorus of chauvinists. The Austrian Social-Democrats came out in favour of the continued existence of the Habsburg Monarchy; and even when in 1916 Friedrich Adler, Viktor's son, assassinated the Prime Minister, Count Stürgkh, who had dissolved parliament two years earlier, it was not greeted as the tocsin of a revolutionary class struggle. A symptom of the general unrest and atmosphere of crisis, it remained a single individual's demonstration against the war and against the absolute régime. The hopes that large numbers of people had placed in the assassin's revolutionary gesture were not fulfilled.

Viktor Adler survived the collapse of the Monarchy by only a short time; he died in 1918, having acted as Foreign Minister of a much reduced Austria for a mere week.

Amongst the reactionary forces in Austria before the First World War German Nationalism was the most extreme. The success of its publicity, which resulted in a German Nationalist party taking firm root in Austria from 1880 onwards, was bound up in part with the apathy and cosmopolitanism of the constitutional party. The powerful nationalistic movements in Europe and in the Imperial and Royal crown lands (especially in Hungary, the Czech and Slovak provinces and in Slovenia) had not hitherto found any counterpart in Austria. A clear Austrian national consciousness seemed to be lacking, though it proved easy to arouse. Thus it was that the efforts of the German Nationalists, with their propaganda in favour of Prussian militarism, Bismarck and the House of Hohenzollern, found a ready echo among large sections of the Austrian population. They preached the superiority of the German nation, anti-semitism and hatred of the Slav world. Liberal capitalists made common cause with the protagonists of German nationalism, who succeeded in giving the impression that they were the guardians of the traditions of the bourgeois revolution of 1848.

Georg Ritter von Schönerer (1842-1921) coined the slogan 'Back to the Reich' and in 1879 founded his own two-man party in the Imperial Council. After the elections of 1901 he was able to enter the House of Representatives with twenty-one party supporters. To his surprise and embarrassment it then transpired that his own wife was Jewish, which made him no longer acceptable to his German allies so that he lost the election of 1907; he withdrew to his estates in the Waldviertel an embittered man. But the programme to which Schönerer and his companions subscribed marks them clearly as predecessors of the Nazi party; and there is no doubt that Adolf Hitler, who lived in Vienna from 1907 to 1913, was indebted to them for his ideas. Hitler had come to the metropolis, whose racial conglomeration appeared to him, as he was later to explain in *Mein Kampf*, as 'blood pollution personified',[15] to study architecture.

23

Rejected by the Academy of Fine Arts on account of his insufficient talent, he managed to exist by selling advertising posters and coloured picture post-cards. He lived in a hostel for men in Brigittenau, one of the most miserable working-class quarters in Vienna. It has been proved that Hitler at the time was an enthusiastic reader of the *Ostara* series of booklets, published under the general title *Bücherei der Blonden und Mannesrechtler* (books for the blond and the male) by Lanz von Liebenfels,[16] a former inmate of the Cistercian monastery of Heiligenkreuz, who propounded racial theories and was romantically infatuated by 'Germanism'.[17]

The 'Break with Rome' campaign of German nationalist ideology, designed to smooth the way towards the union of Austria with Protestant Prussia, began to pervade the climate of opinion in Austria. The publicity apparatus of the 'Reich' lent support to the glorification of Bismarck, Wagner and Karl May, and ensured the popularity in Austria of the book *Foundations of the Nineteenth Century* (1899) by Wagner's son-in-law, Houston Steward Chamberlain, the founder of the 'racial conception of history'. The overt, no less than the disguised, propaganda was effective. About the turn of the century the German ideology of 'Aryanism' came into fashion, even among Jews.

A survey of the political ideologies prevailing in Austria around 1900 shows that liberalism was the formative and pervading influence in most public institutions. Despite some loss of prestige it still operated upon the major part of the upper bourgeoisie, though some sections of this class looked to Christian-Socialist or German-National ideas. The workers almost unanimously aligned themselves with socialism. The two main classes, the bourgeoisie and the proletariat, exercised a strong ideological influence on the lower middle class, sections of which supported the Liberal Party, other sections the Christian-Socialist and German-National, and a small minority the Social-Democratic party. Such was the compound of mutually conflicting forces that formed the domestic political panorama in the Austrian part of the Danube Monarchy and its centre, Vienna, at a time when the tragedy of war and destruction was slowly unfolding.

There was, indeed, an offshoot of the peace movement active in Austria, the 'Austrian Peace Society' founded in 1891. Its mentors were Bertha von Suttner (the Countess Kinsky), whose pacifist novel *Die Waffen nieder* (Lay Down Your Arms) published in 1890, went around the world and earned her the Nobel Prize; Alfred Hermann Fried, Nobel Prizewinner in 1911; and the jurist and international lawyer, Heinrich Lammasch. Bertha von Suttner was a typical liberal, seeing it as her main task to interest the nobility and the propertied class in the idea of peace. She regarded it as her own and the Society's crowning achievement to be received in audience by the Emperor Franz Joseph. The cause of peace appeared at first to register considerable progress. In 1892 the World Peace Congress opened a permanent office in Berne; Alfred Nobel and Andrew Carnegie established foundations for the promotion of world peace; the Czar's manifesto of 1898 subscribed to the main tenets of pacifism. However, the conference of the powers in The Hague in 1899 brought a moment of disenchantment when Germany, by contrast with the other great powers, sent no delegation. Finally, when the First World War broke out, most pacifists shelved their peace propaganda and acknowledged the demands of national defence. Lammasch, member of the Upper House of the Hague Court of International Settlements, was to have been arrested in 1914 at the behest of the general staff, but the Emperor's veto saved him. Later

24

he became Prime Minister during the last two weeks of the Monarchy's existence, but all he was able to do was to prepare the Emperor Karl's abdication, which took place on 11 November. Not until after the First World War did the Peace Movement again come into its own, achieving a provisional triumph in the founding of the League of Nations in 1919.

Among the spiritual movements that arose about this time in Vienna and spread throughout the world was Zionism. About nine per cent of the Viennese population before the war were Jews, many of whom had become completely assimilated. Even if they were debarred from a career in the army or in the civil service, they were free to establish themselves as merchants, doctors, lawyers or journalists. Jewish intellectuals—one thinks of Schnitzler, Freud, Karl Kraus, Zweig, Altenberg, or the two leading newspaper editors, Benedikt and Szeps—dominated the mass media. But the smouldering anti-semitism, to which Lueger owed his electoral triumphs, was about to burst into flame. Theodor Herzl, a writer and journalist born in Budapest in 1860 and brought up in Vienna, was one of the first to question the belief in successful assimilation. As correspondent of the *Neue Freie Presse* he reported on the Dreyfus trial (1894) from Paris, and during the trial experienced at first hand the elemental out-burst of hatred for the Jews. The outcome of this experience was his manifesto, *The Jewish State* (1896), originally conceived as a novel, which led to the foundation of the Zionist movement. Again, in his utopian novel *Altneuland* (1902) Herzl put forward the demand for a national home for the Jewish people in Palestine. The response, even in Jewish circles, was not encouraging, and when Herzl died in 1904 the fulfilment of his project belonged to the remote future. One of his comrades-in-arms was the young Martin Buber. Born in Vienna in 1878 he attended the Zionist congresses at Basel in 1899 and 1901 where he first achieved public recognition. After Herzl's death the leadership of the Zionist movement was taken over by Chaim Weizmann in England, and Buber withdrew from Zionist party activities, devoting himself during the ensuing five years to collecting and editing old and half-forgotten Chassidic writings. To his efforts we owe *The Tales of Rabbi Nachmann* and *The Legend of Baalschem*.

The great tradition of the Vienna medical school dates from the foundation of the General Hospital by Josef II in 1784. With the passage of the years, it increased in importance and, thanks to a succession of remarkable physicians, Vienna soon outpaced Paris, which had led the world in medicine up to the beginning of the nineteenth century. Semmelweis, the discoverer of childbirth fever, the anatomist Rokitansky, the internal specialist and intuitive diag-nostician Skoda, and the dermatologist Hebra who introduced water-bed treatment, are only some of the names of doctors who gained world-wide recognition for the Vienna medical school right up to the 1880s. In the 'heroic' period must be counted the anatomists Hyrtl and Oppolzer, the physiologist Brücke and the psychiatrist Meynert (the two latter were Freud's teachers). There then followed a generation of great surgeons: Billroth, Albert, Zucker-kandl. Theodor Billroth, who directed the first surgical sanatorium (1880), made Vienna the mecca of the art of healing. Famous specialists, who were now beginning to be trained here, attracted hundreds of thousands of patients from all over the world, many of whom remained in the city for months.

Part of the tradition of the Vienna medical school was 'the artistic attitude of medical practice towards science and the patient'.[18] A Viennese Doctors' Orchestra gave public performances. Billroth, founder of the 'Society of

Doctors', was also a brilliant pianist and writer on musical matters, besides being the friend and enthusiastic disciple of Brahms. Between Billroth and his colleague Albert, a Wagnerite, there were often heated discussions about music, opera and the theatre. Bertha Zuckerkandl reports that her husband, the renowned anatomist, on Klimt's initiative held learned lectures for an audience of artists. His demonstrations of art forms in nature, which could be made visible by dyeing little sections of the epidermis and of the substance of the brain, undoubtedly exerted an influence on Klimt and the decorative work of the Viennese ateliers.[19]

Yet, that medical research even in the last decades of the past century still had a long way to go, may be illustrated by many examples. When Emil Zuckerkandl gave his inaugural lecture in 1888 as professor of anatomy and referred to Darwin's theory, there was a call for his dismissal on the grounds that it was an offence to challenge a dogma of the Church.

After the turn of the century Vienna 'in part preserved and in part re-furbished'[20] its old reputation as the metropolis of medicine. Others asserted on the other hand that 'the Aesculapian centre had moved from the Danube to the Spree'.[21] The tradition of the artist doctors persisted, however: Arthur Schnitzler, in his literary work one of the most significant diagnosticians of his time, was also a distinguished laryngologist, while the dramatist Karl Schönherr, and, above all, Sigmund Freud, must certainly be mentioned in this context.

After 1880 further significant achievements in the history of medicine continued to be made in Vienna. Julius von Wagner-Jauregg tried to cure progressive paralysis by malaria inoculations, for which work he received the Nobel Prize in 1927. Krafft-Ebbing, whose *Psychopathia Sexualis* had changed universally held ideas on this subject as long ago as 1886, effected adjustments in legislation (initiated in Austria) to conform with the new discoveries in psychiatry. Emil Zuckerkandl was the founder of topographical anatomy, and in 1904 his anatomical atlas was published. His assistant and successor, Julius Tandler, who made a name for himself in social and public hygiene, was invited to China in the late twenties to organize a public health system. Eugen Steinach, from 1912 head of the Institute for Experimental Biology in the Academy of Sciences, became through his investigations of glandular functions the initiator of the study of hormones. In 1911, the bacteriologist and biologist Karl Landsteiner discovered the theory of blood groups and its application to transfusion therapy, the significance of which was only understood during the First World War. He received the Nobel Prize in 1930. An inventory of the medical achievements of these years must include the discoveries of the neurologist, Sigmund Freud, which in due course, under the name of psychoanalysis, radiated outwards from Vienna and caused excitement and bewilderment throughout the world. When Freud began his work, psychology was in a state of torpor. It looked upon man as a biological machine, measurable by physical and mathematical means, a colourless and standardized entity predestined by nature to a middle-class existence. The discovery of the forces of the unconscious destroyed all fictions and abstractions of such liberal philistinism. The discoveries of psychoanalysis, as Freud explained in a lecture in 1914, were the latest of three upheavals which the human consciousness had suffered since the Middle Ages: first Copernicus' astronomical theories, then Darwin's theory of evolution, and now finally the knowledge that 'man is not even master in his own house'.

26

Psychoanalysis, which was developed during the very last two decades of Old Austria's existence, yet put new life into the science of psychology, has become part of the climate of modern opinion. During the twenty years of his scientific work up to 1898, Freud, the university lecturer, born in 1856, only published twenty articles, among them the *Studies of Hysteria* (1895, in collaboration with Josef Breuer), in which the case of Anna O. was treated and which was to be the point of departure for all further speculations. To the year 1898 belongs Freud's self-analysis; the theory of dreams was composed and became the basis of psychoanalysis.

When his *Interpretation of Dreams* was published in 1900, it was unheeded at first. Nobody noticed this revolutionary work, and the modest edition of 600 copies was not sold out for another ten years. In 1901 appeared the *Psychopathology of Everyday Life*, and in 1903 Freud's first disciples began to collect around him. It was the *Three Essays on Sexual Theory*, published in 1905, that first gave rise to scandal. True, the campaign of abuse in the reactionary newspapers was ineffective, but Freud, who postulated the omnipresence of the sexual impulse, was from now on ostracized. Probably he would have remained a lecturer all his life if an influential patient had not exerted herself on his behalf and thus ensured that the title of professor was finally bestowed upon him. In 1907 and 1908 Freud received visits from Jung and Ferenczy, who accompanied him a year later to the USA, where he delivered lectures at Clark University in Worcester, Massachusetts. Psychoanalysis developed into a world-wide movement, and its influence extended to other fields as well. The 'modern' Austrian painters, for example, and especially expressionism, then in its early stages, were indebted to psychoanalysis for vitally important incentives. Beginning in 1908 psychoanalytic congresses were organized (in Salzburg, Nürnberg and Weimar), and in 1910 the International Psychoanalytical Society was founded with Jung as president. Publication began of the *Zentralblatt für Psychoanalyse* and of *Imago*. To this period belongs the most dramatic episode in Freud's life, the split with his pupils, who now established their own schools. In 1911 Adler broke away from Freud's famous 'Wednesday Society', at which his disciples assembled like a group of conspirators, and two years later he was forsaken by his favourite pupil, Jung. In an essay *On the History of the Psychoanalytical Movement* (1914), Freud took stock of the first chapter of his life and work. Freud's biographer, Ernest Jones, reports that for Freud himself the findings of psychoanalysis were 'contrary to nature'. Throughout his life Freud was undeviatingly middle-class, a representative of liberalism, by nature anything but a revolutionary. He certainly stood aloof from middle-class society, which never forgave him for the loss of its illusions; but still he remained within its orbit. It may be symptomatic that Freud lived for seventy-nine years in the Vienna he affected to hate 'with physical disgust', and which he described as a prison, and yet, being an international celebrity, he would doubtless have been welcome anywhere. It was left to the Nazis to drive him from the city.

Alfred Adler (b. 1870), the founder of individual psychology, also began his scientific work in pre-war Vienna. Having started a private practice in 1900, he soon met Freud and became one of his first followers. In 1907 he published his *Study on the Inferiority of Organs*. He began to develop a critical attitude towards psychoanalysis, seeing in sexuality merely a mask covering the will to power. After the break with Freud in 1911 he founded the society for 'Free Psychoanalysis' out of which the 'Society for Individual Psychology' later developed. In 1912 his principal theoretical work appeared, entitled *On the Nervous Character*.

In 1903, *Sex and Character* by the twenty-three year old Otto Weininger, propounding the theory of psycho-physical bisexuality, caused a sensation. An attempt to systematize the dissolving 'pointillistic' image of the world, this book became one of the key works of the period, and yet, in the same year, the brilliant young author shot himself. It was not merely the split he had revealed between the male and the female principle, but the irreconcilable conflict between his Jewishness and the 'Aryan' philosophy to which he felt attracted that overwhelmed him and drove him to suicide in an orgy of self-hatred.

Jakob Moreno Levy (b. 1892 in Constanza), the father of the psychodrama, spent the formative years of his life in the capital. He came to Vienna, which had acquired a reputation as the centre of modern psychiatry, to pursue his studies, and for a short time before branching out independently he was a student of Freud's. About 1911 he started to assemble groups of children in the parks and to encourage them to perform impromptu plays. The following year he founded the 'Society of Vienna Prostitutes' at whose meetings the first tentative efforts at group psycho-therapy were made, and during the war carried out group investigations in the refugee camp at Mitterndorf near Vienna. He published the results of his experiments in the two theses *Invitation to a Meeting* and *The Testament of Silence* (1915). It was from the impromptu theatre that Moreno later developed his conception of the psychodrama, a method of 'discovering the truth of the soul through action', which has since become a feature of psychiatric treatment all over the world. In our time, which is experiencing a reaction against traditional theatrical forms, the significance of Moreno's theatre of spontaneity and creativity is being fully appreciated for the first time.

An astonishing number of upheavals and new departures occur in Vienna during these years. Revolutionary personalities enter the arena—either in isolation or as founders of associations, movements, societies and schools—and combine to form the image, and the art, of the twentieth century. Whether a Freud, a Herzl, a Schiele, a Schönberg or a Karl Kraus could, in fact, only have emerged in the specific atmosphere of Vienna at the time of the dying Danube Monarchy, is a vain question. Otto Basil gives his answer by pointing out that in principle all these personalities (who have gone down in history as revolutionaries) 'merely transformed certain ultimate potentialities of the paradoxical Kakanian world—potentialities which existed nowhere else—into intellectual realities.'[22] The move forward into the twentieth century presupposed the existence of that 'latent revolutionary condition' in which the essence of the Habsburg Monarchy is reflected.

Revolution embraced too the literature of the period, and here new forms and possibilities of expression were revealed, containing elements of the outrageous as well as the hitherto unsuspected (or overlooked). Nearly all the achievements that were to oust the traditions of the last century and lead to the emergence of new realities in literature were prepared or moulded during the last twenty years of Old Austria's decline.

The increasing role of psychology made the straightforward portrayal of a hero in literature an equivocal matter, and the hero's 'death' found a factual echo in the abolition in 1919 of all titles of nobility. A hitherto unknown extension of the field of creative activity opened up to the writer areas that were once the preserve of the psychologist and psychiatrist, namely the irrational, lying at the root of psychic motivations, and which it was now the business of the writer to comprehend. Dream realities were discovered and explored. The unbroken meditation or 'interior monologue' added new dimensions to the hitherto accepted image of the human personality. Finally through the revelation of the secrets of the pre-conscious and unconscious mind, the material of literature itself—the language—became problematical. 1924, the date of Breton's surrealist manifesto was, after all, not very far ahead.

Responsibility for the word was claimed by certain clear-sighted people to be an imperative necessity, a protective measure in face of 'feuilletonism as a philosophy of life, which coloured the later Kakanian style'.[23] Significant as a reaction to this was the meticulously cultivated art of the aphorism, a typically Austrian form of philosophizing, as well as the linguistic philosophy of Ludwig Wittgenstein (b. 1889), who only came into prominence with his *Tractatus Logico-philosophicus* after the First World War.

After the death of Nestroy (1862), Stifter (1868) and Grillparzer (1872), Austrian literature underwent a period of stagnation, lasting several decades, which was only relieved by Ferdinand von Saar (1833-1906), whose *Stonebreaker* from the collection of *Tales from Austria* (1897) was the first proletarian short story. Dismissed as a naturalist and much misunderstood, Saar had little influence upon the period in question.

In the great European revival from 1890 onwards, beginning in France and embracing all the arts, Austria and Vienna played a leading role. Literature, music, painting suddenly acquired a new image. 'With few exceptions everything developed as if a simultaneous vision had modelled the style of our age. Mysterious links were forged connecting language, colours, forms, tones and attitudes to life,'[24] wrote Bertha Zuckerkandl in her memoirs. Basil has described those decades of efflorescence as 'the final apocalyptic spurt of the Habsburg Empire'.[25] Hermann Bahr (b. 1863), writer, journalist, critic, and later Director of the Burgtheater, whose comedy *The Concert* (1909) is still frequently played today, was the real theoretician of the Viennese 'Moderns'. Having spent many years in Paris where he was in touch with intellectual trends, in 1894 he returned to Vienna and soon became a focus for the new artistic life. On his initiative a literary round table was formed in the Café Griensteidl composed of a circle of writers known as 'young Vienna', to which Schnitzler, the young Hofmannsthal, Altenberg and Salten belonged. Although himself conventional and an offspring of middle-class liberalism, Bahr espoused the causes of Ibsen, Zola, *Art Nouveau* and the *Ver Sacrum* movement: he was also among the founders of the 'Secession'. He followed every artistic fashion, but was always the first to do so, he himself providing the stimulus.

The most important representative of the literature of imperial Vienna was Arthur Schnitzler (b. 1862), whose plays and novels capture the spirit of the age in a masterly fashion. When examples of the young writer's work were submitted to Sonnenthal, then Director of the Burgtheater, he referred to Schnitzler's 'abstruse, incomprehensible thought and feeling, expressed in highly curious language'.[26] But these thoughts and feelings were soon to become universally comprehensible, albeit the occasion of scandals and reprisals against the author. For Schnitzler was not only the master of 'ringing intervals and resounding intermediate tones' (Robert Musil)—such has often been the common judgment—he was also a precursor of Freud, and therefore was certain to outrage the susceptibilities of his contemporaries. As early as

1890, in his cycle of one-act plays entitled *Anatol*, he coined the idea of the unconscious, about ten years before Freud.

According to Stekel, the pupil of Freud, Schnitzler's psychological analyses could be used as real factual material for the purposes of scientific research. The master himself avoided Schnitzler throughout his life on account of a kind of 'distrust of his own double'. Only an occasional correspondence took place between these two men whose careers coincided in the Vienna of our period. In one of Freud's letters to Schnitzler, he writes,

> 'Your determination and scepticism, which people call pessimism, your fascination with the subconscious, with the instinctual nature of human beings, your destruction of the conventional certainties of civilization, the attachment of your ideas to the polarity of love and death—all this affects me with an uncanny familiarity.'[27]

In *Liebelei* (1895), perhaps Schnitzler's best known play, which earned him his reputation as the classic writer of the period up to 1914, he composed a moving requiem to the *süsse Mädel*, those enchanting Viennese girls of the suburbs, who, sought after for short-term liaisons by the upper-class young men of Vienna, enjoyed only a brief period of happiness. Schnitzler's Christine, the most famous *süsse Mädel* in Viennese literature, makes the mistake of taking the amorous skirmishing too seriously and ends by committing suicide.

In his series of scenes, called *Der Reigen* (the round dance, filmed as *La Ronde*) of 1900, he made a sociological examination of erotic behaviour in different classes of society; here the range was extended, and the treatment satiric. The short scenes before and after the darkening of the stage, during which the sexual act is performed with changing partners until the round is completed, reveal the moral conceptions of the time. It was not only in Vienna that Schnitzler's *danse macabre* led to riots.[28] He acquired the reputation of being a scandalous, 'seditious' writer, a fact which many were ready to attribute to his Jewish origin. In later years Schnitzler turned to contemporary problems and in *Professor Bernhardi* (1912) treated the problem of anti-semitism (which has not disappeared in Vienna even today, so that Schnitzler's play scarcely appears out of date, at least not in the German-speaking world). In his novel *Der Weg ins Freie* (The Path to Freedom) the problem of deciding between Zionism and the assimilation of Jews is explored.

Critics were for a long time quite content to assign Schnitzler to the 'non-recurring school of impressionists and naturalists' (Robert Musil), as the world he portrayed came to an end with the outbreak of the First World War. Yet the Schnitzler renaissance in Vienna's theatres, which began after 1945, had surprising results. It was apparent that in his short pieces, *Der Grüne Kakadu* (1899) and *Zum grossen Wurstel* (1904), he had created the self-questioning theatre, in which the boundary-line between play and reality is blurred, twenty years before Pirandello. The audience is drawn into the action; figures in the play make themselves independent. Here we find the roots of the theatre of alienation and of the absurd.

In the short story, *Leutnant Gustl* (1900), which lays bare the hollowness of the military code of honour and in which an imperial lieutenant is presented as a figure of fun (for which Schnitzler was deprived of his officer's rank), Schnitzler anticipated the technique of the interior monologue by the first literary presentation of 'stream of consciousness', the technique of association related to psychoanalysis. (During this period, from 1905, Joyce taught in the

Berlitz school in Trieste, then belonging to Austria, the town in which Freud had pursued his studies, the town where Italo Svevo lived and near where Rilke was to write his *Elegies*. It was not until after 1914 that Joyce began to work on *Ulysses*, the publication of which in 1922 altered the course of literature.) Schnitzler's achievement was not appreciated at its true value until fifty years after it was written. He never had the manner of the world-changer and revolutionary. New forms were thrown off by him as though playfully and incidentally, so that he was long overlooked and relegated to 'the world of yesterday'.

Among the intellectual trends that dominated pre-war Austria, mention should also be made of idealistic philosophy. The literary scene was influenced in particular by Ernst Mach's theories of 'Empirio-Criticism'. Mach's theory of perception and the trend initiated by him, which considered everything existent as sensation, provided the philosophic backbone to the attitude of an entire epoch. Ernst Mach (1838-1914) was professor of philosophy at the university of Vienna from 1895. In 1898 he had a stroke, gave up his chair but continued with his philosophic work, his best known book, *Knowledge and Error*, appearing in 1905. Having achieved public recognition, he held a seat in the upper house. So strong was the influence emanating from Mach and his doctrine that even Lenin considered it necessary to criticize the direction taken by Viennese philosophy (*Materialism and Empirio-Criticism*, 1908). And, indeed, a philosophy that interprets the world as the conception of each separate individual does appear to make the class struggle, the life struggle, insignificant. As distinct from materialism, idealistic philosophy is compatible with a religious way of thinking; it covers certain class interests.

In Austria, too, voices were raised in refutation of empirio-criticism and idealism—which culminates, ultimately, in solipsism. Ludwig Boltzmann (1844-1906), Mach's successor from 1902 at the university, posed the ironic question: 'Only our sense perceptions are given to us, we are told, but if we are consistent, we should ask the further question: are our sense perceptions of yesterday also given to us?' (*Popular Writings*, 1905). Friedrich Jodl's *Criticism of Idealism* appeared posthumously in 1920.

For many Symbolists and Neo-Romantics, indulgence in the cult of the emotions and in the complete egocentricity of a period which saw events merely as 'the foam of things' (P. Valéry) was simply a transitory stage. Their literary productions failed to survive the collapse of the Empire. Richard Beer-Hofmann's mannered prose in *Der Tod Georgs* (1900), which clings to the decorative imagery of *Art Nouveau*, might serve as an example. He too sees the world of masks and marionettes in which 'nothing really happens', but unlike Schnitzler he fails to penetrate farther in order to discover new realities.

One of the most important *Art Nouveau* writers was Richard von Schaukal (b. 1874), who in his aphoristic *Life and Opinions of Andreas von Balthesser* (1907) made the principal Austrian contribution to the literature of dandyism in a manner recalling the scintillating wit of Oscar Wilde. His text of *Pierrot and Columbine* (1902), illustrated by Rezniczek, Franz von Bayros and Heinrich Vogeler, was scarcely noticed by his contemporaries and is now forgotten. The novel of Vienna's *fin de siècle* was *The Garden of Knowledge* (1895) by Leopold von Andrian (b. 1875) who in his youth was a friend of Hofmannsthal. *The Festival of Youth* (the intended title of the work) which Andrian's anaemic young Baron glorifies, his hedonistic isolation – one of the ideals of the time–

and a pan-psychism exactly illustrating Mach's doctrines, all culminated in the crisis of identity that befell a whole generation. Beyond this generation Andrian had no further influence, and his literary production soon afterwards died out completely.

On the other hand Hugo von Hofmannsthal (b. 1874) succeeded in breaking out of this paralysing solipsism. He made his literary début in Bahr's 'young Vienna' circle of poets, where as a seventeen year old grammar school boy he wrote, under the pseudonym of Loris, poems and short plays the mood of which fluctuated between enjoyment of life and readiness for death. Along with Schnitzler he must certainly rank as the most representative writer of the Monarchy and its style of life. His early symbolic and mystical pieces, which are really poems, such as *Der Tod des Tizian* (The death of Titian, 1882) and more especially his dance of death comedy *Der Tor und der Tod* (The fool and death, 1893), mirror the psychological condition of his generation.

In 1898 the first performance of a Hofmannsthal play, *Die Frau im Fenster* (The woman at the window), took place in Berlin, directed by Otto Brahm. In 1902 appeared the short prose work, *A Letter*, a 'document registering despair of language' (Hermann Broch), which marked a general disintegration of values, extending even to language. Lord Chandos, the fictitious writer of the letter, had 'completely lost the capacity to think or say anything coherent'. At the root of Hofmannsthal's crisis of literary expression lay an increasing scepticism about the powers of language, a knowledge of the inexpressible, and a realization of the impossibility of complete communication. This gave rise to lines which are among the most beautiful in the German language. He attempted to deal with the problem of communication by orienting himself by classic models. He sought to forge through drama a link with real life and with actual speech. His writings for the theatre really began after the turn of the century, as well as his cooperation with the great 'stage magician', Max Reinhardt. From now on his *oeuvre* appeared, clothed in baroque, mediaeval or Venetian garments. In 1903 *Elektra* was first produced by Reinhardt in Berlin; in 1905 followed *Venice Preserved* (after Thomas Otway's play of that name); in 1910 a version of the English morality play, *Everyman*, the 'play about the rich man's death', which since 1920 has been part of the tradition of the Salzburg Festival, of which Hofmannsthal was a co-founder. He felt attracted, too, to the practical work of the stage; as early as 1903 he planned to direct his own theatre, and shortly before the collapse of the monarchy, thanks to the intervention of his friend, Andrian, became intendant of the Imperial Court Theatres, thus openly becoming part of the Austrian establishment.

Hofmannsthal's plays are scarcely ever performed today, except for the Salzburg *Everyman* which is to be reckoned primarily among the city's tourist attractions. It was in opera that Hofmannsthal found the medium in which he could realize his ceremonial conception of theatre, and in which his name survives. In 1906 he met Richard Strauss and out of this meeting arose that unique partnership whose products were to become landmarks in a brilliant operatic renaissance. They remain today in the repertoire of opera houses the world over. In 1909 *Elektra* was performed as an opera, in 1911 *Rosenkavalier* followed, then in 1912 *Ariadne auf Naxos*. The ballet, *Josephslegende*, was produced in 1914 and *Die Frau ohne Schatten* in 1915, although the first performance did not take place in Vienna until after the war in 1919. The correspondence between Strauss and Hofmannsthal exemplifies to perfection

32

the problems of partnership between composer and poet; it continued right up to Hofmannsthal's death in 1929.

The only one of Hofmannsthal's plays to be set in the present is the comedy without music, *Der Schwierige*. Themes that echo like leitmotifs throughout Hofmannsthal's works–knowledge of the inexpressible, the problematic quality of all action–are treated in this 'Austrian social comedy', as the poet called it, in the happiest and most relaxed manner. 'The mere fact of stating something is indecent,' says Hans Karl, Count Brühl, the hero of the play, who, through exaggerated scepticism and consideration for others, shuns making a decision and thus almost misses the opportunity of achieving happiness for himself and the woman he loves. *Der Schwierige* epitomizes much that belongs to the essence of Austrian life, which reached its peak of florescence in the last years of the monarchy. The most successful of all his plays, it was completed in 1917 after years of preparation, and was not published until 1921, in Munich.

Hofmannsthal's most important prose work, *Andreas*, was largely written during the years 1912 and 1913. A novel about the journey to Venice of a young Austrian from Vienna, it remains a fragment, a *Bildungsroman* of a very special kind in process of developing; how it would have ended is impossible to predict, since only extracts are preserved. It resembles in this respect so much work, perfect in conception, but left unfinished–a type of fragmentary creation in which the annals of Austrian art are extremely rich. *Andreas* was published posthumously in 1932 with an epilogue by Jakob Wassermann who ranks the work alongside Goethe's greatest writings.[29]

An important rôle, especially in the literary life of Vienna in the *belle époque*, was played by the salons, where the intellectual élite of Europe came together, to determine world history. The great ladies of society set the tone: Pauline Metternich, the patroness of countless charitable events; Josephine von Wertheimstein, at whose salon Hofmannsthal in later years was often a guest; Bertha Zuckerkandl, who included the medical profession as well as politicians in her circle; and Alma Mahler-Werfel, whose association with Mahler came about through the offices of the '*Hofrätin*' Zuckerkandl, and who continued the tradition of the Viennese salon right up to the years preceding the Second World War. Hofmannsthal used to receive in his house in Rodaun near Vienna such eminent contemporaries as Bahr and Schnitzler, Rudolf Kassner, Rilke, Gerhart Hauptmann and Thomas Mann.

By contrast with the official literary salons of this period, now approaching its end, there was a growing tendency to stress the non-conformism of the artist, and more particularly the poet. Even Hofmannsthal had felt the double existence of the poet, vacillating between his vocation and his bourgeois profession, as something 'impossible and immoral'. The writers who broke away from the traditions of the nineteenth century lived, materially and spiritually, an insecure existence on the edge of chaos. Their attempts to find a foothold in bourgeois society were in vain; they lived in complete anonymity and often only became known after their deaths.

Even Rainer Maria Rilke (b. 1875), uncrowned prince of the poets of the age, lived in borrowed castles. Born in Prague (he has been called 'the most sublimated form of Austrian'), he wandered from one adopted country to another. He married in 1901, tried to settle in the artists' colony at Westerwede near Bremen, but finding no regular work was unable to support his young family, and after a year took to wandering again. In 1902 we find him in

Paris as secretary to Rodin. The north, Capri, Venice, and Duino were further stations in his travels, when he enjoyed the hospitality of a series of distinguished noble families in their castles and villas. Always yearning for a settled existence and for favourable conditions in which to work, hyper-sensitive, waiting upon poetic inspiration as upon divine grace, Rilke, the renowned author of the *Stundenbuch* (1905) and the *Weise von Liebe und Tod des Cornets Christoph Rilke* (1906), was constantly plagued by the problem of where to spend the coming winter. In his novel, *Die Aufzeichnungen des Malte Laurids Brigge* (1910), one of the books that mark the breakthrough of modern literature and which, along with Kafka's and Musil's 'models of insecurity' (in the words of Gerhard Fritsch), heralded the opening of a new century, he wrote: 'O what a happy fate to sit in a quiet room in an inherited house, surrounded only by tranquil, settled things.' How temporary the 'quiet rooms' and the 'settled things' were the poet already suspected, as he enjoyed in luxurious independence the favours of a social order in dissolution, often completely without means of his own, and was passed on from one cultivated aristocrat to another, repaying them with dedicatory notices.

It was only in the castle tower in Muzot, rented for his benefit, that Rilke, after many critical years, was able in 1922 both to complete the *Duino Elegies* and the *Sonnets to Orpheus* and to find a home for the last years of his life. Rilke, whose points of orientation were rather Berlin and Munich, felt an insur-mountable aversion for Vienna. In 1907 we find him in the course of a lecture tour staying with Hofmannsthal in Rodaun. In 1916 he spent a half-year in Vienna, including several weeks of infantry training. After being released on intervention from higher quarters, he stayed on some weeks longer as Hof-mannsthal's neighbour in Rodaun, together with the painter, Lou Albert-Lasard, who painted his portrait. Rilke's mistrust of Vienna and his acute perceptiveness for everything important happening there is clearly expressed in a letter to Lou Albert-Lasard when the news of Franz Marc's death reached him:

> 'Here, too, many people knew him well, and the news spread rapidly. But what difficulty they all have here in "knowing" anybody; how strenuously everything "new" is stressed simply because it is new, and how quickly a wave of the usual frivolity closes over it again – nothing, nothing . . . Now I shall take a good look at Kokoschka and see if I can get to hear Schönberg's music. This is all, as it were, wasted here in this atmosphere . . . Where is it in fact?'[30]

During these years Franz Kafka (b. 1883) was living and working anony-mously, and apparently aloof from all contemporary events, in Prague. Cutting himself off from literary talk, he had no contact with his famous Austrian contemporaries. His prose, composed outside office hours (spent in the Workers' Accident Insurance Company for the Kingdom of Bohemia), received only in the twenties the encouragement of a small circle of literary connoisseurs. In 1913 he came to Vienna for the first time in his life, only for a few days, as delegate to an International Congress for Rescue and Hygiene. He attended at the same time a Zionist conference which happened to be in session.

And yet Kafka, whose influence extends to the literature of the present time and who has lost nothing of his topicality, is the 'poet *kat'exochen* of the decline of Kakania'.[31] His mysterious and cryptic parables, interpretations of which have repeatedly been attempted – and from a variety of angles –

suggest the hierarchic structure of the Monarchy and its bureaucratic institutions. For example, into the 'traumatic fabric of an archaic religious fantasy of punishment' in his story, *In the Penal Colony* (1914), Kafka has woven according to Basil the practice of public executions as they were still practised in Franz Joseph's time. He continues:

> 'The Kafkaesque top-floor offices and stifling little bureaux, the sinister methods of a corrupt subordinate officialdom, characterized by servility to those above; the hopelessness for the normal citizen of ever getting as far as the high or the higher courts in the Imperial and Royal set-up; the system of secret agents, informers, and beaters-up, the rising pyramid of the judiciary, ever more rarefied towards the top, and of the castle authorities themselves; these are nothing but puzzle-pictures of absolutely real, completely literal conditions, institutions, surroundings and customs in Kakania.'[32]

Gustav Janouch, who knew Kafka personally and was the author of the book, *Conversations with Kafka*, also rejects the idea that one should 'mythologize and thereby obscure' Kafka, a reproach directed against Max Brod: 'Franz Kafka is not a miracle descended from heaven, but a great man, equipped with a seismographically acute mind, able through his symbolic language to point a way through the undergrowth of doubt and anxiety.'[33] The poverty of vocabulary and the sobriety of Kafka's language– by contrast with the other writers of his generation–is explained by Klaus Wagenbach as due to the poverty and purism of Prague German.[34] And Rilke, an extremely fluent Prague poet, used to study dictionaries in the Paris Bibliothèque Nationale in search of rare words. Basil on the other hand has compared Kafka's dry, hermetic manner with Imperial and Royal officialese of the period. The immateriality of the world of Kafka's novels, he claims, has 'an extraordinary counterpart in the immateriality of the official Austrian forms of expression'.[35] The comparison throws a new light upon the notoriously prosy 'legalese' of Old Austria.

Kafka began writing in 1898, but his earliest extant work, *Description of a Fight*, was composed in 1904. From 1908 onwards he began publishing his works in periodicals. The earliest of his major works, *Judgment*, *Metamorphosis*, and *America*, were written in 1912. The first book, *Meditation*, appeared in the same year. In 1914 *The Trial* was committed to paper. In Vienna the advent of Kafka had clearly not yet been registered.

In the lyrical poetry of Georg Trakl (b. 1887) too, there is a full awareness of the decline of an age. The very titles of his poems– *Twilight and Decay*, *Revelation and Decline*, *Dream and Derangement*–trace out the area around which he circles and in which his personal tragedy is realized. In 1908 this pharmacist's apprentice from Salzburg (who had begun to take chloroform as an accompaniment to his early attempts to write poetry) was studying pharmacy in Vienna. He led the lonely life of a provincial lad, in miserable lodgings, far from the high-brow salons of the élite. His sister, Grete, to whom he was inseparably bound through an early incest experience, followed him to Vienna. Trakl felt guilty on account of the unnaturalness of the bond, and the words 'blood-guilt', 'degeneracy', 'decay', constantly recur in his work, signals of a private concatenation of events which magically express the circumstances of the time.

During the Vienna years, torn between cosmic anxiety and servitude, between the euphoria of creativity and the euphoria of narcotics, Trakl discovered the form of expression best suited to his talents. In 1909 the *Neues Wiener Journal* published three of his early poems. In the ensuing years which he spent mostly between Salzburg and Innsbruck, alternating between drunken excesses, nihilistic despair and vain efforts to settle to a bourgeois existence, Trakl felt more and more drawn to Vienna. In 1912 he was to have taken up a post there in the Ministry of Labour, but he stood it for only two hours. The following year we find him working for a month as an official of the War Ministry. By now, alcohol and drugs had so undermined his health that he could no longer follow a regular profession, and through lack of money he was forced to sell his favourite books. He determined upon a desperate attempt to break out, perhaps to find a job as army pharmacist in the newly created state of Albania or in the Dutch Indies (Kafka too had planned to flee from Prague and emigrate to South America), but all his plans came to naught. In Vienna he had contacts with Karl Kraus, Loos and Altenberg (with whom he undertook the only journey of his life – to Venice in 1913); with Kokoschka, according to the latter's statement, he painted the picture, *Die Windsbraut (The Tempest)*.

In 1913 appeared Trakl's first (and in his lifetime his only) publication in book form: *Poems*, a selection by Franz Werfel. He was able to see the galley-proofs of his second volume, *Sebastian's Dream*, but by the time it appeared in 1915 he was already dead. The First World War, just broken out, claimed an early victim. Sent to the front in West Galicia, Trakl is said to have been charged after the battle of Grodek with the care of about a hundred severely wounded soldiers in a barn. In his despair he tried to commit suicide, was removed to the garrison hospital in Cracow for observation of his mental state, and put an end to his life with an overdose of cocaine. He never received part of the 100,000 crowns, presented by Ludwig Wittgenstein to assist Austrian writers and artists in need and of which Rilke and Trakl were each to receive a share.

Trakl's *Helian* (1913) is considered by Basil as 'one of the most shattering revelations in German lyric poetry. The form of this poetry suggests a sort of preserved eternity.' His *Dramatic Fragment* (1914), the poetry of classical expressionism, Basil regards as the 'most perfect psychodrama in the German language'.[36] Both remained unknown until after 1918.

The mercilessness with which the destinies of such people as Trakl and Egon Schiele (another who died young) were fulfilled in the final phase of the Monarchy is seldom acknowledged as part of its mystique, and therefore merits particular attention. Heart of the Empire, and therefore also of its frustrations, was naturally Vienna – 'official Vienna'. Otto Wagner spoke of the 'ignoramuses in artistic matters who hold unfettered sway' and there are no lack of examples in the literature, music, painting and architecture of the time of unrealized possibilities and of the prematurely abandoned. Bertha Zuckerkandl refers to the archives of the National Library, where, for instance, Otto Wagner's untried plans are to be found, as 'a graveyard of works un-realized, criminally impeded, or of unborn masterpieces. Such graveyards are to be found in every country, but nowhere covering such vast areas as in Vienna, a city which has begotten geniuses again and again and then de-molished them.'[37] And Girardi, alluding to the fact that the Viennese made constant difficulties for Gustav Mahler during his life, but buried him with honours, coined the expression: 'The Viennese have always been great at interments.'[38] This delightful tradition has persisted to the present day.

The avant-garde innovators of the time were acclaimed only in their old age, if they lived to experience recognition at all. In the first decades of the century, as they set about conquering the city, which in the words of Hermann Broch was the city of 'decoration par excellence' and whose gaiety was 'correspondingly weak-minded', they were outlawed or ridiculed. The new movement, then being heralded, was expressionism, which reached its apogee only after the dissolution of the old European order. In Austria a phalanx of painter-poets inaugurated expressionistic literature 'long before its official beginning'[39]; for example, Kokoschka's poem *Die träumenden Knaben*, and his play *Mörder, Hoffnung der Frauen* (Murderer, Hope of Women) written in 1908 for the theatre of Hoffmann's Kunstschau; Schiele's moving diary, written in prison; Gütersloh's *Tanzende Törin* (1911), whose prose already displayed elements of surrealism. Expressionistic painters illustrated works by writers they felt akin to or did portraits of them. Kokoschka illustrated Albert Ehrenstein's *Tubutsch* for Herwath Walden's magazine *Sturm*, published in Berlin, and Schiele did a portrait of the young poet Hans Flesch-Brunningen which appeared on the cover of Pfemfert's *Aktion* dedicated to his work. The only novel by the artist Kubin (b. 1877), *Die andere Seite*, written in 1907 and published two years later, is 'the first great vision of Kakania's end'.[40] It is an account of the rise and fall of the dream city of Pearl in the Kingdom of the Other side, slumbering its time away without day or night. From his vast empty palace a magician holds sway over his subjects who are compelled to share his whims and sufferings in the form of spasms and convulsions. The attempts of an American millionaire to open up the dream kingdom by the application of rational methods end with its destruction and the crumbling away of everything material. It is the world of Kafka we find anticipated here, in more plastic and comprehensible form.

The other key work of modern literature whose publication falls into our period is the novel *Die Verwirrungen des Zöglings Törless* (Young Törless) by Robert Musil (b. 1880). In this distillation of Musil's years as a cadet at the military college in Mährisch-Weisskirchen (Rilke attended the same college, and some years later Erich von Stroheim), Musil was not interested in describing milieu or realistic action, but in evoking the systematic coercion that allowed barbarity and brutality to break through the façade of civilized bourgeois behaviour:

> 'It then became possible for a door to lead from the bright, everyday world, which was all he had hitherto known, to another world, a dim, surging, passionate, naked, destructive world. It became possible not only for there to be a bridge connecting those people whose lives alternate regularly between office and family as if within a transparent and stable building of glass and iron, and those others – the outcasts – bloody, dissolute and filthy, blundering through intricate corridors full of bawling voices, but for the two kinds to rub shoulders secretly, and the bridge to be passable at every moment of the day.'[41]

When it appeared in 1906 this prophetic book, which Musil had written 'out of boredom' in 1902, created a sensation through its 'amoral treatment' of the subject. It was not noticed at the time that the cruelty of the young people in young Törless' circle, their desire to perform 'great and bloody deeds', to gain absolute control of others, whom they would cause to bark like dogs and grunt like pigs, 'heralded the terrorism of the decades to come'.[42] In 1906 Musil wrote a dissertation on Mach's doctrines and attempted to make a living in Berlin as free-lance writer. But he was one of those dogged by misfortune; after the failure of his next work, *Alliances* (1911), he returned to Vienna to try his luck in some bourgeois occupation. His main work, *Der Mann ohne Eigenschaften* (The man without qualities), the novel of Kakania, the state 'that somehow just drifted along', mentioned as a project in his diaries as early as 1905, did not appear until 1930, and remained a fragment.

The most important record kept of Kakania's final phase and death agony we owe to Karl Kraus (b. 1874). Satirist, lyric poet and critic, Kraus, who made the demolition of the Café Griensteidl in 1894 with its wealth of literary associations the occasion for publishing a pamphlet, *Die demolirte Literatur* (in which he attacked the 'young Vienna' impressionist circle and acclaimed the Berlin naturalists), founded in 1899 *Die Fackel* (The torch) which was to become a Viennese institution. *Die Fackel* became a bitter rival of the *Neue Freie Presse*, and fiercely denounced feuilletonism and the misuse of words. Kraus, in establishing the paper, was totally indifferent to his financial interests and accepted no advertisements in order to safeguard his absolute independence. In his lonely struggle against corruption, abuses in the administration of justice and the general decline of morals, made manifest in his view by the rottenness of language, Kraus was driven into more and more extreme positions. From 1911 onwards he wrote every number of *Die Fackel* from the first page to the last entirely on his own. Language for him was the sole criterion; grammar was his ethic. He would stand alone against the whole world if his convictions made it necessary. It was said of him that he would spend longer over a single word than others over a whole novel. As his method for unmasking the empty phrase is by quotation, he lived in a world of paper and news, obsessed with cataloguing the contents and rearranging them to a satirical end.

But Kraus invited persecution; he enjoyed seeing himself in the rôle of the martyr. Inevitably he was soon at loggerheads with everybody. He brought an action (and lost, for once!) against Bahr, whom he accused of being prejudiced, as a freemason, in his dramatic criticism; he was also on bad terms with Schnitzler and Musil. Later he was to attack Max Reinhardt and his 'stage tricks', and to secede from the Catholic Church to which he had been converted, in protest against its collaboration with the Salzburg Festival. A misogynist and a lone wolf, he was nevertheless an excellent exponent of ideas, and his lectures, which he delivered in all the major towns, made him famous.

When the First World War broke out, even intellectuals in Austria were carried away by the chauvinistic war propaganda, emanating from all camps and all parties. Men of letters composed verses and articles glorifying the deeds of the central powers. At this historical juncture Kraus rose to his full stature. From countless minute observations he distilled the spirit of the war and held it up to ridicule, extracting his material from the press. Usually no commentary was called for, so that there was practically nothing the censors could object to. In this way between 1915 and 1918 his tremendous satiric and demonic indictment of war, *The Last Days of Mankind*, was written. Fragments of it were printed in *Die Fackel* and it was printed in definitive form in 1922. This Mars-drama, which could only be performed, according to Kraus, on ten consecutive evenings, presents an apocalyptic panorama of war: it gives a cross-section of all social classes from the Emperor downwards. For every episode, every sentence spoken or written by the actors, there is documentary evidence.

Even in the first year of the war difficulties arose in feeding the population, and maximum prices were fixed by law. As the first hospital trains arrived, garbled accounts reached home of the fighting in the front line. Journalists reported from the safety of the base area. Between hunger demonstrations the cult of Vienna and the Emperor continued to be celebrated. Bad news was kept from Franz Joseph himself, and only censored newspapers were laid before him. Operettas were performed endlessly to divert attention from the generally wretched conditions of life. Lehar toured the western front with the *Count of Luxembourg*. Then, in 1916 the old Emperor died. It was the end of an epoch. For a short time the 'mixture of court ceremonial and fuss', blood and *Gemütlichkeit*[43] which formed the essence of the monarchy, continued to operate, but the long predicted, long anticipated dissolution became a reality: 'It was all a dream. It ended like a film, all waltzes and bloodshed.'[44]

The Monarchy was no longer what it would like to be–'an asylum for all the national splinter groups cast by history into Central Europe' (Franz Joseph). Even its 'despotism tempered by slovenliness' (Viktor Adler) took on new forms. The farewell to Old Austria, to imperial Vienna, was a rapid process. In a letter, written on the occasion of Schnitzler's sixtieth birthday in 1922, Stefan Zweig wrote:

'The unforgettable types which he created and which one could see daily, as recently as on his fiftieth birthday, in the streets, the theatres, the drawing rooms of Vienna, almost formed by his vision, have now disappeared from real life. . . . *Das süsse Mädel* has become a whore; the Anatols play at the stock exchange; the aristocrats have fled; the officers have become salesmen and agents. Conversation has lost its grace and ease, and has become hoarse; love-making has been vulgarized and the city itself proletarianized.'[45]

The myth of Vienna and Kakania could begin to flourish.

On 28 December 1895 the brothers Lumière gave the first public show of moving pictures. This was the birth of the cinema, which developed in a short time into one of the major arts and mass media. The first cinema performance in Vienna took place in 1896, but the production of native Austrian films began relatively later than in other countries: the first efforts of the photographers Anton and Luise Kolm and Jakob Fleck date only from 1906. In 1907 a scene from Oscar Strauss's *Waltz Dream* was filmed, and a phonograph was used during projection. Thus the 'Singing screen' had its first performance. In 1908 Heinz Hanus made the first picture feature film *From 'Step to Step' in the Prater*.

Austrians played an important part in the development of the technique of the cinematograph. In 1895 Theodor Reich demonstrated the camera he had built, together with his own films, in London, but his invention failed to gain acceptance and was forgotten. In 1905 Heinrich Peschka patented his experimental coloured and plastic films. In 1907 Musger's experiments with a film apparatus incorporating a mirror adjustment led to the invention of the slow-motion picture.

And yet in conservative Austria the film was long despised as a trivial art form. In 1908 cinema audiences were made subject to the vagrancy laws and even in 1911 the *Cinematographic Review* felt obliged to make the following gloss on its activities:

'It is quite untrue that the cinema constitutes a threat to physical safety, to morals and to the welfare of the public in general. As for the further assertion, that the complete darkness of the cinema endangers the morals of the audience, this shows that the accusers are badly informed on the true facts, since the darkness in cinemas is by no means complete.'

In 1912 actors of the Volkstheater in Vienna were refused permission to act in films, since it was 'a breach of professional etiquette', while dramatists were asked not to write scripts for the cinema.

Nevertheless the rise of the new medium was not to be arrested. Count Sascha Kolowrat began to be interested in films from 1910 onwards. For this well-known industrialist and sportsman (he was one of the first Austrians to take his pilot's certificate; he flew balloons and took part in motor-racing) the new preoccupation was originally a mere pastime. He began with documentaries and films of expeditions in Algiers and Tunis, but was soon devoting himself wholeheartedly to his interest in cinematography. His later war documentaries, on the battle of Isonzo, for example, were used in the USA as teaching films before the entry of that country into the war. He also began to produce feature-films and tried to attain international standards by attracting famous actors from the theatre. In 1913 *Der Millionenonkel* was produced with Girardi in the leading role.[46]

In 1912 Kolm and Fleck founded Vienna Art-Films, following a general European trend to produce films based on works of literature. The filming of Grillparzer's *Ahnfrau*, Raimund's *Verschwender* and Anzengruber's *Pfarrer von Kirchfeld* took place during these years. In 1912 Felix Dörmann, the librettist of *Waltz Dream*, set up his own productions, writing, producing and playing in his own films – the first attempt at film *auteur*-ship.

The most important writers of the time also began to interest themselves in the cinema. Schnitzler in 1913 wrote the script for the first film of *Liebelei*, taking great pains over an 'interpretation in terms of the film'. He was anxious to omit the usual title flashes that interrupted the picture in the silent film, speech being replaced by 'mime, pantomime and optical effects'. From Schnitzler's diaries, access to which could only be made available by the terms of his will forty years after his death, it is clear that during the last years of his life he went almost daily to the cinema in a serious attempt to come to grips with the essence of the film. He left about thirty original adaptations of work for the cinema.

Hofmannsthal was also much occupied with the cinema. In 1913 he composed a film scenario from his ballet, *Das fremde Mädchen*, and the film was shot in Sweden. Ten years later followed the scenario for the filming of *Rosenkavalier*.

For Max Reinhardt, who came into contact with the new medium through the Art-Film movement, the film remained only a marginal activity, and he referred to it scornfully as the 'flim' from 'flicker'. In 1912, at the Vienna Rotunde and Kreuzenstein Castle, he shot the film *Das Mirakel* from Karl Vollmoeller's pantomime; in 1913 followed *Die Insel der Seligen*, filmed in Italy, and in 1914 *Venetianische Nacht*, also from a pantomime by Vollmoeller; the story of the journeyings of the student Anselmus to Venice and the figure of his officious servant Pipistrello remind one of Hofmannsthal's *Andreas* fragment. However, Reinhardt's almost unknown silent films mark no advance on filmed theatre, and he saw in the cinematograph at the best a sort of 'travelling' method of direction that would enable uniform productions of a drama to be made all over the world by reference to a model performance.[47]

In 1914 Kolowrat built the Sascha Film Studios in Sievering. Completed despite the outbreak of the war, they started operations in 1915. It was the beginning of the short heyday of the Austrian film industry. The ban on the importation of foreign films enabled home production to flourish, and even in the famine year 1918 a hundred feature films were made. Vienna had the chance of becoming a European film centre. Kolowrat got his directors, Alexander Korda and Michael Kertesz (who changed his name to Curtis when he went to Hollywood) to make a series of ambitious films, but the inflation in 1923 put an end to the dream of an Austrian film empire. The first of the great Sascha films of 1918 was called *A Sunken World*.

In the same year the young Viennese painter and officer, Fritz Lang (b. 1890), first emerged as a scenario writer. He later acknowledged his debt to Egon Schiele[48] (and owned one of the largest Schiele collections). It would be worth investigating how much of the atmosphere of the Vienna of that age found its way into the work of the world-famous film director. François Bondy has pointed to the influence of Schiele upon the satiric and mercilessly analytical vision of the world in Erich von Stroheim's films (b. 1885), the first of which, *Blind Husbands*, was made in 1918.[49] It was the prelude to his *Vienna trilogy*, consisting of *Merry-go-Round* (1922), *The Wedding March* and *The Honeymoon* (1926-8). In Hollywood perfect reconstructions of imperial Vienna arose, photographic documents of its decadent grandeur, put together with an obvious amalgam of love and hate. *The Merry Widow* (1925) also belongs to this series. Nearly all Stroheim's films, which are among the most important in the history of the medium, survive only as fragments; they were wantonly destroyed by his producers and enemies. He thus fulfilled a typically Austrian destiny, even far away from the homeland.

The power of the film and the power of the myth surrounding Vienna and Kakania may be vividly seen in an episode that occurred in a film studio in post-war Vienna and reported by Bela Balasz in an article entitled *Ghosts in Vienna* (*Der Tag*, November 1922). A film was being made about the Emperor Karl, the last Habsburg monarch, and for the court scenes fifty genuine officers of the Imperial and Royal army had been engaged.

'It was only a scene in a film studio, and yet I have never seen anything more eerie. I saw how a costume could terrorize the soul of its wearer. I saw how uniforms emerged from the locked cases of the museums like prisoners breaking out of gaol. It was no longer theatre, ghosts were abroad. When an undistinguished young actor, who played the Emperor Karl because he really resembled him, entered the studio, the director bawled him out good-humouredly, telling him not to step out of focus; but without effect, it quite failed to shake the erstwhile officers out of their dream. There they stood, overcome, with trembling lips, before their "ruler", although in their former life they had perhaps never had the chance of appearing before him in person. This was the greatest moment of their lives. It was no comedy, it was mass psychosis. The clothes they drew on over their bodies obscured their minds. The uniforms were fetched, still warm, from the grave; the past was still too much alive. If one is unwilling to revive it, one must fix strong locks on the museum doors.'

I would add that it would be well to lock the doors of the museums of the 'criminally impeded' – for the sake of the intellectual and artistic peace of Vienna today. As Cocteau has said, the greatest plagiarist is the past.

Adolf Opel

THE DEMYSTIFICATION OF ARCHITECTURE

The Ringstrasse and Otto Wagner

The introduction has shown, as indeed the later development of this study will also show, the inter-relations that existed within this microcosm. For instance, the surgeon Billroth read the score of Brahms's First Symphony, and pointed out to the composer its relation to Beethoven's Ninth. Schnitzler, the first writer to use the stream of consciousness in German, was a friend, possibly not surprisingly, of Freud, but at one time he had an international reputation as a laryngologist. Loos was not only a fervent and practical supporter of the young Kokoschka, but also of Schönberg. It is difficult within all these interactions and cross-fertilizations, to say who was the greatest or the most important figure. Mahler? Klimt? Although, to some extent, such animadversions may seem unreal, or even irrelevant, yet one figure stands out: Otto Wagner's achievement was the most massive, and probably the most durable. Without any shadow of question Otto Wagner left his stamp on Vienna in a way that no single architect has yet achieved. This is an extravagant claim for one of whom few abroad have even heard the name, let alone in Vienna. One thinks of Haussmann's Paris, or Viollet-le-Duc's Toulouse, or even of Herbert Baker's Delhi. Quantitatively a more valid comparison is with Wren and the City of London, since fifty of Wagner's most important buildings still survive in Vienna, include thirty-six metropolitan railway stations, and bridges and viaducts for forty kilometres of tracks. As well as these massive constructions he was responsible for the control stations and sluices that regulate the Danube Canal. Outside Vienna, he built a synagogue in Budapest, which was almost his first building.

Wagner used the most modern materials available, corrugated zinc, copper sheets, aluminium, and prefabricated concrete or marble cladding. He is even more relevant to the argument of this book, for not only does he bridge the whole period, but precisely at the moment of the Secession's foundation he changed his style completely. This might be considered mere eclecticism, a cloaking of historicism with the new *chic* or *Art Nouveau*, or, more precisely, *Jugendstil*, but for a successful architect of the Empire establishment it was in fact something far bolder. Firstly, his conversion was to a heretical sect, one that was very far from being accepted; indeed he adopted the *Jugendstil* in spite of, not because of public opinion. Secondly, he was able to understand its underlying principles so that he could employ its sparing uses of plant forms in decorations and detail. Furthermore, like all great artists, he continued to develop so that, while his church at Steinhof, although extremely modern in many ways, was still imbued with *Jugendstil* ideas, his Post Office Savings Bank was entirely functional, with the merest hint of decoration in the aluminium angels. All in all Otto Wagner epitomizes the burst of artistic activity in this period, all the more significantly in that he was creative enough to develop without caring for the consequences, or indeed for the loss of popularity and reputation.

This is perhaps not easy to understand at such a distance in thought and time from the Vienna of these two decades, but one fact and one distinguished critic's opinion can speak for Wagner. When, at the end of 1898, the Archduke Rainer, co-founder of the Museum of Applied Arts some thirty-five years before, withdrew his patronage, a new board was appointed by the Minister of Public Worship and Education to include Oberbaurat Professor Wagner, 'the most important representative of modern thought in Austria'.[1] In a revealing passage, Werner Hofmann describes those that were the real pioneers of this time. He puts Otto Wagner and his doctrine of realistic architecture, which, he points out, became more and more evident in his later work, before Freud's discoveries, Karl Kraus's social-critical opinions on language, or even the moral aesthetics of Adolf Loos.[2]

Otto Kolomann Wagner was born in 1841 in Penzing near Schönbrunn, then a village just outside Vienna. His father was a lawyer, and he was educated first at the Academic Gymnasium and then at the Benedictine boarding-school at Kremmünster. He was directly influenced in his formative years by four architects who were all involved in the building of the Ringstrasse, the most important feature of nineteenth-century Vienna, and which gives it its present-day character.

On 20 December 1857 an imperial patent in Franz Joseph's own hand had ordered the demolition of the fortifications around the old city, the real reason being to prevent the citizens barricading themselves inside the city as they had done in 1848. Beyond the fortifications lay an area 600 paces from the wall, in which it was decreed, after the second siege of Vienna in 1683, that nothing might be built. On this new ground a ring avenue four kilometres long and fifty-seven metres wide was laid, and the Ringstrasse ceremoniously opened in 1865.[3] It enclosed the old city on three sides (along the fourth, from north-west to south-east, runs the Danube Canal), and where important streets from the Josefstädter Strasse to the Mariahilfer Strasse converged onto the Hofburg, potential insurgents were confronted by a stone wall at least one metre high with a fence of cast iron three metres high, behind which troops could easily defend the centre.

To walk along the Ringstrasse is to survey nineteenth-century Viennese architecture as Wagner would have seen it. Historicism had its own tenets and iconographical rules: a parliament building was associated with Athens and law-giving, a town-hall with the guilds of northern France and Flanders, while universities recalled the Renaissance and Florence of the Medicis. The *Ringstrassenstil* has been described by the historian Hugo Hantsch as that of 'liberalism and economic optimism, expressing at the same time the break-up of a period no longer governed by a unifying way of life'.

Theophil von Hansen (1813-91) was born in Copenhagen, and trained as an architect there and in Athens. His Heinrichshof, an apartment block opposite the opera house, largely destroyed in 1945 and later pulled down, was built between 1861 and 1863 in a Renaissance historicist style, and Wagner was one of the first to move into it. Wagner was such an able student of civil engineering at the Polytechnic Institute (now the Technical University) that Hansen advised him to go to the Royal Building School in Berlin. Hansen later built the Academy of Fine Arts at which Wagner was himself a pupil from 1861 under August Siccard von Siccardsburg and Eduard van der Nüll and at which he was later to teach. Wagner also worked for a short time with Ludwig von Förster, one of the architects who had submitted plans for the Ringstrasse, and who like others won a prize but like others did not see them

From Meyers Konversations-Lexicon
(Vienna 1897)
Photo Gert Rosenberg

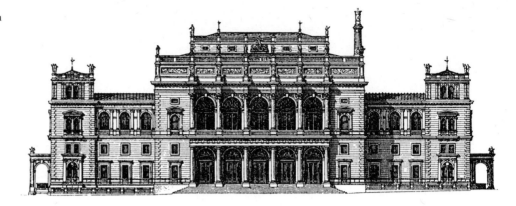

Theophil Hansen
Stock Exchange

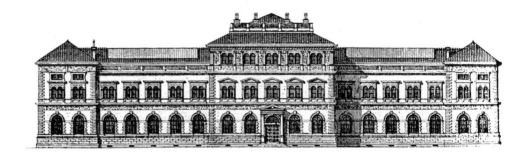

Heinrich Ferstel
Museum für Angewandte Kunst

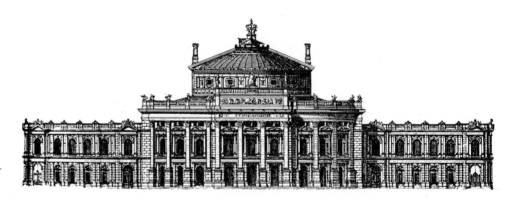

Karl Hasenauer and Gottfried Semper
Burgtheater

carried out, as had also happened to the designs by Wagner's two teachers at the Academy. With Hansen, Förster designed the splendid Army Museum near the arsenal (1850-6) in the 'Moorish-Lombardic' style.

The first building at the north-west end of the Ringstrasse is the Rossauer barracks in the 'Windsor' style, completed in 1870 to designs by a colonel and a major. It is a large, gloomy, red and pink toy castle famous for the omission of any lavatory facilities. On the opposite side is Hansen's Börse, a Renaissance-style, orange terracotta-brick Stock Exchange, completed in 1877.

The town-hall was the most important commission of Friedrich Schmidt, a Württemberger, born in 1825, who assisted in the completion of the Vienna Stephansdom. The town-hall, a bleak, towering imitation of a Flemish guild-

46

hall, was built between 1872 and 1883, to the dismay of the aristocratic circles, on the site of a military parade ground. Later, when the Ringtheater burnt down in 1881 just before the second performance in Vienna of *The Tales of Hoffmann* and 386 persons were killed, Schmidt built the *Sühnhaus* ('house of expiation'), including a chapel, on the site. It was paid for with monies from the imperial private purse, and the rents went to various charities (Freud had his first practice in it). It was pulled down after severe damage in 1945.

In 1853 an attempt was made on the Emperor's life, and his brother, Archduke Maximilian, later to be the unfortunate Emperor of Mexico, initiated a fund for a votive church (1856-79). One of the entrants was Schmidt, but the competition was won by Heinrich Ferstel, a Viennese, twenty-nine years of age. His design was of a French Gothic cathedral in miniature, with two spires flanking a rose window, but whose interior is dull compared with the strikingly deceptive exterior. It was in no way Neo-Gothic, but a copy of St Nicaise in Rheims destroyed during the Revolution. It stands in sight of his Italian Renaissance New University building of 1873-84. Like Wagner, Ferstel was a pupil of Nüll and Siccardsburg, and his least unimaginative building is the Museum of Applied Art and the attached school of 1868-71, at the further end of the Ringstrasse, again in Italian Renaissance red brick with majolica medallions and red and white bands of sgraffiti decoration. The school and museum are separated by a fountain with a mosaic by Salviati of Venice dated 1873. The interior has a covered cortile not unlike those by Barry. Of Ferstel it might be said that he created nothing original, but none of his buildings is offensive. His architecture epitomizes the historicism which confronted the young Wagner, and which it became his task to break through.

Further along the Ringstrasse, opposite Schmidt's Gothic cloth-hall Rathaus, is the new Burgtheater by Karl Hasenauer (1833-94) and the Hamburg architect, Gottfried Semper (1874-88), with an extravagant façade flanked by huge wings containing nothing but grand staircases. This gives it a theatre-like appearance, and the ceiling decorations have some of Klimt's earliest works, particularly the large *Theatre in Taormina* and *Globe Theatre* (1888). Further along, Hansen's Parliament, built as the Imperial council chamber (1873-83), is a long Greek classical block with Corinthian columns, and a pedimented entrance portico reached by high, curving carriage ramps. This building was so multi-purpose that Hansen was able to propose a version of it to the Athenians as their Academy building. The Viennese said that in the Parliament one could hear nothing, in the Rathaus one could see nothing, while in the Burgtheater one could neither see nor hear, and as so often with new theatres considerable alterations had to be carried out immediately after it was opened.

After the fire at the Ringtheater the regulations for theatres were considerably tightened, with the direct result that both the Burgtheater and the opera house stand on island sites, which adds to their importance as monuments besides providing quick egress to the street and access for fire-engines.

Alongside the Parliament the small Palais Epstein is another not unpleasant Italianate essay by Hansen (1870-3) in which caryatids support a portico with a stucco and faience façade, now somewhat obscured by a tram-station.

Opposite the Hofburg and at right angles to the axis of the Ringstrasse, an imperial 'new forum' was planned. It was to stretch from Montoyer's neo-classical Ceremonial Hall across the Ringstrasse to the Imperial Mews on the far side of what is now the Maria-Theresia-Platz, and, although not entirely completed, it remains probably the most important complex of monumental Germanic nineteenth-century town-planning. Outside the Ringstrasse stand the two museums of art and natural history, whose principal architect was Karl Hasenauer, another pupil of Nüll and Siccardsburg. Linking the museums to the Hofburg was to be a new wing to contain the state and reception rooms, lacking in the original palace. Opposite this, on the Heldenplatz, there was to be a further block, or at least, a matching colonnade with a concave exedra as in the completed wing. Semper was called in to complete the exterior of the museum blocks, and complained bitterly that he had to do a great deal of the detailed drawings himself. He was also involved with work in the Neue Burg, which dragged on into the First World War, and the costly expense at such a time so annoyed the young Emperor Karl that he only visited the site once. In fact, the new wing was never completed as planned and now houses part of the National Library and various museums. The first designs by Semper and Hasenauer for the Neue Burg were dated 1871, the second 1881, and building began in 1881-94 under Hasenauer. In 1897-9 Emil Förster altered the garden front, the windows on the main front, and the stairs into the gardens. Friedrich Ohmann, a *Jugendstil* architect, took over and was responsible for the grandiose palmhouse, and finally, in 1907-13, Ludwig Baumann completed the exterior and the extremely intricate and contorted main staircase. Although broken by the severe classicism of Peter de Nobile's Burgtor of 1824, the new forum is imposing enough, and the two museums with their domed stair halls, between which stands Maria Theresa's monument, form a conspicuous and characteristic centre to nineteenth-century Vienna.

Beyond Hansen's pink terracotta Academy of Fine Arts (1872-6), also in the Italianate Renaissance style, and containing an important ceiling, *The Fall of the Titans* (by Anselm Feuerbach), stands the opera house. Imposing rather than handsome, it was soon described as a 'sinking crate', because Siccardsburg had assumed the road level was to be considerably lower, so that the building would have appeared to stand slightly higher on a modest plinth. Van der Nüll's decoration had elements of Venetian and Spanish-French Gothic, Florentine and French Renaissance, and Neo-Classicism. Not surprisingly this eclectic mix-up was not very well received, in spite of the cooperation of the best known artists. Typically, two bronze Pegasus groups were found to be too heavy to crown the arcaded entrance front, so they were sold to Philadelphia and replaced by more elegant works. The criticisms made of the building caused van der Nüll to commit suicide and Siccardsburg to die either of grief or a heart attack in 1868. The building was completed by F. Schönthaler in 1869, being opened in May of that year. This Staatsoper, almost more than anything else in Vienna, exemplifies the hazards of official art, for the demands of grandeur have met in such an extreme form that anything other than a sense of occasion has been lost. In it, the heartless ceremonial and ruthless etiquette of the régime has been petrified and turned to stone. There was only one new feature, namely that, unlike the Paris and Dresden opera houses, the auditorium foyers and scenery tower were all contained under a long, convex copper roof.

Further east along the Ringstrasse behind the Hotel Imperial (built originally as a palace for the Duke of Württemberg) stands Hansen's Musikverein concert hall (1867-9), which possibly due to its classical Renaissance interior, is somewhat of a relief after the opera house. Further on, beyond the Stadtpark, stands Ferstel's Museum of Applied Art. On the same side stands Ludwig Baumann's former War Ministry, the latest and the most boring of all the Ringstrasse constructions. Its only interest to us is that both Wagner and Loos submitted designs but Baumann (who, as mentioned, was involved in completing the Neue Burg) won the competition. It was completed in 1913, the last year of imperial peace. Opposite it on the Georg Coch-Platz is Wagner's important and forward-looking Post Office Savings Bank (1904-6). Finally the ring is closed on the edge of the Danube Canal by an adult education centre, the Urania, built in 1910 by Max Fabiani (1865-1962), an underrated Yugoslav, who worked for a time with Wagner. The Urania is not particularly conspicuous, except for the rebuilt Olbrich-like observatory tower, but his Artaria building for the map and music publisher on the Kohlmarkt of 1902 must have influenced Loos when he built the nearby shop on the Michaelerplatz in 1910. The lattice top halves of the windows, with their slight bays, suggest an English accent, and were used by Loos again in the Michaelerplatz while the strong profile of the cornice is a courteous reference to Wagner. Another secessionist detail is the decorative openwork metal cornice of Fabiani's office-block faced with yellow and green tiles in the Ungargasse. It was designed for the builders, Portois and Fix, who were responsible for the interior of the still standing house of Demel, the famous pastry-cook and *Konditorei*.

We are perhaps still too near in time to view the Ringstrasse with the necessary critical detachment. The architects were technically advanced, but their constructions were clad with a series of less than imaginative costumes from a standard wardrobe. No one can deny that the general effect has an imperial grandeur, but, while splendid, it is not beautiful. Historicism was ideal for the conservative builders of the new capital and forum, but generally it was no more inspired than later essays under the Italian and German fascist empires. All the more remarkable therefore is the breakthrough by Wagner and his younger contemporaries while still within and dominated by the Habsburg empire.

There was nothing particularly bold about Wagner's early designs up to the Villa Wagner of 1886-8, except his decorations for Makart's procession for the imperial silver wedding celebrations of 1879 (in which Klimt was also involved) and for the reception of Princess Stephanie of Belgium in 1881 on the occasion of her arrival in Vienna to marry Crown Prince Rudolf. His first villa, built in 1863, almost outside Vienna on the Hüttelbergstrasse, at first glance appears to be Roman or Pompeian with a high entrance portico approached by a double stair. Four columns reach to a flattened roof with extremely wide eaves as practical protection from snow. To the right and left two colonnades of pergolas, whose columns were surmounted by pepperpot finials, were filled in in 1900 to make studios or conservatories decorated with coloured secessionist glass. On closer appraisal, however, one appreciates that the villa really owes little to anyone. Wagner, though not averse to decoration, was never to let his buildings disappear behind the fancy-dress of historicism.

In his monograph on Wagner, Heinz Geretsegger commented that he demystified art.[4] Wagner himself said that there must be a break with the idea that churches and town-halls be Gothic, parliament buildings and museums Greek, and private houses Renaissance. In the comments on his pamphlet, *Plan for the General Regulation of the City of Vienna* (1893) he stated that the

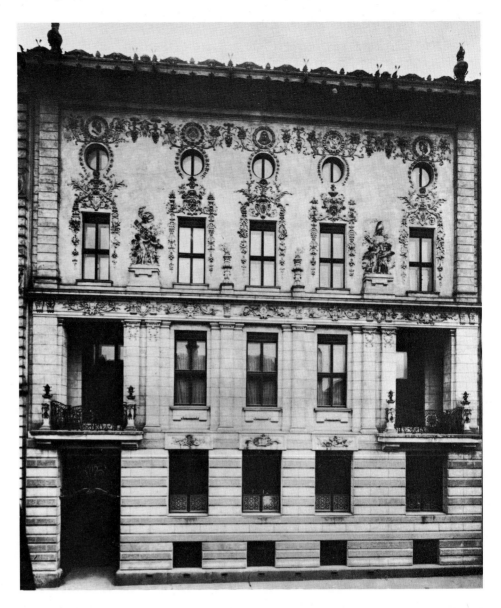

architect must work from three principles: he must grasp the functional requirements; he must use material that is both durable, and easily worked and maintained; and his design must be simple and economic. If these rules were followed, the form would emerge of its own accord. Although his early architecture could not be said to be entirely functional, if that is taken to mean without decoration, yet it functioned well and still does. He was also one of the first architects to appreciate the importance of statistical data.

From the first Villa Wagner onwards, his work was to have more and more the imprint of his original personality. If an 'alien quality' has been the first thing that some people have noticed about his work, Geretsegger and Peinter have commented that this has blinded critics to his highly original technical qualities. This is borne out by his next building, the Palais Wagner (later Hoyos, now the Yugoslav Embassy) on the Rennweg (1890-1). Outwardly, this has the same type of discreet decoration as the so-called *Hosenträger*

50

(trouser braces or suspenders) apartment house of two years before, so-called because of the strap-work scrolling between the windows. Inside, the plan reveals a careful arrangement so that the master's rooms and his studio were kept entirely separate from areas which could be used by servants. Wagner was always building houses and apartment blocks on a speculatory basis and for this reason was constantly moving his own home.

In 1893 Wagner won one of the two prizes for the regulation of the City of Vienna. In the next year the artistic association of the Künstlerhaus, of which he was a member, proposed him to be artistic adviser to the Vienna Transport Commission, formed as a result of the Vienna Transport Act of 1892 which stated that the regulation of the River Wien, the Danube Canal and the metropolitan railway were to be treated as one operation. Wagner gained the day, in spite of British and French competition, and from 1894-1901 he was engaged on the Nussdorf dam on the Danube Canal and with no less than six lines of the metropolitan railway. The combination of engineering and architecture has stood without any significant changes for seventy-five years. Apart from the railway running just below street level from Schönbrunn to the centre, Wagner was responsible for the covering-in of the river along the Wienzeile and the removal of the Naschmarkt vegetable market from the Karlsplatz to the new space won above the river. He envisaged the Wienzeile as a grand access road to Schönbrunn.

The Nussdorf dam, besides being handsome to look at, employed new techniques, and only in 1972 were any major alterations necessary. The administration block, with jutting eaves, a flat roof, a functional observation bay window and a control post on the roof itself, is unmistakably his. A vast undertaking, it used 40,000 blocks of granite in the abutments. Characteristic of his later style for this kind of work is the control block of the Kaiserbad dam in the centre of the city, built in 1906-7, for which white marble blocks were bolted onto the walls and the roofing over the crane driver's cabin is made of corrugated copper; a simple strip of cobalt blue tiling, throughout which run three stylized waves of white to symbolize the tamed Danube, provides decoration.

His court pavilion on the metropolitan railway, as well as other stations, also uses corrugated copper roofing, while a feature of most stations was the exposed T and I girders. With the passion for change that is strangely characteristic of the otherwise so conservative Viennese, many of the stations have been altered, perhaps paying off Wagner for his many alterations to the face of the city. Nevertheless his railings featuring a central rosette or patera motif can be seen as far afield as Dubrovnik, and his railway in most of its essentials still forms part of the Vienna scene, and now carries far more people than originally planned.

A department store (1895) on the Kärntnerstrasse and the Anker building which still survives on the Graben both had uncompromising curtain walls of glass from the ground to the top of the first floor. The Anker building has in addition a glass pavilion on the roof built as a photographic studio, and looking like a miniature palmhouse.

Wagner hoped that the Wienzeile would become an important axis for traffic, which to some extent it has. Along it, at numbers 38 and 40, he built his first secessionist buildings in 1898-9, at the time he joined the newly founded society. Together with number 3 Köstlergasse inside the corner they form a coherent group. The furthermost, number 40, is the Majolica House. Like

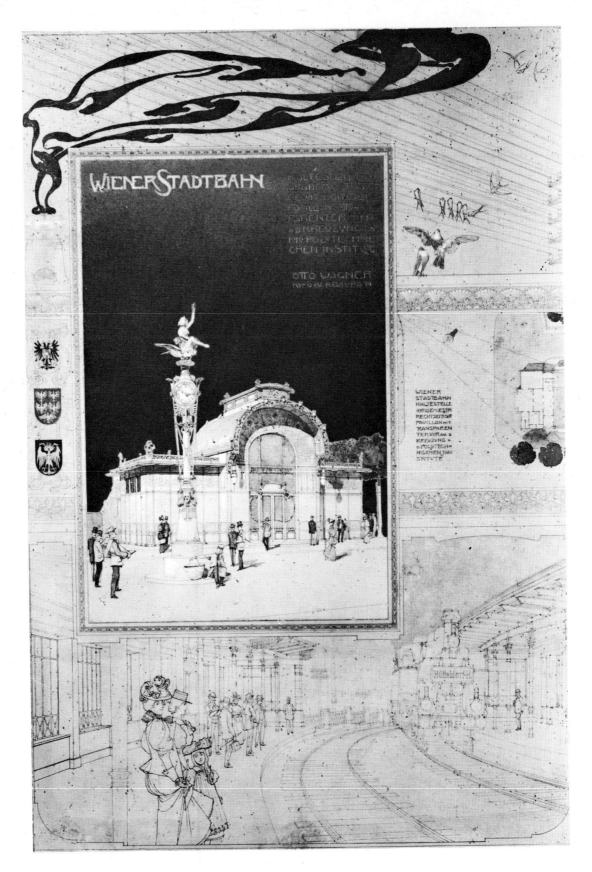

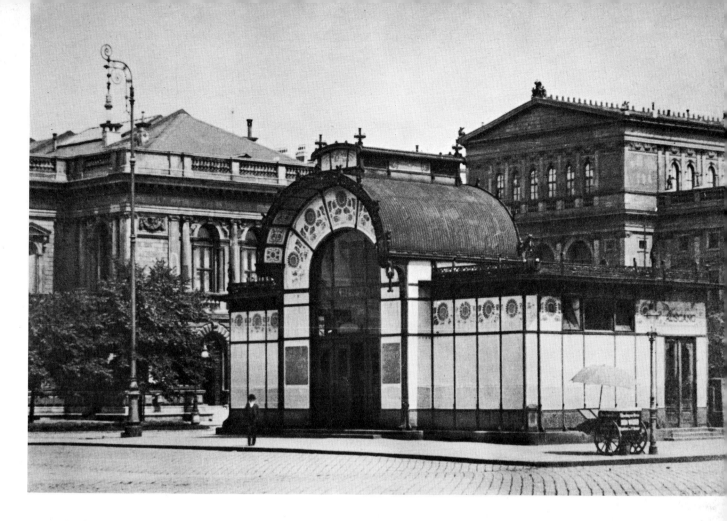

several of his buildings, both earlier and later, it has an extremely severe façade by virtue of its plain windows without lintels. (Later in 1910 Loos's apartment store on the Michaelerplatz was to be criticized for having windows without 'eyebrows'.) All three blocks have the characteristic projecting eaves, while number 40 has a decorated cornice with a vestigial modillion bracket. Number 40 derives its name from the fact that the whole front above the second floor balconies was faced with a warm, terracotta-coloured majolica on which a red flower design, about half a metre in diameter, branches out from the centre over the whole façade. Between each window of the top storey a formalized bunch of red and blue flowers surrounds a lion's head in high relief. Wagner's intention was that the whole front could be sluiced down for cleaning by the fire-brigade. In fact majolica is a fairly unusual cladding material for Vienna, although, as we have seen, Fabiani's Portois and Fix building of two years later, made use of it. The Majolica House has withstood the cold winters of Vienna far better than most buildings, whose stucco and plasterwork facing is easily undermined by frost and damp. Nevertheless, Joseph August Lux, Wagner's constant chronicler and biographer, hoped that it would be forgotten on the grounds that it was a less successful building than much of Wagner's other work. Number 38 next door towards the city was linked to it by a tier of balconies with majolica greenery in the reveals and recesses. The façades were rendered in dead white. Between the uppermost windows sprays of golden palms with chains of golden rain fell, halfway down the façade, and above them and under the stylized palms were golden medallions. Their artist was Koloman Moser (1868-1918), a founder member

Otto Wagner
Stadtbahnstation 1898-9
Cast and corrugated iron stone cladding, in Karlsplatz (in the background stand the Künstlerhaus and Musikverein)
Photo Austrian National Library

Opposite:
Otto Wagner
Studio Drawing of the Stadtbahnstation, Karlsplatz 1899
68 × 49 cm./27 × 19 in.
Historisches Museum der Stadt Wien, photo Museum

53

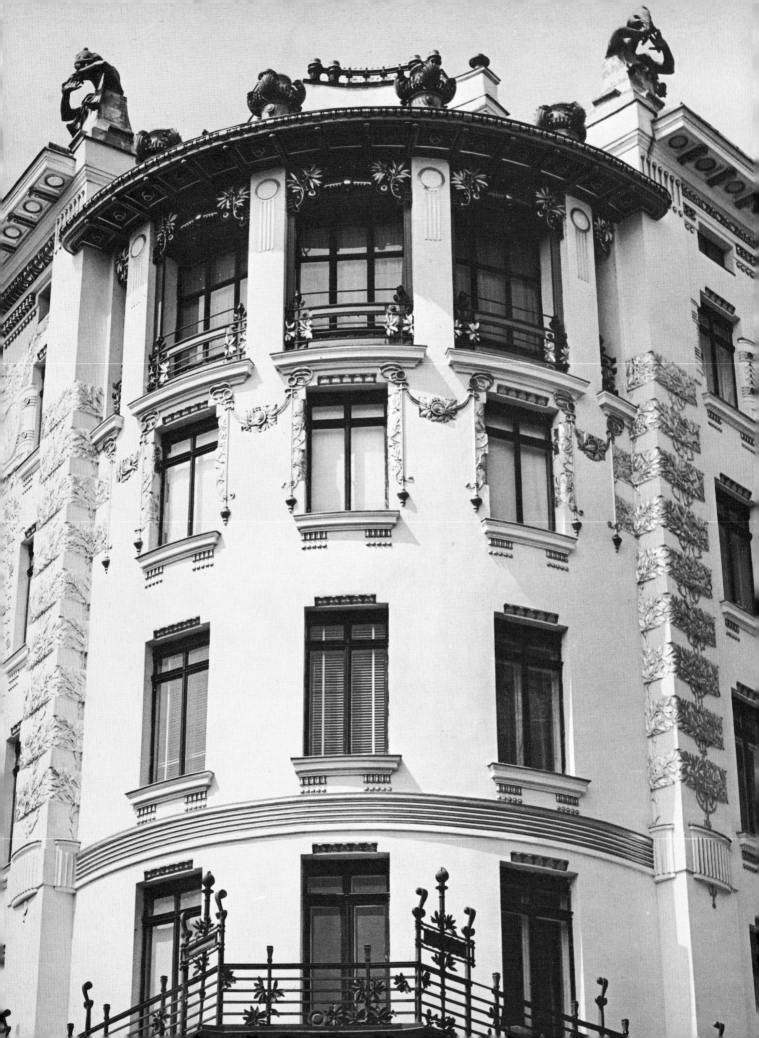

of the Secession. Four half-length, gilded sitting figures by Othmar Schimkowitz (1864-1947) surmounted the corner of both this house and that round the corner. Both artists were to collaborate with Wagner again, on the Steinhof church. Moser designed the stained glass windows, while the sculptor also made the acroteria for the Post Office Savings Bank. From 1929-30 Schimkowitz was president of the Secession.

In both 38 and 40, the oval staircase spirals round a well straightened at the centre for a lift. The *Jugendstil* iron-work in shining white metal has 'poppy heads' picked out in red with blue enamel slashes. The stairs sweep round in an agreeable incline, with only modest risers, which is remarkable considering the restricted use of space. It is a great advance on the apartment house at Stadiongrasse 6 of 1883, when the stair in the entrance hall, although on a grand scale, requires the whole depth of the building to rise to half the height of the first floor. In the Wienzeile buildings, Wagner adhered to his principles of new techniques and simplicity of materials, but their appearance not only broke with tradition, and affronted the conservative establishments of which he was supposed to be part, but they affirmed his adherence to the breakaway ideals of the Secession.

Quite apart from this conflict Wagner could have been thought to be a disappointed man, for he produced many more projects and designs than were ever carried out. In the early days he had sent in designs for the Berlin Reichstag and cathedral, and in 1900 had made an important series of designs for the Karlsplatz. Ironically, the only new buildings other than the Secession building of his pupil Olbrich to be completed on the Karlsplatz was his own station for the metropolitan railway, which was later altered and has now been removed, and a modernist museum built in 1959 on the very site that he had proposed for his own Kaiser Franz Joseph City Museum. In 1905, he competed for the Peace Palace in the Hague, for the War Ministry building in 1907-8, for various libraries and museums, and in 1917, with a certain bizarrerie, for an Armistice Church. The most ambitious series he designed for a rebuilt Academy of Arts and a second design for the City Museum on the manoeuvre field of the Schmelz. In 1902, however, he did win the competition for the Church of the Lower Austrian Mental Institution, and in the next year, by fulfilling the requirements specification for the Post Office Savings Bank. This was built in two phases, first from 1904-6 on the longer side of a trapezoid area freed by Wagner's own regulation of the Stubenviertel, second between 1910 and 1912 behind the main banking hall.

The Post Office had demanded stability, so for the first time Wagner faced a building with sheets of white Sterzing marble, using bolts of aluminium at the corners, decorated with Schimkowitz's winged figures, over life-size, at the corners of the main façade. These were in aluminium, as were the now famous cylindrical hot-air blowers in the banking hall, the casings from the girder pillars in the same area, and the thin columns supporting the marquise that protected the entrance. The banking hall is vaulted with a glass ceiling suspended on bars. Above it, fixed beams support a glass roof, a special feature of which was a built-in air heating system to melt snow. To give light the well is lined with white tiling decorated in black, and all areas visible to the public are faced with marble or glass. For the offices, Wagner designed adjustable partitions and used beams of reinforced concrete for the ceilings. All the furniture and detailing was to a standard design and most of it is preserved, including the black and grey committee room still intact with its stylized

Opposite:
Otto Wagner
Wienzeile 38 1898
With figures by Othmar
Schimkowitz, medallions by
Kolo Moser
Photo Gert Rosenberg

55

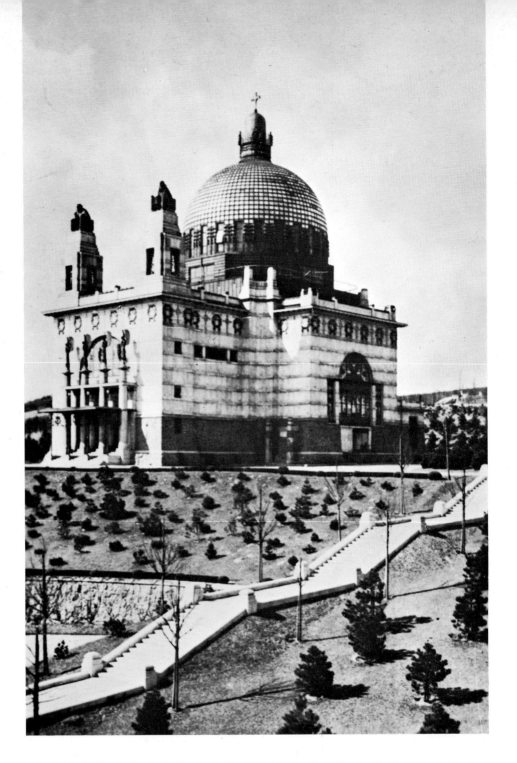

portrait of Franz Joseph. The attic floor is faced with black glass. In the corridors a discreet use of chequered black mosaic tiling matches that of the light well. The public staircase, which has his usual low risers, has an upright at right angles to the traffic with almost the only colour in the whole scheme – ten centimetre squares of bright blue glass, and aluminium bolt heads, stair-rails and air ducts. The functional banking hall, which used unclad girders and glass flooring to light the basement, still looks new today. Furthermore the space was so well thought out that, in spite of increasing demands upon it, the building remains adequate for its function.

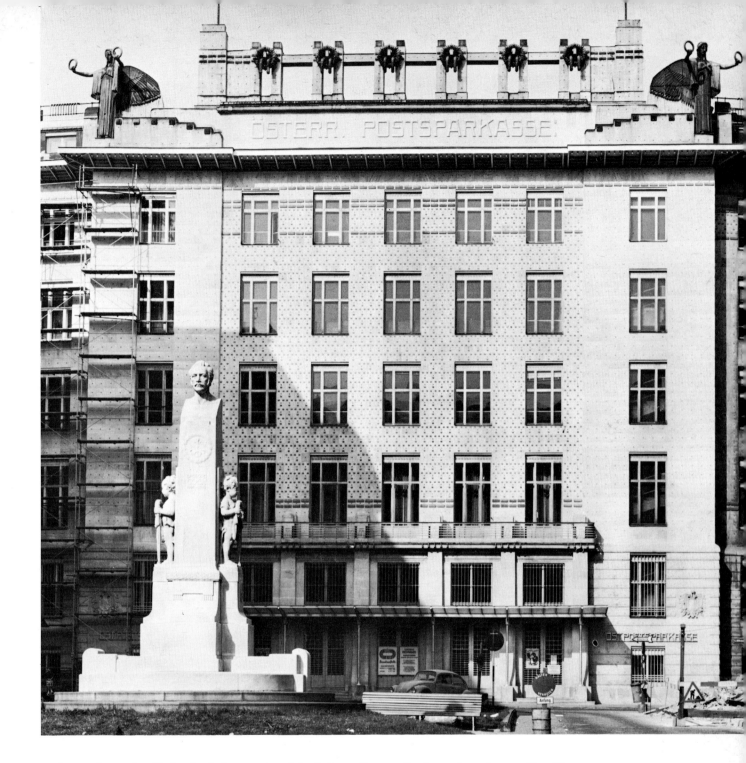

Apart from the Kaiserbad dam control building of 1904-8, the only other occasion on which Wagner was able to use marble sheets bolted to the façade was the church in the Vienna mental hospital at Am Steinhof. This stands at the top of a fairly steep slope on the edge of the Vienna woods, and in his original designs Wagner suggested that the various pavilions be arranged to fall like steps in front of the hill. Although his designs were consulted, he did not in fact build the pavilions. The church was completed in two years from 1905-7, but some of the interior mosaic decoration was not finished until 1913.

Based on a Greek cross plan, with a centrally built block, a projecting west

Otto Wagner
Post Office Savings Bank 1904-6
Main front
Photo Gert Rosenberg

Otto Wagner
Design for Neustiftgasse 40 1909-10
Rendered stone and black tiles
Photo Austrian National Library

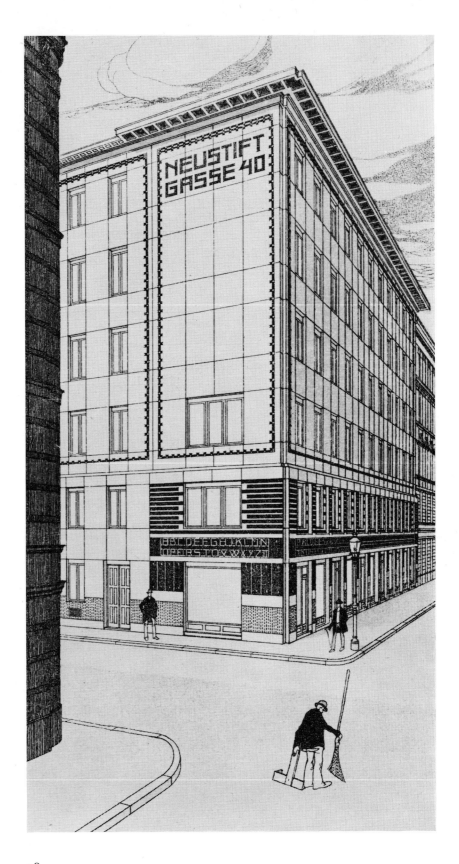

end leads to a portico flanked by two towers and topped by massive statues of sitting saints. Above the whole width of the church a gilded copper dome, surmounted by a lantern, rests on a drum, but inside the effect is quite different, for there is a false dome half the height of the whole with accented corner groins, and a barrel-vault over the prolongation to the portico. This is to provide adequate acoustics, while allowing the exterior to make the maximum impression from a distance. In order to prevent glare the lighting comes only from Moser's stained glass windows on each side. The festive entrance has a somewhat Roman canopy of narrow bronze pillars with two garlands at the heads, and these are repeated on a gigantic scale as a frieze interspersed with crosses of copper running below the strongly projecting cornice. In the technical detail Wagner was thorough: there are concealed heating ducts; the holy water was piped 'to prevent infection'; there were separate entrances to right and left for male and female patients. The pews were only four places wide, so that the nurses could reach patients easily. There was an almost imperceptible slope down towards the altar, which was itself raised high above the congregation. The copper dome was built on a light girder construction over a wooden shell. The false ceiling was built on a framework of narrow T girders, with small, square composition (Rabitz) panels retained by gilded copper bolts. The copper tiles of the dome had a lip to fend off hail, and the marble cladding was held in place with copper screw bolts. Although not as decorative as some of his unexecuted designs for churches, it was to some extent a projection of his theory of the modern church in the round, a combination of the Pantheon and a gasometer, and of which there are some fairly splendiferous examples in Vienna, built inside of a brick framework, like *vol-au-vent* cases.

The church enhanced Wagner's reputation, yet his last four buildings, though extremely advanced and interesting, are modest. Beginning in 1910 he built an apartment house in the Neustiftgasse, which had a flat and studio for himself, a studio for Josef Hoffmann and a studio for part of the Wiener Werkstätte. It has a plain rendered front enlivened only by black glassed, tiled strips. The door has an aluminium lower section, and the stair rails were so 'modern' that it is hard to believe that the block was not built in the twenties. As with the Wienzeile buildings the block was continued with a further wing into the Döblergasse in 1912, so that it merges with the first section as if one.

From 1910-12 he built the Lupus sanatorium. It looks slightly less 'modern', that is to say it is more decorated than the apartment block in the Neustiftgasse and has a somewhat Egyptian look.

Wagner was sixty-nine when he started his last Neustiftgasse block of flats. In 1914, at the age of seventy-two, he was thinking of going to Australia for which he had been asked to plan a capital, but in April 1918, being too proud to seek or eat food from the black market, he died of erysipelas and malnutrition. His work lives, and of his pupils the best known are Rudolf M. Schindler in America, who worked for Frank Lloyd Wright for many years and became his chief assistant,[5] Josef Olbrich, Josef Plečnik and Josef Hoffmann.

The Secession: Olbrich and Plečnik

Josef Maria Olbrich was born in Troppau in Austrian Silesia (Opava) on 22 December 1867. When he died in Düsseldorf on 8 August 1908, thirty-one, his working life had been only ten years. From 1890-3 he was a pupil of Karl Hasenauer at the Academy of Fine Arts in Vienna, at a time when Hasenauer was occupied with the Neue Burg. In 1894, thanks to winning the Rome prize of the Academy, he travelled through Italy and North Africa, and in the year after, visited France, England and Germany. Beginning in 1893 he worked in Wagner's studio for five years, mostly on the railway project. One of the founder members of the Secession in 1897, it was he who was chosen to design the Secession building. On 27 April 1898 the foundation stone was laid on a site given by the city of Vienna, and six months later, on 12 November, the Secession's second exhibition was able to be held in its own building. Since the first exhibition had been a considerable financial success, and the artists involved gave their services free, not only were costs kept to a minimum but the building went up extremely rapidly. It is remarkable that a young architect should have obtained such an important commission, for as Olbrich said, it was his dream house. The first sketches showed two strongly pronounced columns projected in front of the entrance, but these receded and disappeared altogether as the gilded cupola gained in importance in his projects. The result is a series of cubes with four stacks surrounding the cupola. The whole was

Josef Olbrich
Wiener Secession photograph c. 1905
With Arthur Strasser's *Marc Antony*
on the right
Photo Austrian National Library

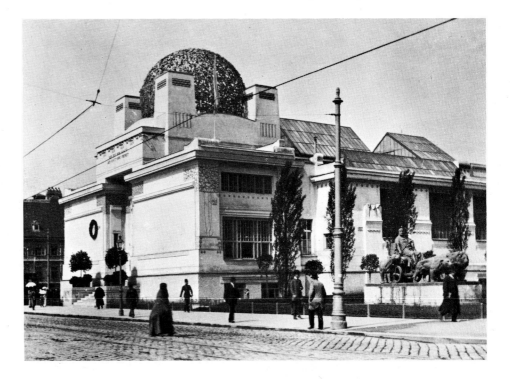

rendered in white stucco, and picked out with gilded and incised decorations, not unlike Wagner's Wienzeile number 38 nearby. Originally, there was a frieze of dancing girls in sgraffito by Kolo Moser on the back of the building but this has since disappeared. The cupola measures five metres in diameter, and is made of gilded open cast-iron work, with 3,000 laurel leaves each thirty centimetres long and 700 berries about the size of a fist. It was known at once as the 'gilded cabbage'. The interior provided for both side and ceiling lighting, and contained movable partitions, so that the exhibition spaces could be adapted as required. In 1899 Olbrich wrote of it in *Der Architekt*:

> 'It was to have walls white and shining, holy and modest. A serious dignity such as crept over and shook me as I stood alone before the unfinished sanctuary of Segesta. I only wanted to hear my own sensibility and see my own warm feelings congeal into cold walls. I had to see my house as I had dreamed it.'

It is a long march from the Greek temple of Segesta in the quiet hills of western Sicily to the noisy Friedrichstrasse of Vienna, yet Pevsner considers this building to be one of the pioneer works of modern design. It had an immense impact. Various critics have pointed out its influence on Sullivan's Wainwright Grave (Pevsner), Townsend's Whitechapel Art Gallery (Schmutzer), some of Mackintosh's plans (Howarth), and some of Mendelson's drawings of 1914 (Sharp). There is a deliberate air of mystery about it. Dark red marble stairs lead steeply into a white cleft, flanked to right and left by real laurel bushes – an idea that possibly goes back to Olbrich's drawing of a tomb seen in Posillipo (1893 or 1894). Minerva's owls in threes form part of the outer decoration. Over the door is written a motto 'To every era its art, to art its freedom'. Immediately above the bronze-clad doors glower three masks designed by Georg Klimt. Despite these decorative elements the building is very much anti-historicist, and intentionally contrasts with the *Ringstrassenstil* of the Künstlerhaus across the Karlsplatz, from which its members had broken away.

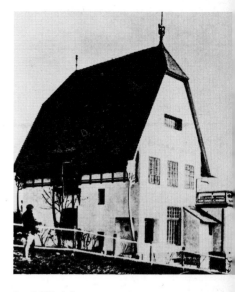

Josef Olbrich
Villa Bahr 1900
Linzerstrasse 22, Vienna XIII
Photo Historisches Museum der
Stadt Wien

Apart from a grave for the Klarwil family in the Döbling cemetery, Olbrich worked on only three more buildings in or near Vienna, all of them villas. The first was the Villa Friedmann at Hinterbrühl in 1898, in which high-pitched gable roofs and projecting eaves crown an upper, partly glazed, balcony, endowing the house with a distinctly 'Chinese' appearance. This was followed in 1899 by the house for Dr Stöhr in St Pölten, which has arched triple windows beneath a rounded roof, and 'English' lattice-work windows. (This rounded roof antedates Loos's one in the Sauraugasse by fourteen years.) In the same year Olbrich did a number of designs for interior decorations, including the 'Wiener Interieur' for the World Exhibition of Paris (1900). His last Viennese building was the villa for Hermann Bahr, the author and director of the Burgtheater, just outside Vienna in Ober St Veit, completed in 1900. Ludwig Hevesi described it then:

> 'It is a genuine house in the country, where village and town mingle together, not an imitated Swiss chalet, an Italian villa, a Mansard hotel in miniature from Meudon, or a chalet from Trouville, and least of all the castle of a German robber knight in a nut-shell. It really appears to grow from the living earth, like a farmhouse and the acacia tree.'

Despite this, it has affinities with not a few of the types against which Hevesi

61

was protesting. It was all but square with a high-pitched, half-hipped gable roof of light pink tiles, decorated with one or two green glass stripes, and a gable window. The most notable features were a kind of barge board at each gable repeated half-way down the house which was carved and painted green with red blossoms to represent the branches of bushes whose stems sprouted out from the base of the walls and rejoined their branching tops. Olbrich demanded and obtained whitewash-rendered plaster, despite the local builders' objections as they were used only to coloured washes. The curve of the carving joined the floor to the roof and held the whole design together. Alas, the house is unrecognizable today, since all that remains of its original design is the line of the roof.

Also in 1899, Olbrich attempted his first industrial design, a suite of glasses and a jug in colourless glass for the firm of Bakalowits in Vienna. In the same year Wagner tried to get him appointed to a post at the School of Applied Arts in Vienna, but he was called to be a founder member of the artist's colony in Darmstadt by the enlightened Grand Duke Ernst Ludwig of Hesse, the patron of international *Jugendstil* and *Art Nouveau*. In 1904 Wagner again suggested Olbrich's name for a professorship at the Academy of Fine Arts in Vienna, but the post went to Ohmann. His further career–designs for houses, jewellery, ceramics, an Opel motor-car, the Hochzeitsturm and exhibition buildings in Darmstadt (1905-8), and the department stores, now the Kaufhof, in Düsseldorf (1906-8)–is distant in place if not in spirit from the Vienna of the Secession.[1]

Less spectacular, but no less important than Olbrich, was the Slovene, Josef Plečnik, who was born in 1872 at Gradisce near Maribor (Marburg), and died in Ljubljana in 1957. Having trained as a furniture designer in Graz, he became Wagner's pupil at the Academy in 1894-5 and again in 1897-8. From 1901 to 1909, he was a member of the Secession, and practised as an architect in Vienna from 1900-11. In 1920, he was called to lead a master class at the newly founded faculty of architecture at the University of Ljubljana, where he continued to build particularly interestingly, especially churches.

During his period as an architect in Vienna, he produced three important works. The Zacherlhaus on three sides of a block on the Brandstätte in the inner city of Vienna was commissioned by Johann Zacherl as a business and apartment block, and was built from 1903-5 in association with J. Tölk. The façade was faced with blocks of natural, warm, brown-pink stone, marked with pairs of parallel ribs, about fifty centimetres apart, and each pair separated by a space of about one metre. The windows were without sills or lintels. A band of metal decoration on the attic floor carried on upwards to a pronounced cornice, while above the mezzanine floor, a decorative band of light metal balustrading gave the effect of a vestigial balcony running round the block. In much of this there are signs of the faithful pupil of Wagner, particularly in the simple treatment of the façade and the use of cladding. Far more modern is the bold round curve of the right-hand front, which has, high above the attic floor, a round tambour. The whole is set off by a single gigantic figure, suspended on the main façade, of the Archangel Michael by Ferdinand Andri, president of the Secession at the time.

Plečnik's parish church, the Heiliggeistkirche on the Schmelz, built in 1910-11, was a rigorous essay in new forms, and an early example of purely reinforced concrete construction. Indeed the front is so severe that it looks as though it has been built entirely from a young giant's toy building blocks. For entrance

62

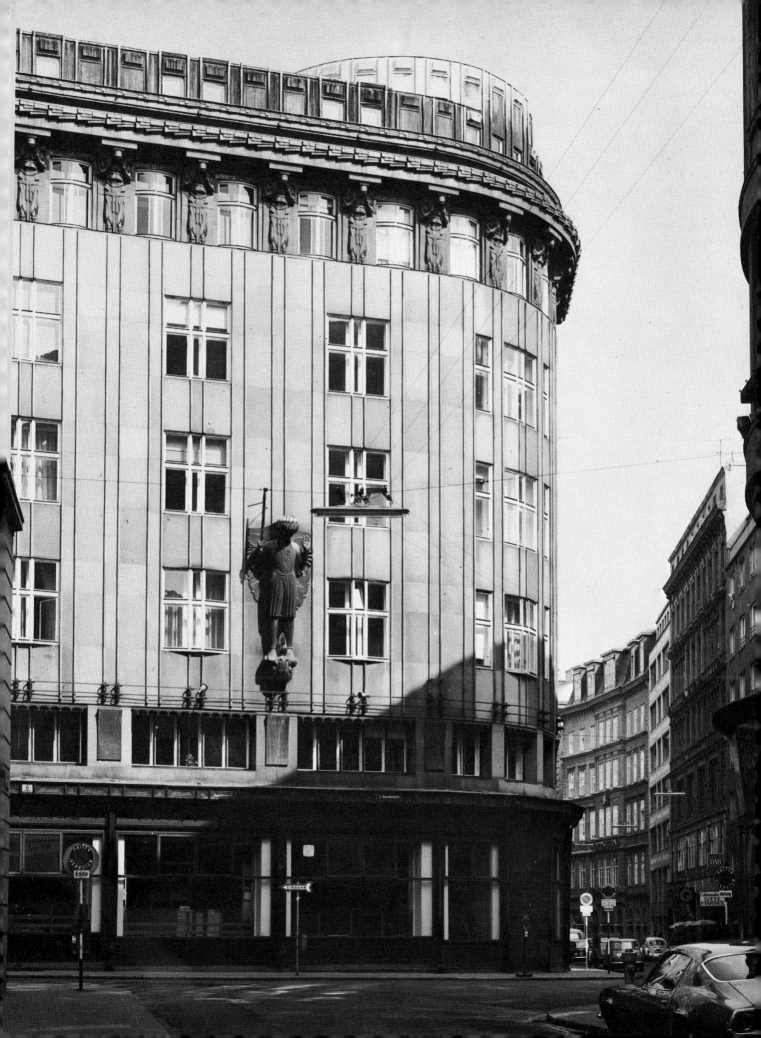

it has a stylized portico with octagonal pillars leading into a simple porch. Inside the equally uncompromising basilica there is an unsupported gallery on both sides, and an organ and choir loft. The balustrade supports square columns with a minute cornice at the roof. The ceiling is broken up with square cross beams. The chancel is approached from right and left and the altar area divided from the nave by an open rail, like a ship. The modern techniques combined with a neo-classical interior, are strangely countered by the crypt below the altar, which has a low ceiling supported by octagonal columns with capitals and bases in a primitive northern Gothic. In such a place Hunding could have worshipped on conversion to Christianity, and Plečnik here looks back nervously to the historicism which his master had forbidden. The church has been considerably altered since in the way that only piety knows, but quite apart from that, the complex was never completed as planned. There should have been a tower thirty metres high at the side, behind it a vicarage, and a hall on the other side.[2]

In the same year, Otto Schönthal (1878-1961), a pupil and collaborator of Wagner on the Post Office Savings Bank and the architect of the Friedens-brücke bridge in Vienna (1926), built the Villa Vojcsik at number 375 Linzerstrasse not far from the Wagner villas. It has the flat eaves and roof of the master, but delightful, almost wilful, *Jugendstil* motifs. There are rounded doors, grilles like mangers from a stable, but less useful, abstract ornaments, and realistic swags of greenery.[3]

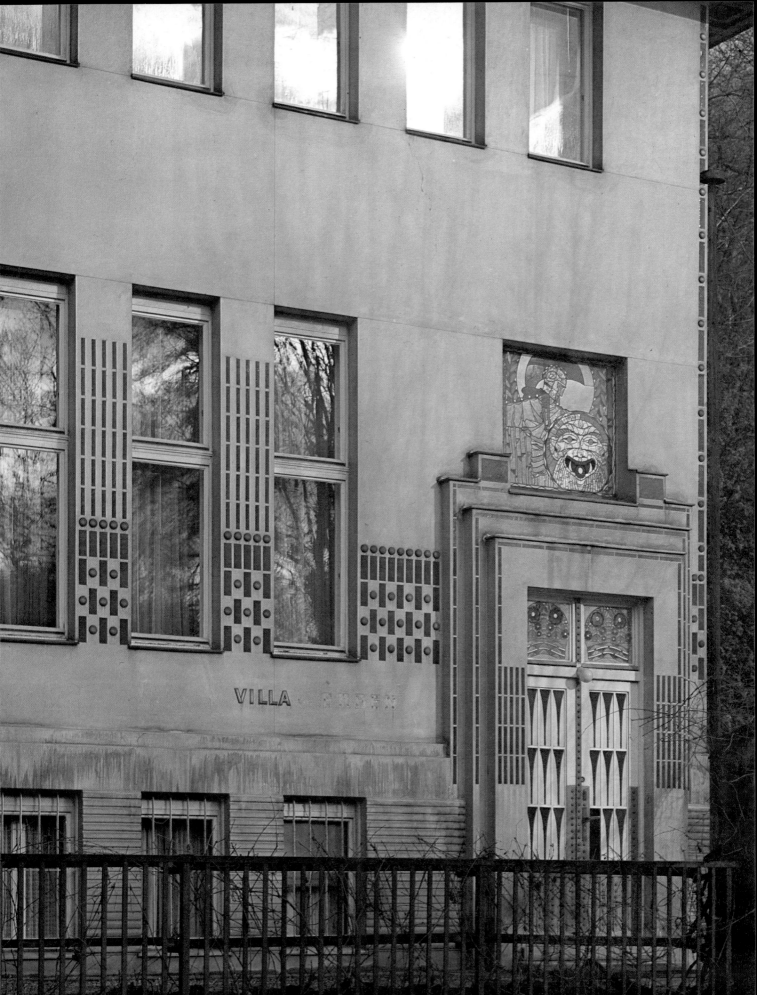

Josef Hoffmann and the Palais Stoclet

Josef Hoffmann lived until 1956. When he died, Wilhelm Mrazek said:

> 'The last representative of a great era had departed from his chosen sphere of activity. The City of Vienna hardly rewarded this loyal allegiance, and the generation that came after 1945 hardly knows his name.
>
> 'And yet, Vienna as a whole, to the exclusion of anything else, is alive in his creations and in the achievements of the Wiener Werkstätte. Both his and the Werkstätte's style is the Viennese one, which . . . sprang from an intrinsic relation to the tasks of the period, and from an understanding and awareness of the good and the beautiful in the old tradition.'[1]

The beliefs and ideas of the Secession coalesce in Hoffmann, and no single architect or interior decorator and designer is more typical of this epoch. His fabulous Palais Stoclet in Brussels, which houses Klimt's *Tree of Life* mosaic frieze, was the best *Gesamtkunstwerk* to be both realized and preserved (1905-11). His influence as a designer is still felt in Vienna even if not acknowledged. A coffee-set designed by him is still available from the Augarten porcelain manufacturer, and glasses and decanters from Lobmeyr (and incidentally a service by Loos as well). Hoffmann's finest glass service, with straight stems and upright sides inclining almost imperceptibly inwards, engraved with a formal design and filled in with black, can no longer be made as all the workmen with sufficient expertise have gone.

Hoffmann was born in Pirnitz (Brtnice, Moravia) on 5 December 1870. When Hasenauer died in 1894 and Wagner became the new professor of the Academy, he not only inherited Olbrich as his assistant, but Hasenauer's most promising student, then in his final year. (In turn, Wagner recommended Hoffmann to follow him as professor, but without success.) Hoffmann spent 1896 in Italy on a scholarship and worked for a further year in Wagner's studio which then numbered about seventy architects, engineers and draughtsmen. Then, from 1899 to 1937 Hoffman taught as a professor at the Vienna Kunstgewerbeschule. His activity as an architect started with the Purkersdorf sanatorium in 1903-5 and continued with little interruption; his last building being a block of flats for the city in 1952. Together with Kolo Moser and the young merchant, Fritz Wärndorfer, he founded the Wiener Werkstätte in 1903, which survived until 1932. He was a member of the Secession from 1897 until 1905, then again from 1938 to 1939 (when it was closed), and from 1945 until his death; from 1948-50 he was president. In 1912 he founded the Austrian Werkbund. The year before his death in Vienna on 7 May 1956 the Ministry of Education founded a Hoffmann Prize for Architecture in his honour.

While his villas in Vienna still remain, not one of his interior decorations has survived intact, mostly due to the astonishing Viennese passion for destruction and change. His greatest monument is not in Austria but in Brussels, and now it is not even possible to reconstruct his Austrian interiors, since the furniture, carpets, silver, decorations and textiles, which were all designed to harmonize, are dispersed. It is symptomatic of Austria's attitude to him that there is no adequate study of this many-sided, indeed dominating, figure.

Renate Wagner-Rieger, discussing Viennese architecture from late historicism to the Secession, that is from about 1880-1914, speaks of Wagner and his followers' 'proto-cubism'. In Loos's houses up to the beginning of the war she finds Biedermeier motifs, as in Hoffmann's villas of the same period. She follows Hoffmann's progress from an imaginative *Jugendstil* in his first designs, to a radical severity in his exhibition pavilion designs. 'During the first decade of the twentieth century, Hoffman changed this radical attitude for another, discernible in the design of his great *Gesamtkunstwerk*, the Palais Stoclet, in which there is mild expressionism, extending towards Neo-Classicism with a Viennese, Biedermeier touch.'[2] Hoffmann's architecture is worth examining in the light of these remarks, especially the Palais Stoclet. The Brussels palace was inextricably connected with the formation of the Werkstätte, and if we follow its development to the end in 1932, we shall indeed find a strong current of what we may call Neo-Biedermeier running through Hoffmann's own ideas and the artistic concepts of the Werkstätte, however outwardly modern they may have wished to appear.

To explain this, it is necessary to give a definition of Biedermeier.

'Originally it described a style of furniture, then also genre painting, and later the way of life of the whole period of the *Vormärz* (from 1815 to the 1848 revolution). The characteristics of Biedermeier "are often found in Europe generally, but above all in the Austria of Metternich's period" (W. Kayser). The most important cultural sphere of Biedermeier was the home. Furniture and smaller objects were practical, simple and unpretentious, their lines clear and slightly curved; materials and wall-papers were flowered and striped, everything was bright and friendly. Trinkets, clocks and delicate genre pictures increased the charm of this specifically Austrian domestic style.'[3]

This might almost be the work programme for the Werkstätte, and the origins of Hoffmann's liking for fluting, and tight bunches of flowers, which he used to decorate his architecture and which are seen in Michael Powolny or Berthold Löffler's pottery, are thus not too difficult to unearth.

Hoffmann's first building was also his most uncompromising. The Purkersdorf sanatorium was built just outside Vienna from 1903-5 as part of the activities of the Werkstätte, but only two years afterwards it was altered by the addition of another floor, thereby removing the flat roof and the majolica decoration. Even the chairs were designed by Hoffmann and one of them can be seen in the Museum of the Twentieth Century in Vienna. The building was five years ahead of Wagner's Lupus sanatorium and had a functional interior. The entrance front is asymmetrical with cube masses rising in two steps to right and left, while the ward front is kept extremely simple. Latticed windows flank the entrance.

Three of the four villas next door to each other in the same street, and which include Hoffmann's earliest work, are the most interesting, not least because Adolphe Stoclet must have seen the two first when deciding to commission Hoffmann to build for him. In the Hohe Warte on the edge of the dip to the west which drops into the valley leading to Heiligenstadt, Hoffmann hoped to build an artist's colony. The first house was the Villa Moll for Carl Moll in 1900. Next door the Haus Henneberg (1901) was built for the printer and

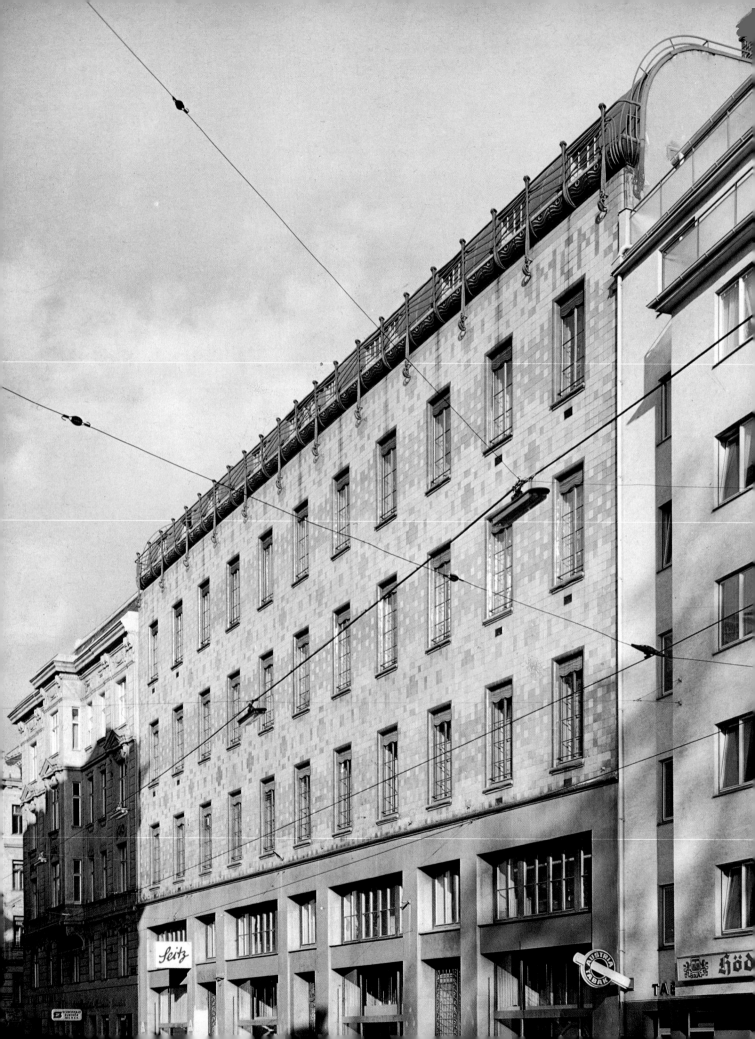

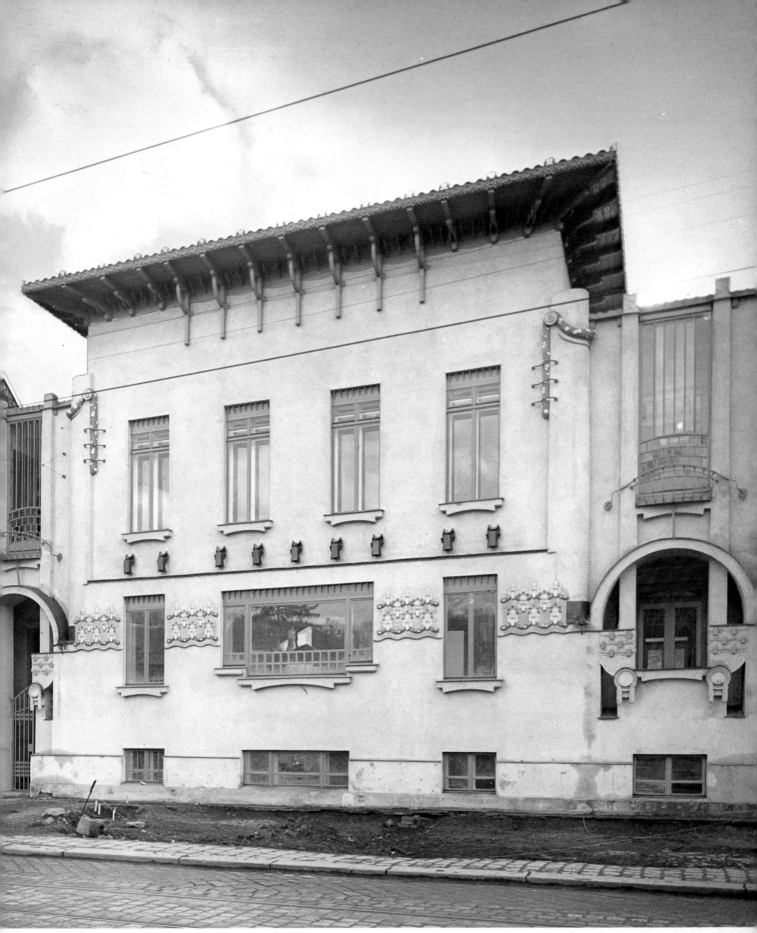

Left:
Max Fabiani
Portois und Fix building 1900
Ungargasse 59-61, Vienna III
Photo Hendler

Above:
Otto Schönthal
Villa Vojcsik 1901
Stucco with majolica decorations,
Linzerstrasse 375, Vienna XIV
Photo Hendler

Japanese print collector, Hugo Henneberg. It had complete furnishings by Hoffmann, and also a cupboard by Mackintosh, while in the hall hung Klimt's portrait of Marie Henneberg (1901-2). The completely asymmetrical treatment, with small windows scattered over the front and the modest door moved to the side, are not far from the Glasgow school and more especially Voysey, whose work had been seen in reproduction in Austria. These two buildings now demand the eye of faith from the devotee, but Haus Ast, next door to the right, is vital and shows Hoffmann at his best (1909-10). It later became the Villa Mahler-Werfel, lived in by Gustav Mahler and his wife (who was to marry the writer Franz Werfel), and now houses the Saudi-Arabian Embassy. It consists of a two-storey block on a basement floor. Five lines of arched windows run in thin strips with floral moulded bands round them and surmounted by tightly carved bunches of flowers, and a rounded decorated cornice leads to dormer windows in the roof above. The whole frontage, including a round bay at the side, is faced with fluting, except the rough stone rusticated casement

Josef Hoffmann
Haus Ast, later Mahler-Werfel 1909-10
Photo Gert Rosenberg

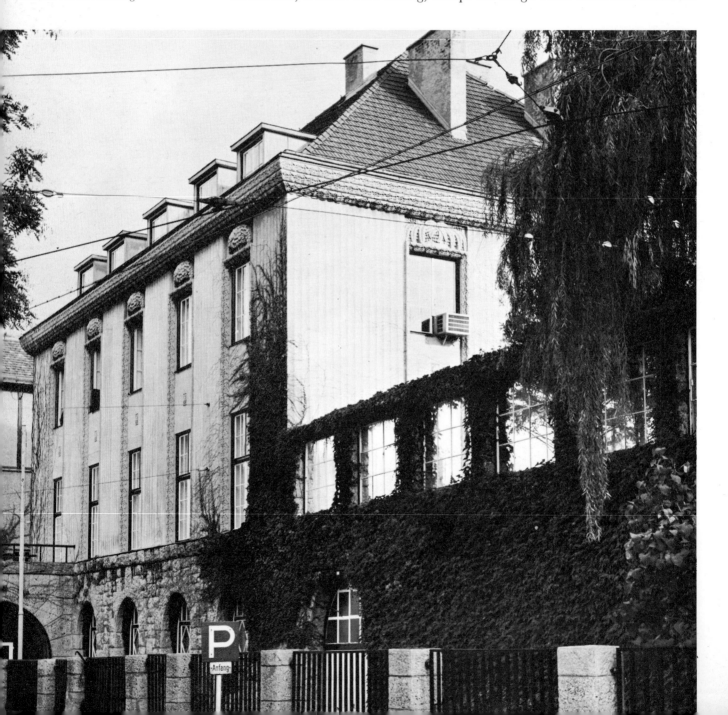

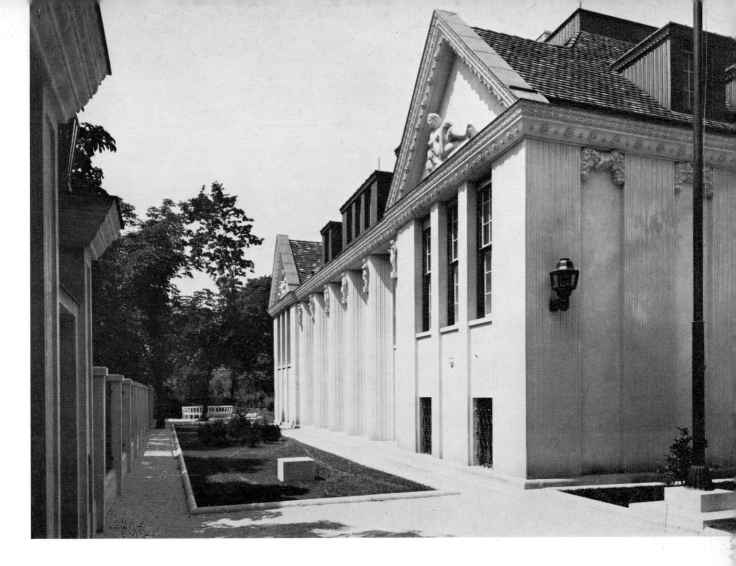

floor. Finally, in the Gloriettegasse near Schönbrunn, Hoffmann built Haus Primavesi, later Skywya (1913-15), Otto Primavesi being the second financier after Fritz Wärndorfer to spend his whole fortune on the Werkstätte. It was intended for parties and receptions. A half-basement floor leads to sashed windows on the main floor, and once again dormer windows peep out between formal pediments with a single lying figure isolated in the centre of the tympanum. The moulding of the cornice has a formal decoration. The gable ends rise above flat, fluted pilasters, with swags of flowers in place of windows on the side elevation. Five rounded and fluted pilasters with a small figure suspended at the top instead of a capital stretch across the entrance. There were also matching garden pavilions and a pergola. This neo-classical variation on a Biedermeier fantasy is unique in Viennese architecture, and, I suppose, the nearest parallel to the Neo-Queen Anne and Neo-Georgian in England of the time.

Loos was unwilling to admit any debt to Hoffmann's villas, and yet in their simplicity they somewhat foreshadow Loos's early work. Hoffmann's Haus Beer-Hoffmann (1906) in the nineteenth district, and Haus Bernatzik (1913-14) are both cubes with gables at forty-five degrees and dormer windows. Rounded doors or, in the latter case, a rounded bow give a certain relief, but they are almost as severe as Haus Knips of 1924-5 (Sonia Knips sat for one of Klimt's earliest portraits), which was intended as a place of relaxation, or his apartment block of the same year for the city of Vienna in the same district.

Josef Hoffmann
Haus Primavesi 1913
With sculpture by Anton Hanak,
in Vienna XIII
Photo 1915, Austrian National
Library

71

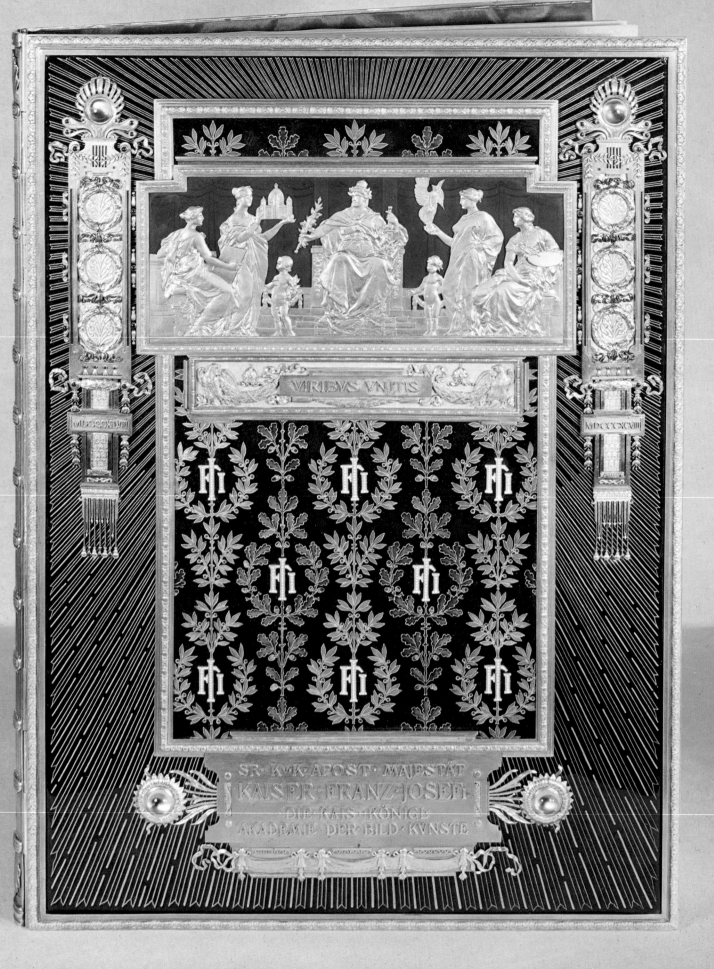

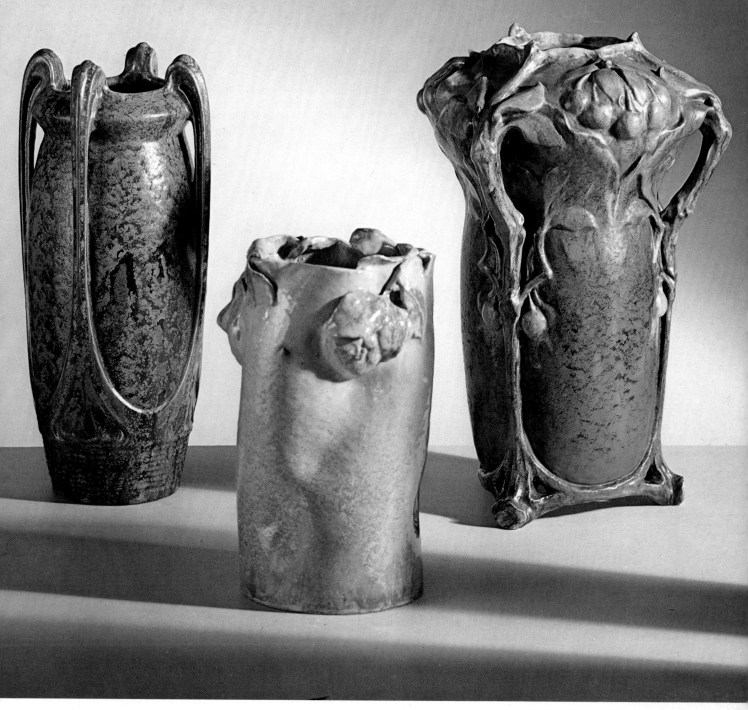

Otto Wagner
Cover of Address from Academy of Fine Arts for Imperial Jubilee 1898
Silver, silvergilt and enamels with inlaid tortoise-shell,
30 × 39.5 cm./12 × 15½ in.
Austrian National Library, photo Library

Fachschule Teplitz
Vases 1903-4
Glazed pottery, 26, 37.4 and 39.6 cm/
10¼, 14¾ and 15½ in. high
Österreichische Museum für
Angewandte Kunst, photo Museum

It was as an exhibition architect that Hoffmann was able to exercise the greatest freedom. The list of exhibitions he displayed at is long and in itself justifies Hofmann's position not only as the stylist of the Secession, but also as the embodiment of his country's image abroad. Indeed his fame outside Austria, as is so often the case with distinguished Austrians, was if anything greater than at home. For the Secession he was responsible for the interior decoration in the first, fourth, fifth, eighth and fourteenth exhibitions, and for rooms in the twelfth, seventeenth and eighteenth. (A feature of Olbrich's building was, as we have seen, that individual designers could arrange the interiors, as they still do.) In the twelfth exhibition (1902) his room was a simple arrangement of wicker garden chairs and flowers. At the fourteenth, his room housed Klinger's monumental marble statue of Beethoven (now in Dresden) and, apart from wall decorations by Alfred Roller and Adolf Böhm, it contained Klimt's Beethoven frieze. The approach to the central sculpture was to the left through a hall where high on the wall and winding round a corner hung decoration which has become almost more famous than the object of the exhibition.

In 1908 Hoffmann built the exhibition halls of the Kunstschau, the ultimate demonstration of the breakaway Klimt group, as well as an inexpensive country house for it, that proved he did not have to work on the expensive scale of the Stoclet, Ast and Primavesi houses. In 1911 he designed the Austrian pavilion for the International Art Exhibition in Rome, which included a Klimt room with the, by then, notorious *Jurisprudence* in it. In 1914, he built the Austrian hall at the famous Cologne Werkbund exhibition, a variation on Haus Primavesi with strict ribbed pillars and severe pediments at the end of the roof.[4] He was also responsible for the Austrian pavilion of the World Exhibition in Paris of 1925, and for the Venice Biennale in 1932.

In 1913 a room designed by him and executed by the Werkstätte was exhibited in the Austrian Museum of Applied Art. In the same year he designed a room for the Geneva house of Ferdinand Hodler, some of the furniture from which is now exhibited in the Hodler room in the Musée d'Art in Geneva.

It remains to discuss his greatest achievement, the Palais Stoclet.[5] More than once it has been compared to a precious piece of furniture, a box that holds valuables.[6] Faced entirely with grey Belgian marble framed with thin bands of metal moulding, it is indeed somewhat like a box of semi-precious stone bought at some titanic Asprey or Cartier. Inside, *verde antico* marble in the vestibule, black and white marble in the main hall, Portovenere marble in the dining room, and malachite inserts in the all but Roman bathroom, not to mention translucent onyx in the small sitting room, indicate that this is in every way a palace.[7]

The young Belgian Adolphe Stoclet had married the daughter of the Parisian art dealer Arthur Stevens, brother of the society painter Alfred. In 1903 they came to Vienna where their third son was born. They obviously visited the progressive exhibitions of the Secession, and apparently were introduced to Hoffmann by Carl Moll, into the garden of whose villa on the Hohe Warte they had penetrated. According to Hoffmann he met them in his studio and was immediately commissioned to build a house for them, to be on the site of the Haus Ast, as yet non-existent. But the next year, 1904, Stoclet's father died, and returning to Brussels to the world of banking and high finance, he demanded from Hoffmann a house worthy of his art collections and in which he could entertain and give concerts. He never told his family what the

74

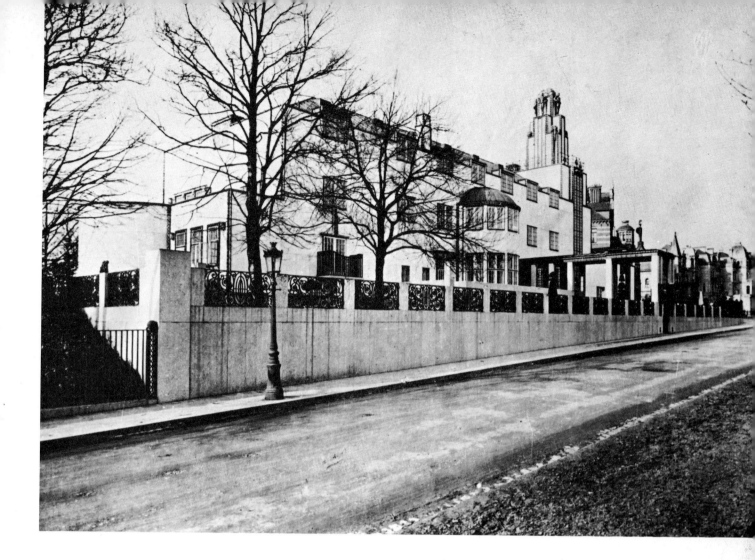

palace had cost (although Hoffmann himself did not make a great deal out of the commission as the contract was with the Werkstätte) but it was un-important to one whose ties matched his wife's Poiret dresses, and who enter-tained Diaghilev, Stravinsky, Cocteau, Anatole France and Sacha Guitry, among others whose names are recorded in the silver bound guest-book designed by Hoffmann. When Stoclet died in 1949, within one month of his wife's death, he remained faithful to Hoffmann until the end, because in his will he asked to be buried with a black and white silk handkerchief designed by him.

Just as the original designs for the sanatorium were relatively simple, so it was with the basic idea for the Stoclet house. A rectangular block three storeys high has on the right of the front a long staircase window leading to a rectangular block on the roof and above it a small tower. In the centre a long, narrow open arcade leads up steps to the entrance. To the immediate left a bow window two floors high topped with a curved roof lights the main hall. On the left side wall a rectangular addition and a curved end form part of the music room. To the right of the entrance a bridge surmounted by a roofed pergola leads to the offices. The front facing the garden is fairly simple in plan: two 'prow-like', angular protuberances containing the study and part of the dining room open out on either side of a contrasting concave fronted block above a terrace, which is thus enclosed on three sides. This mass of rectangular

Josef Hoffmann
Palais Stoclet, Brussels 1906
Street front
Photo Austrian National Library

Page 76:
Josef Hoffmann
Wiener Werkstätte Jewelry 1905-10
Brooches and buckles of silver and
semi-precious stones
Private collection and Österreichisches
Museum für Angewandte Kunst,
photo Museum

Page 77:
Carl Czeschka
Wiener Werkstätte Jewelry 1905
Gold with opals
Österreichisches Museum für
Angewandte Kunst, photo Museum

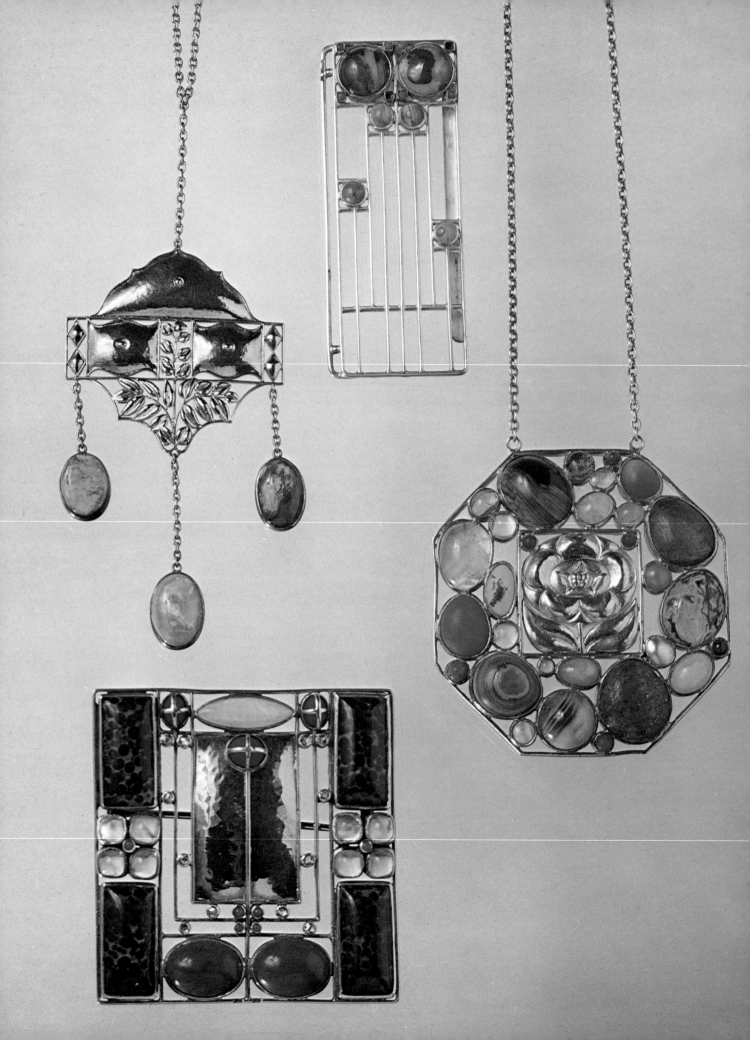

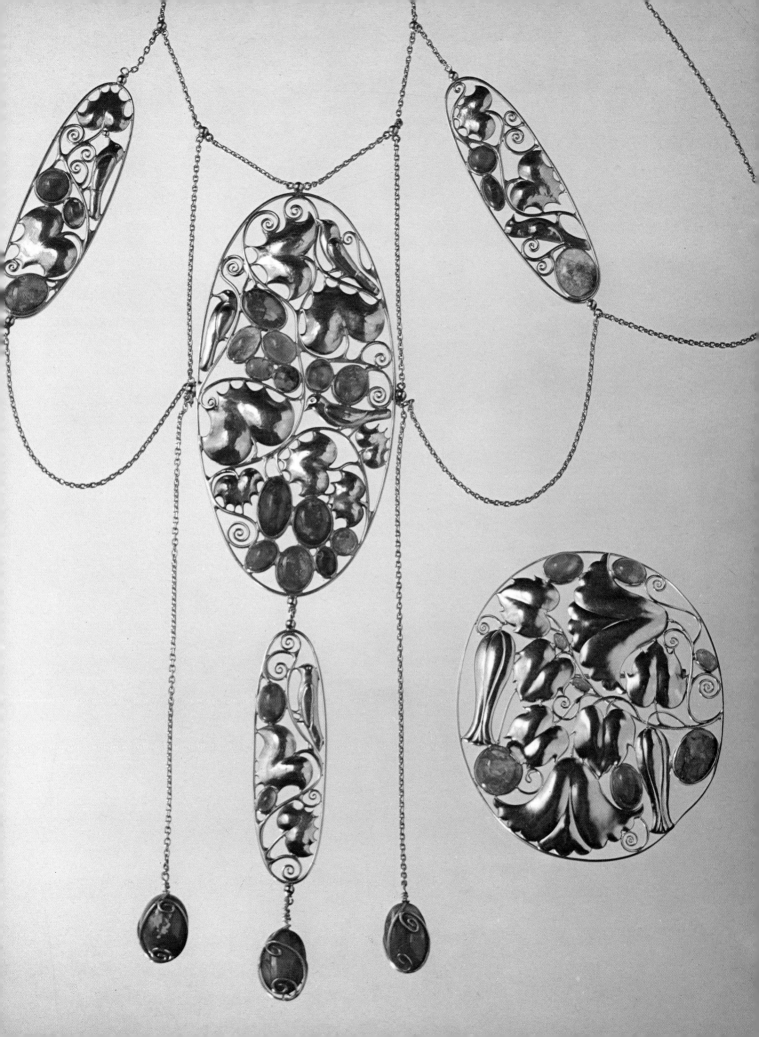

blocks lightened by the tower at the end has something of the appearance of a ship, though this must have been far from the designer's mind. The thin moulding frames, which have no structural purpose and are not even used to emphasize height or length, give the whole complex a mysterious quality made all the stronger by the entrance, with its deliberate preparation by stages for the even more numinous interior. Over the entrance is a statue of Pallas Athena, so much loved by the Secession; at the corners and top of the tower are tightly carved bunches of flowers, the topmost bouquet being flanked by four figures by Franz Metzner. Metzner (1870-1921) collaborated with Bruno Schmitz on the heavily Germanic monument of the battle of Leipzig, and was a teacher and colleague of Hoffmann's from 1903-6 at his school, and from 1903-5 a member of the Secession. It is perhaps being wise after the event to suggest that his monumental figures are incongruous, and even if this criticism is justified, then they are the only jarring note in the whole. From the bouquets the mouldings cascade downwards, garlands of running water turned to metal.

The air of solemn mystery associated with a temple of the arts which this certainly was, continues when one penetrates the interior. The small dark vestibule of *verde antico* marble with a white and black floor prepares the visitor for the formal solemnity of the great hall, which is entered by turning to the left. Straight ahead springs the ceremonial staircase down which the Stoclets used to come to meet their assembled guests. Thin 'marble-clad' square pillars run through to the ceiling of the first floor which appears as an open gallery above, with some but not all of the edges picked out with a very narrow gilded moulding. In the bay to the visitor's left and thus towards the front of the house stands a small fountain with a sculpture by the Belgian Georges Minne, well known through his contributions to the Secession up to 1905. Under and beyond the stairs was a small sitting room with a chimney piece of transparent onyx held in place by thin bands of metal moulding. On the right of the long axis is the music room with a small stage, the dark effect of whose marble flooring sets off a shrine framing Fernand Khnopff's painting *I lock my door upon myself*. The study off the music room and facing the garden, is small with oak panels. Across the hall, opposite the music room, is the long dining room.

It can hardly be doubted that this is the greatest artifact of the Werkstätte, Hoffmann or possibly even Klimt. On a chequered floor runs a long carpet with a rose motif, and in the middle a narrow table with eight chairs on each side and chairs at the end to seat up to twenty. The chairs and table are of dark macassar wood, as are the long service cupboards on either side, upon which stand silver ornaments echoing the tower outside. The walls are covered with honey Paonazzo marble. Above them, along the whole wall, run Klimt's marble mosaics *Expectation* and *Fulfilment* (200 × 740 cms). At the end entirely on its own and reaching almost to the ceiling in a stepped marble recess is an abstract mosaic (183 × 93 cms).[8] Klimt received the commission for these on 12 October 1906, the Werkstätte obtained the order to execute the mosaics to Klimt's designs in 1909, and they were in place by 1911. His working drawings are in tempera watercolour, gilt and silver bronze, chalk pencil and white wash on paper. His instructions are very precise: 'Material enamel–enamel–mosaic (green)–material enamel for the flowers. Leaves beaten metal (greenish a bit curved)–enamel or glass-mosaic.' Or, 'The spots marked with silver are (possibly) to have mother of pearl inserts' etc. The mosaics were carried out under Klimt's supervision by Leopold Forstner (1878-1936), the founder of the Wiener Mosaik-Werkstätte, in copper sheeting, silver-plate, coral, semi-precious stones, gold mosaic, and coloured faience on a white marble base. On the left of the whole feature shows *Expectation* a young woman looking to her right into the distance, with her hands in a horizontal 'Egyptian' pose, and her bare arms covered with rich bracelets 'behängt mit Steinen' as Klytämnestra says of herself in Strauss's *Elektra*. Her robe is built up of superimposed triangles of gold. She is balanced by a small formal tree, and behind both there is a larger tree with obsessively repetitive spiral branches. On the wall opposite *Expectation*, a man in a robe of flat gold ovals on a pink background bends with a bare shoulder over a girl with closed eyes, her head turned back and up towards him. Klimt was to use this wonderfully suggestive idea again but reversed in *The Kiss* (1908), one of his most stimulating and exciting paintings. The swirling trees of life are decorative in the best sense. The severe but brilliantly shining narrow abstract reminds one, as do the formal poses of the figures, that Klimt had been to Ravenna for the first time in 1903 and had sent back to his mother a postcard of the interior of S. Vitale. The gilded, towered gates from which the sheep emerge in the spandrels above the apse in S. Apollinaire in Classe are an instance of the Byzantine sources enriched, if such a suggestion is possible, by Klimt's own imagination.

After these sublimities, the intimate octagonal breakfast room, which had a carpet with white dots on black and yellow, in order to hide any dropped crumbs, must be a return to the everyday. Reached either through the dining

Josef Hoffmann
Dining Room, Palais Stoclet, Brussels
With frieze by Gustav Klimt (1909)
Photo Austrian National Library

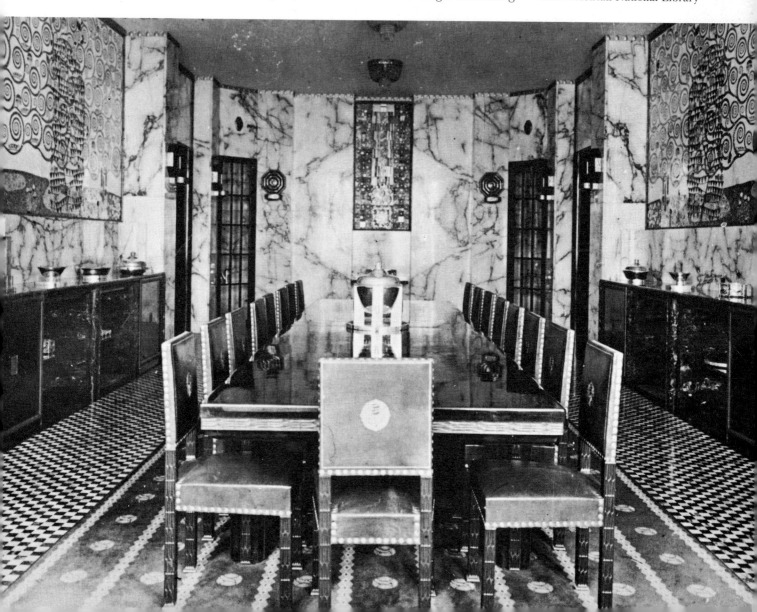

room or beyond a door leading to the service passage, it is conceived entirely in the spirit of the Werkstätte. The symmetrical rose decoration, carved in low relief and picked out in white and yellow paint, has a hint of Morris wall paper. It only remains to mention the panelled master bedroom with its barrel vault offset by convex curves above the ceiling-high panelling, the far more successful bathroom, in which a veined marble bath stands enthroned on a black dais motif, while a thin triple line motif, and malachite inlays decorate the marble walls, and a nursery with a frieze by Ludwig Jungnickel.

In the Werkstätte, the business manager, Wärndorfer, who had to bear the brunt of the law-suits which followed the building of the Purkersdorf sanatorium, after this episode demanded that the architectural department should be removed from the Werkstätte. He too had gone with Hoffmann to visit the Brussels site for the Palais Stoclet. The idea of founding an artist's cabaret had been mooted in the Café Central by someone without the capital, and Wärndorfer, encouraged by Peter Altenberg, Carl Hollitzer, and Egon Friedell, who took on the artistic direction, founded the 'Fledermaus' in the Kärntnerstrasse in 1907. Partly owing to a column in the middle of the room which had to remain because of police regulations it was difficult to see the stage.

In spite of the illustrious names of those associated with the venture–Peter Altenberg, Hermann Bahr, Franz Blei (the first German translator of André Gide), Hanns Heinz Ewers and the like–it closed by 1910. A short flight of steps led into the small bar-room, and a white balcony, with slender pillars, a motif very similar to that used in the hall of the Stoclet house, and boxes below, surrounded the theatre. Indeed, like the Stoclet dining room, a bright ceramic frieze about two metres high surrounded the bar. The artists involved were C. O. Czeschka, who also designed the programme covers and posters, F. Delavilla, Hoffmann, Klimt, Oskar Kokoschka, Bertold Löffler, who designed the famous 'Fledermaus' poster, Emil Orlik and Josef Eduard Wimmer. Löffler and Powolny executed both their own tiles and presumably those designed by the other collaborators.[9]

Opposite:
Kolo Moser
Textile c. 1902
Design for Johann Backhausen und Söhne
Österreichische Museum für Angewandte Kunst, photo Museum

Adolf Loos and Building Without Ornament

The handful of buildings Adolf Loos left in Vienna, of which three were directly connected with the tailoring trade, and two were cafés, does not immediately suggest one of the pioneer architects of the twentieth century, nor his importance as a front-line publicist and lecturer. Yet, Edith Hoffmann in her biography of Kokoschka (1947) wrote:

> 'The most important figure in Kokoschka's early years was the architect Adolf Loos, whose name should rank among the most famous in the history of modern art. He was the forerunner of those who have introduced modern building in all countries—it is, indeed, not too much to say that he was one of the originators of the modern style on this side of the Atlantic, not only in architecture, but in the whole art of living. Although he devoted an exceptional intellect and enthusiasm to questions of taste and culture, he shared the tragic fate of so many Austrians, of being persecuted in their own country and unrecognized abroad.'

Adolf Loos
Café Capua Johannesgasse
photograph 1913
Photo Historisches Museum der
Stadt Wien

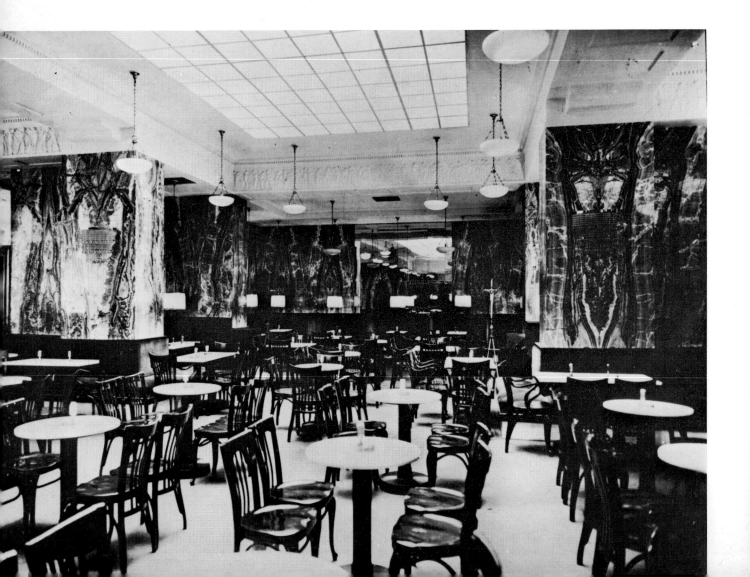

Henry Russell Hitchcock has ranked Loos with Perret, Wright and Behrens as the four most important architects of the first generation of this century. In 1936 Nikolaus Pevsner could say, 'Loos is one of the greatest creators in modern architecture. In spite of that he never became known, during his lifetime, to more than a small circle of admirers.'[1]

Loos was born on 10 December 1870 in Brno, the son of a mason-sculptor who died when he was ten, his mother taking over the business. During his military service, he managed to become lieutenant of the reserve, and was then mostly trained in the polytechnic at Dresden. When he suddenly decided that he wanted to go to America, his mother agreed to pay the fare if he would renounce his right to the family inheritance. This he did, and then spent three years in New York, Philadelphia and Chicago, where he visited the World Fair in 1896, living hard and working some of the time as a mason, his apprenticeship in which Loos completed on returning. He also brought back a fanatical admiration for Anglo-Saxon habits and the English way of life.

An outsider, a maverick almost, with a turbulent private life, he married four times, and his third wife, Elsie Altmann Loos, hints that he had a liking for 'small women'. Always extremely well dressed with trousers pleated at the sides, which he believed to be the style approved by King Edward VII, 'he was tall and well built, with broad shoulders, narrow hips and long legs. He had strong worker's hands, and a high brow, kindly eyes, a small fine nose and a thin-lipped mouth gave him a strong profile.' He could argue at length about food and even the correct way to peel an orange. In spite of his attacks on Viennese *Gemütlichkeit*, he attended the Hofkapelle with the nobility on Easter Sunday, had a liking for animals, including dogs and pet monkeys, and paid regular visits with Elsie Loos to the Spanish Riding School.

Although his name is linked with Josef Hoffmann as a pioneer of modern design in Austria, he disliked the Werkstätte and what it stood for, and demonstrated this hatred by his idea of founding a museum of what would now be called kitsch, a *Hausgreuelmuseum* to house all the products of the Werkstätte. His friends in the Vienna cafés he frequented were Peter Altenberg, Karl Kraus, Schönberg, and the young Kokoschka whom 'he adored and loved like a son'. Kokoschka painted him in 1909, drew him twice between 1910 and 1916 for *Sturm*, published by Herwarth Walden to whom Loos had introduced the artist in Vienna, and drew him again and did a lithograph both in 1916. Loos, for his part, had Kokoschka dressed by one of Vienna's exclusive tailors, Ebenstein; he later got him into a smart dragoon regiment during the First World War and had him photographed in red trousers, blue tunic and golden helmet. (His own uniform made by Knize was based, unbelievably, on the American one with huge pockets.) His help to the young painter not only consisted in making him presentable but also in securing him commissions, and introductions to influential people. After the war he presented works by Kokoschka to various public collections.

He also had a great talent for speaking and this is Kokoschka's description of a lecture.

'It is hardly comprehensible today that an architect, who had hardly ever been given the chance to build what he visualized, could at his will pack the great Viennese music hall with 5000 bewildered listeners, whenever one of his classic jeremiads *Ins Leere gesprochen* ("talks into the void") was advertised. He stood for culture, but where he differed from a professed appreciator of the beautiful was that, as a modern thinking man, he rejected the belief that in the machine age social life must of necessity do without culture. To him social history was not an agglomeration of accidents, and consequently man's thoughts were the perfection of his social being, of his material life. Logically, Loos became a reformer. He saw modern barbarism conditioned by the way western man acts, earns, eats, sleeps, worships, copulates.'

Emmie Loos has also written of this phenomenon.

'His lectures were unforgettable. I heard them year after year and was never tired of them. He spoke about eating, sitting, walking, standing, sleeping. He wanted to teach people how to live. He spoke about living, shopping, and housekeeping. He taught us how to dress. He spoke about art and music, about the present and the past. He spoke about foreign countries. He spoke and one forgot one's surroundings. He fought against the Viennese cuisine. He hated boiled puddings, white sauce, and gulasch and he often spoke for hours about foreign cookery.[2] His lectures were always sold out and, though new people came, there were year after year the same listeners who were never tired of hearing Loos speak.'

Loos was a fighter ahead of his time, and therefore misunderstood. He stood up for Kokoschka after the performance of one of the first expressionist plays ever, *Hoffnung der Frauen*, at the Kunstgewerbe Schule in 1907, at which there may have been a scandal during the première. Anton Webern has recalled that he did the same after a concert where Schönberg performed works by himself and Zemlinsky.

It is completely in character with Austria's neglect for her most distinguished progeny and of Loos in particular that the first collection of his writings should appear in France in 1921, since no German speaking publisher could be found. His *Ins Leere gesprochen* include a series of articles for the *Neue Freie Presse* written in connection with the Kaiser Franz Joseph Jubilee exhibition of 1898, but also other essays, especially 'Die Potemkinsche Stadt' which appeared in the same year in *Ver Sacrum*. This famous attack on the *Ring-strassenstil*, the Renaissance and Tuscan fronts of brick and tiles stuck on façades, ends, 'Whether one tries to build wooden huts of canvas cardboard and paint, in which the happy peasants live, or construct sham stone palaces from tiles and cement rendering, in which feudal lords appear to rule, the principle is the same. The spirit of Potemkin sways over Viennese architecture of this century.' This was indeed the thesis of my exposition of the Ringstrasse and the scene that confronted Wagner as a young architect. *Trotzdem* ('Nevertheless') first appeared in Innsbruck in 1931. It included his often quoted article 'Ornament and Crime', and was probably given first as a lecture in 1910. This appeared in French, Hebrew and Japanese, before being printed in Prague in 1929 for the first time in German! An editorial introduction pointed out that Loos was an exponent of *neue Sachlichkeit*, or the new realism,[3] long before the phrase had ever been used, and yet he had never been called to a university chair up to that time, which was only a few years before his death in 1933.

Loos opened his own school of architecture on the Rennweg in 1906, warning his pupils that they would have a hard time working for him. He was particularly fond of Richard Neutra, who had been with Wagner at the

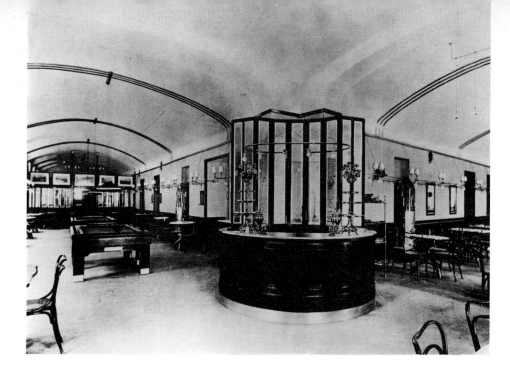

Adolf Loos
Café Museum photograph 1899
Photo Historisches Museum der
Stadt Wien

Academy, and said that he was the only student with real talent and the necessary gift to be a great architect. Others included Finetti from Milan, and, after the war, Adolf Breuer and Heinrich Kulka who left for New Zealand, and Robert Hlawatsch who went to Hamburg. When Loos had a post in the housing estates development department from 1920-2, his students worked there in the mornings. In 1930 he was involved with the most important of these estates, the Werkbundsiedlung in the fifteenth district, which had four houses by himself and his pupils, Wagner-Freynsheim, Neutra and Rietveld, as well as early works by Clemens Holzmeister, later to be the architect of Ankara, and Ernst Plischke, who emigrated to New Zealand in 1939 returning to a professorship at the Academy after the end of the Second World War.

Loos's architecture has three strong characteristics, a use of rich materials in the place of decoration, metal lattices often bowed, and, in his later villas, an interplay of strong cubes on different levels in the interiors as well as in the spatial treatment of the elevations.

His first shop and fitting rooms (1898) for the tailor Goldmann have disappeared and his Café Museum (1899) has been altered beyond recognition. The first had long, floor-length cupboards, and above it a bowed lattice decoration. The Café Museum was ascetically simple, with Thonet chairs and a central dresser feature with dark framed mirrors. Fortunately the interior of the American bar of 1907 (now called the Loos Bar) off Kärntnerstrasse surives intact. Like the Goldmann shop, it is a remarkable solution to the problem of minute space, with mirrors just above head-height carrying the strong dark columns and marble coffered ceiling to infinity. The bar is richly furnished with leather and mahogany panelling, and again Loos used Thonet chairs for their simplicity and good design. In 1904 he built his first house, the Villa Kharma in Montreux, the owner of which shot himself in prison having just received a long sentence for, significantly enough, photographing small girls. Loos's gift for working on a small scale continued with the Knize tailor's shop on the Graben of 1913. The square front is treated with strong slabs of black Swedish granite with uprights curving in towards the entrance, and the interior walls and stairs up to the larger show-rooms are of light brown cherry wood.

85

Max Fabiani
Artariahaus 1901
Kohlmarkt 9, detail
Photo Gert Rosenberg

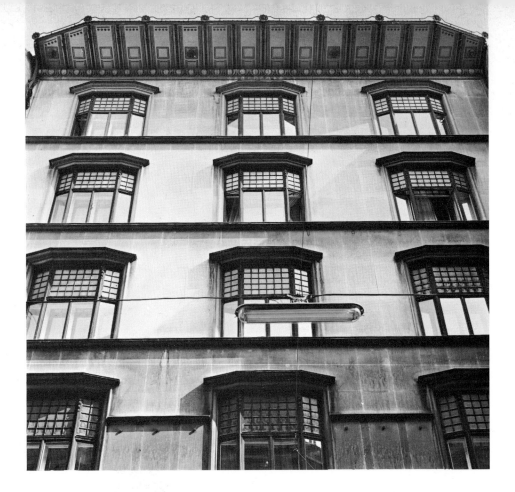

Adolf Loos
Michaelerplatz 3 1910
Photo Gert Rosenberg

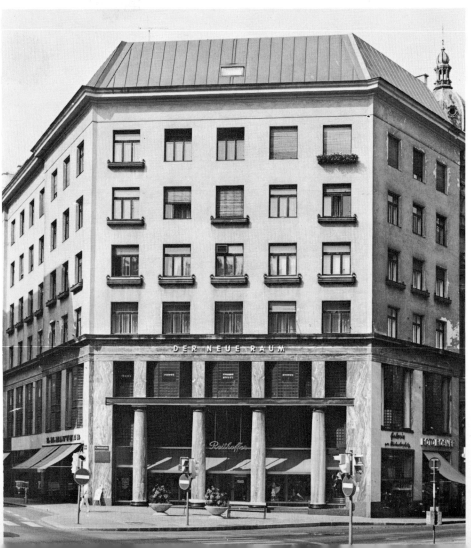

The Looshaus on a corner site of the Michaelerplatz in the heart of Vienna, was built for the outfitters, Goldmann & Salatsch, in 1910, as a result of a competition to see who could use the space most economically. For the apartments above he used a plain front of rendered cement that differentiates them strongly from the shop below faced with green cipollino marble. The entrance portico is recessed behind four Tuscan columns; inside, above, and to each side there are bowed lattice bronze windows. The treatment of the side entrance to the apartments is particularly noble, simple and characteristic, with bronze fittings and stair-rails, and walls covered with yellow marble. The building owes not a little to the nearby Haus Artaria of Fabiani (1901), as we have seen. As soon as the scaffolding was down there was an outcry. Since the site is very prominent, facing across to the Hofburg, it was suggested that it should be pulled down at once as an affront to the imperial house, and it is said that Franz Joseph never used the Michaelertor again. The windows had no 'eyebrows', but no one seemed to have noticed that by then few of Wagner's windows had lintels, let alone sills. The controversy was even echoed in *Die Wienerinnen*, a comedy by Hermann Bahr. It was the only commission of any size that Loos was to fulfil.

In the same year, 1910, in the thirteenth district, Loos built Haus Steiner for another tailor, completely without ornament, with small windows of various sizes, and a curved roof to the front (which has since been altered) and a flat roof on to the garden. Haus Scheu (1912) also has various window openings, including long lattice stair windows, and an arrangement of rooms which was almost open space. With its different levels and chunky appearance it showed how his ideas were to develop. The house of the Sauraugasse of the next year was covered with a semicircular gable. Different levels in the interiors were important features of his later villas built after his 'exile' to Paris, where his Maison Tzara of 1928 is his monument. His most interesting flats and buildings, such as the Haus Müller (1930), were those in Czechoslovakia of the thirties, when his ideas and style came to full fruition.

Elsie Loos has a tragi-comic account of how Loos fitted up a demonstration house in a housing estate. The furniture was built-in, the kitchen and living room open plan. Housewives commented that there was nowhere to cook; one man complained that he could never get his double chiffonier up the stairs; some visitors expected marble stairs like the Belvedere Palace. Also, the Loos couple and their students had filled the house with books, pictures, ashtrays, cushions, kitchen pans, and even vases filled with flowers, but by the first evening the visitors had taken all the ashtrays, books and vases. This parable on the failure to communicate might stand for Loos in his lifetime.

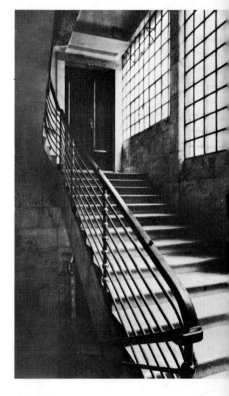

Adolf Loos
Staircase of the Building on the Michaelerplatz
Photo Historisches Museum der Stadt Wien

Overleaf:
Otto Wagner
Stairwell 1898
In Wienzeile 38
Photo Gert Rosenberg

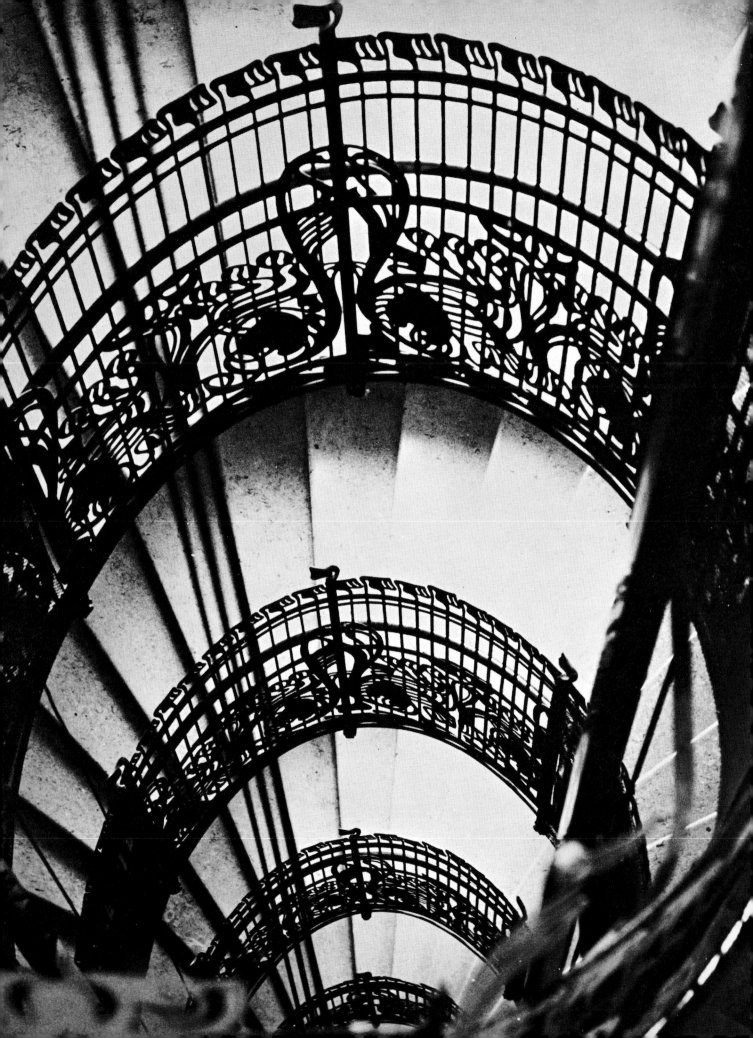

APPLIED ARTS

The Wiener Werkstätte

In exactly the same way as the embryo Victoria and Albert Museum in London began in Marlborough House, some ten years later, in 1864, a museum of Austrian art and industry was started in the Ballhaus of the Hofburg. It was the first of its kind on the continent, though there was a tradition of encouraging industrial design going back to Metternich and even to Joseph II (1741-90). Rudolf von Eitelberger, who was also the first professor of art history at Vienna University, was its first director. In London in 1862, he had not only seen the standards of design in industrial art at the third World Exhibition, but in particular, he had visited the South Kensington Museum and, attached to it, what was to become the Royal College of Art; he reported on these things in full to the Prime Minister Archduke Rainer. In 1871 the Emperor opened Ferstel's Museum of Applied Art with a school of design next door. Industrial firms allied themselves with the attempts at improvement in design, including J. & L. Lobmeyr, the glassware shop, and Philip Hass & Söhne, the upholsterers and fabric firm both still active today. When Arthur von Scala, who had been director of the Oriental Museum, was appointed director in 1897, the attempt to modernize and improve design became even more intensive with the result that Archduke Rainer resigned and, as we have seen, Wagner came on to the board. Scala issued a periodical *Kunst und Kunsthandwerk*, which appeared until 1921, and organized a series of advanced exhibitions. He was known for his almost fanatical devotion to things English, but his main interest was in the commercial products. It is worth mentioning that the museum policy succeeded so well that a further addition to it towards the River Wien was made in 1906-9 by Ludwig Baumann. Despite it being rather dull, Baumann went on to become the unworthy winner of the competition for the War Ministry building.

Next door a number of teachers associated with *Gründerzeit* ideas, those of the speculative period of Germanic art, were followed in 1899 by the new director, Felician Freiherr von Myrbach, an army captain, painter and illustrator, who brought with him Josef Hoffmann, Alfred Roller, the stage designer and an innovator of fundamental importance, Kolo Moser, the designer associated with the founding of the Secession. From the Werkstätte came Rudolf Larisch, a graphic designer and modernizer of lettering, the silversmith Carl Otto Czeschka (1878-1960), and the sculptor Arthur Strasser (1854-1927), creator of the bronze *Marc Antony drawn by lions* (1899-1900) in front of the Secession building (originally only the provisional site for it). It is virtually his only known work.

Isolated from these artistic movements, the activities of Michael Thonet (1796-1871), who first produced chairs in Vienna for the second-rococo Ballroom of the Liechtenstein Palace in 1843-6, had been so fertile that by 1900 the Thonet factory was employing 6,000 workers and twenty steam machines, making 4,000 pieces of bent-wood furniture daily. By 1910, sixty factories in Austria were employing 35,000 working on the lines of the Thonet invention.

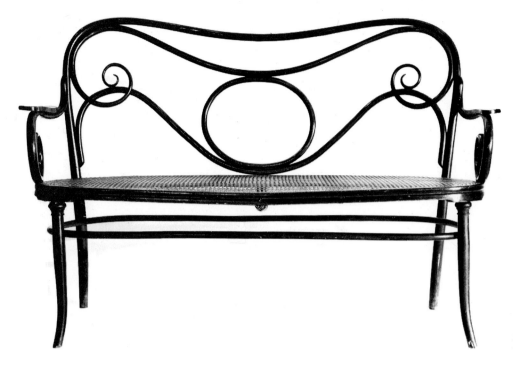

Michael Thonet
Settee no. 8 in production from 1860
onwards and reproduced in 1873
catalogue
Bentwood, 139 cm./55 in. long
Photo John Sailer

It is characteristic of Vienna that the only permanent, and albeit modest, Thonet display is in the Technical Museum, and not in one devoted to furniture design. There are still Thonet stools in Loos's American Bar, and hat-stands in cafés and restaurants; some of the original designs are still available from the factory, whilst old Thonet rocking-chairs and the like are sought by collectors.

The story of the Secession in 1897 belongs to that of painting for it was primarily a painters' association, with sculptors and architects as members. In the very first exhibition there had been a '*Ver Sacrum* room' called after their new publication, for whose layout and design the young Josef Hoffmann was responsible. The International Exhibition in Paris of 1900, whose main theme was 'Electricity', not only brought Wagner a legion of honour for his designs for Group VI (Engineering) and his display for the Imperial Gardens department, but the modernity of the secessionist exhibits was an enormous success. Indeed there was a danger that manufacturers were ready to accept the latest style as a mere ephemeral fashion. In the spring of 1900 Hoffmann wrote a letter to Myrbach at the museum urging him to visit Charles Robert Ashbee's Guild of Handicrafts on his next visit to England. He also told Myrbach that he intended at the autumn Secession exhibition 'to present a survey of modern industrial art. It would be worthwhile indeed, sometime, to show real English industrial art in Vienna. It would be a hard blow to the Museum. One has so far seen nothing but Old English objects or English expert articles.' Since the parallel to the Old English was the Old German style of furniture suite which had been popular since the 1860s, he was therefore touching a sensitive area. He also felt that Scala was giving too much prominence to the purely commercial.[1]

The autumn exhibition of 1900 was arranged by Hoffmann and Moser, and devoted principally to interiors. Ashbee, Charles Rennie Mackintosh and his wife Margaret Macdonald, and her sister Frances MacNair, Henry

Charles Mackintosh
Music Room in Haus Wärndorfer 1902
From *The Studio* XVIII November
1912
Photo University of
Glasgow Museum

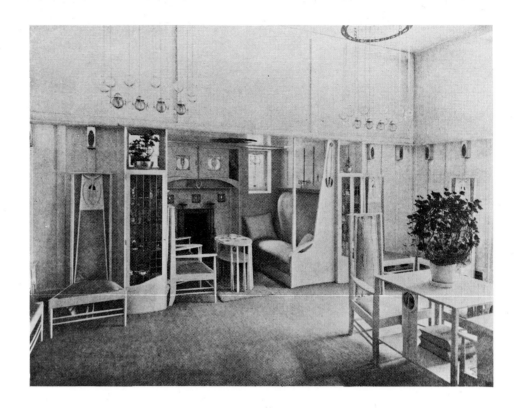

van der Velde and the 'Maison Moderne' from Paris were all represented.
There were vases and furniture by William de Morgan, and pictures by
Walter Crane and Burne-Jones.[2] The Viennese found Ashbee's furniture
severe, but the black and white of Mackintosh appealed to them; the Minister
of Education bought a sideboard by Kolo Moser, and Fritz Wärndorfer
commissioned a dining room from Hoffmann and a music room from Mackintosh for his villa in Währing to the west of Vienna. Hoffmann and Moser met
Ashbee and the Scottish artists, and followed this by visiting Scotland and
Ashbee's guild of craftsmen at Essex House in London.

In May 1903 at the lunch table in a café where Moser and Hoffmann met
regularly to complain about the crafts situation in Vienna, there occurred
a decisive discussion. According to Hoffmann, Fritz Wärndorfer, who had
just returned from London and knew the Morris movement, appeared and as
a joke asked the pair how much they needed to start a crafts guild. When Moser
said that 600 kronen would be enough, Wärndorfer produced the money from
his wallet. They were astonished but went out at once, found a small flat in the
Wieden district, and furnished it with tables, cupboards and chairs, significantly choosing Biedermeier furniture on the grounds that it was not only of
good design, but in the last genuine style before eclecticism set in. This was
done in an hour, but all the cash had been spent. They confessed what had
happened to their protector who laughed, said that he would discuss it with
his mother, and in a few days collected 50,000 kronen with which they moved
into a factory building at 32 Neustiftgasse in the autumn.[3]

The newly constituted Wiener Werkstätte had an artistic direction committee of two headed by a commercial manager, Wärndorfer himself. He was
to remain in charge until 1913, when his place was taken by the banker Otto

92

Primavesi who generously supported the workshop until his death. In spite of a financial crisis in 1925-6, its twenty-fifth birthday was celebrated with ceremonies and an important publication, *The Wiener Werkstätte 1903-1928– Modern Design and its Progress*, designed by Mathilde Flögl to Hoffmann's ideas, and with a cover by Vally Wieselthier and Gudrun Baudisch. There was also a shop in the Kärntnerstrasse for fashions and textiles, and a branch in Zurich from 1917-19. Other branches were in Marienbad and Breslau, and as late as 1929 Hoffmann suggested opening a branch in the Friedrich-strasse in Berlin. Yet in spite of the efforts made by Primavesi's widow, Mäda, the company closed on 14 October 1932, and the stock was sold at auction.[4]

The aims of the Werkstätte by no means appealed to everyone. Loos was a deadly enemy, as we have seen, partly, as Hoffmann suggests, because Wärn-dorfer never asked him to collaborate, but then neither did the Tuscan columns and the window treatment on the Michaelerplatz building conform to Hoffmann's ideas. In 1902 Eduard Pötzl (1851-1914), the influential editor of the *Neues Wiener Tagblatt*, published *Heuriges*, a collection of his articles that serve as a fair example of the articulate opposition to the principles of the Werkstätte and the Secession. He had already complained of the Old English influence in Scala's exhibitions, which was 'as boring as fake Renaissance side-boards and divans, dreary Boule, and degenerate public-house baroque. We will soon get tired of the English style, if it becomes uniform in a thousand homes.' In the Secession exhibition of 1900 he found four dangerous tendencies:

'1.   The threshing-machine style, imitated from Van de Velde, by all the Secessionists at home and abroad. In my eyes it is the elephantiasis of furniture.
2.   The ice-box style. [He particularly disliked blue clothes cupboards which he considered to be more suitable for the kitchen. However no one has heard of a blue ice-box.]
3.   The steel-safe style.
4.   The travelling-trunk style used for small decorative cupboards and the like.
5.   The lath style used for chairs and stands.
These repeat themselves again and again until it makes one sick. It is a style for halls, bathrooms and bowling alleys, not for the homes of people seeking ease and comfort in their dwellings. The Mackintosh collection filled a whole room, in which there was an absolute orgy of lack of imagination and tastelessness. One has to have seen this hellish room for it is beyond the possibility of description. It was a torture chamber. Everything grimaced, showed its teeth, [one wonders whether he had ever seen a Pre-Raphaelite painting] and squinted. Nothing was made in accordance with either heavenly or human ideas. The standing clock in the corner looked like an octopus, the dressing-mirror like a fair-ground swing-boat in the Prater, the wall covering like a frame for hanging tripe.'

Also, Pötzl gives a delicious account of a secessionist ball starting at the un-likely hour of noon, at which the ladies wore vine leaves over their dresses, and a blond young gentleman in a frock-coat leant on a thyrsus, or staff:

' "This staff is a symbol, Sir. It signifies that we should all be naked or merely hung about with calves' feet and fennel. But our time is not sufficiently

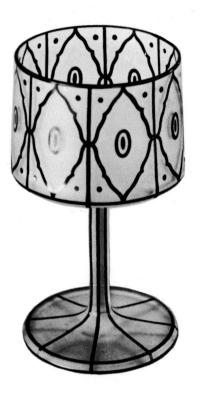

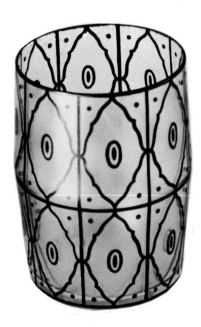

Dionysian for such freedom – alas.''

"You are right," I replied. "Pure humanity is, so to speak, to be met with only in the steam baths. Calves' feet, in our excessively modest society, are boiled, and fennel is strewn on bread rolls. It is all very sad." '

Despite this, the Werkstätte proceeded, and Hoffmann has recounted how carpenters were found. He goes on: 'It was often remarkable how Moser, although he was a painter, found his way into the secrets of construction, and recognized wrongs born of bad habits. In the metal-work department we were delighted to make small objects of perforated sheet-iron, often with glass inserts.' These included fruit baskets, bowls, flower holders, sugar and biscuit bowls. These extremely simple objects, which were popular and sold well, went as far in size as an umbrella-stand. Although their existence is all but ignored, except by collectors, they are among the most advanced designs produced by the group. There were also enamel and leather workers. Hoffmann particularly liked a book-binder called Beitel, who knew Morris's work and ideas. He taught them how to do marble and batik papers which were used in the small boxes made by Moser. Wall-papers were designed by Maria Likartz, Mathilde Flögl and Vally Wieselthier, and, up to his death in 1923, Dagobert Peche. These designers, besides Kitty Rix, Reny Schaschl and Hilde Jesser, were all involved in the lace textile and fashion side. Towards the end there were more than forty glass designs, mostly by Hoffmann himself. Many of these designers and Peche in particular were responsible for a wide range of ceramic work in polychrome glaze. By the time the group programme was published in a small elongated brochure in 1905, there were more than a hundred workers and thirty-seven masters and craftsmen signing with their own monograms.[5]

94

Working alongside the group was the Wiener Keramik workshop founded in 1906 by Michael Powolny (1871-1954), a professor at Myrbach's school, together with Berthold Löffler (1874-1960), who had studied under Moser. The strongest characteristic of their appealing work is the swirl of brightly coloured flowers, which swathe the objects. The state schools of glass and ceramics produced excellent work at the time, especially the ceramics school at Teplitz.

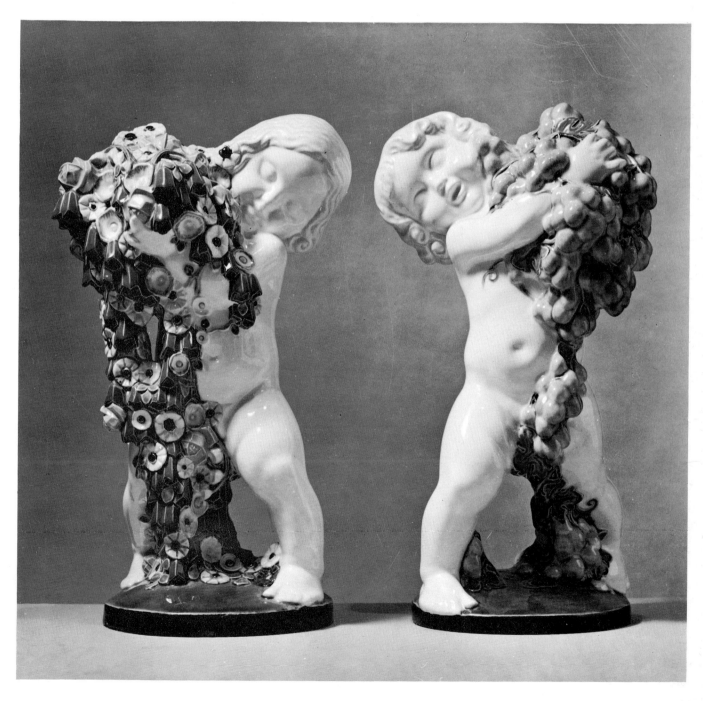

Kolo Moser was born on 30 March 1868. Born the son of the porter at the Theresianum, Vienna, at that time Austria's boarding school for the nobility, he passed into the Academy of Fine Arts and supported himself with fashion designs. He was a member of the 'Siebernerklub' which met in the Café Sperl, a group of young students, including Hoffmann, Olbrich, and Josef Urban (1872-1933) who later founded the *Künstlerbund Hagen* in 1900 and was architect of and, from 1918 until his death, chief designer at the New York Metropolitan opera house. The club was collectively responsible for illustrating several books. Moser was a founder member of the Secession, and, called to teach by Myrbach in 1899, was made a professor the year after his appointment. In 1902 he started to design for the State printers. He was a great friend of Carl Moll and of Hermann Bahr, and he married his pupil, Edith von Mautner-Markhof, a member of one of the richest and most influential families concerned with the arts in Austria. He designed for Otto Wagner, in particular the windows of the Steinhof church. In 1906 he resigned from the Secession along with the Klimt group, and, more decisively, in the same year he left the Werkstätte on the grounds that the public were making impossible demands on it. According to Hoffmann he wanted to devote himself entirely to painting after his marriage, but his short life prevented this, his original leaning, from being fulfilled. He died on 18 October 1918 in Vienna. Not only did his touch enlighten the early numbers of *Ver Sacrum*, with which he was associated from its foundation in 1898 until its end in 1904, but he was one of the leading designers of the time. His landscape stamp designs of 1906 for the Austro-Hungarian Post Office in Bosnia-Herzegovina made him one of the first artists responsible for the fame of Austrian stamp design.

The severity of the English and Scottish inspiration, the ideas of Hoffmann and, in particular, Moser kept the designs of the Werkstätte to strictly geometric forms until 1906. Indeed Wilhelm Mrazek has called the striving for geometricization the Hoffmann-Moser style of 1903-15. However this changed with the arrival of a pupil of Moser's, Eduard Josef Wimmer (1882-1961), who designed in all fields including fashion, and who worked for a time at the Chicago Art Institute. Even more decisive was the arrival in 1915 of Dagobert Peche (1887-1923), a designer from 1912 onwards in the field of applied art, who had studied architecture with Ohmann. From 1917-19 he was head of the Zürich branch, and until his early death a leading influence on the house style. 'We felt that each of his designs was something precious, inspired and wonderful, and we could hardly wait until he came forward with new ideas,' Hoffmann records. His main concern was with ornamentation, on a high level, and with almost aristocratic intentions, yet full of fantasy. The beautiful was to be an end in itself. It is hardly surprising that this kind of prettifying should have infuriated Loos. To quote Mrazek again, in a highly significant passage:

'This style, whose repertory of ornamental forms was to dominate creative work in Austria's and Germany's art for some years, was diametrically opposed to the architecturally conceived structure of Hoffmann's world. With its playful, relaxed grace it lightened the sober earnestness of new realism, restored elegance to a system of mere usefulness, and answered the creative intentions of the numerous woman-artists in the Wiener Werkstätte. Peche's linear rhythm, his extravagant colour harmonies, his fantastic forms, their subtlety and ease were traits whose fascination even Josef Hoffmann could not deny entirely. Eventually the predominance of these

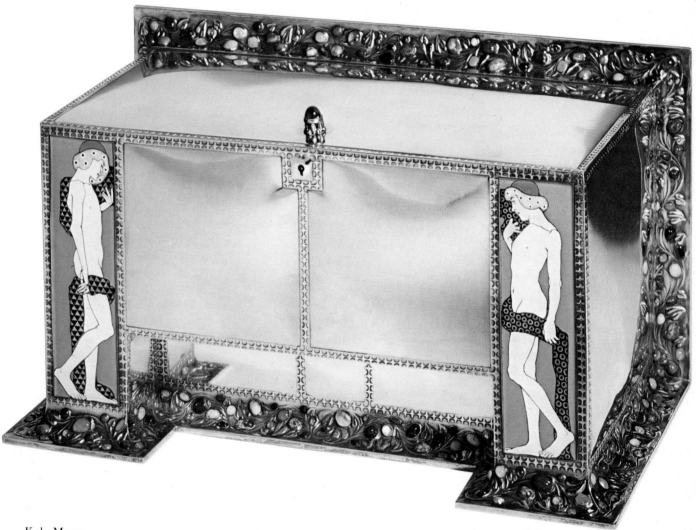

Kolo Moser
Wiener Werkstätte Casket 1905-6
Silver, semi-precious stones and
enamel, 23.6 × 42.4 × 24.4 cm./
$9\frac{1}{4} \times 17 \times 9\frac{3}{4}$ in.
Österreichische Museum für
Angewandte Kunst, photo Museum

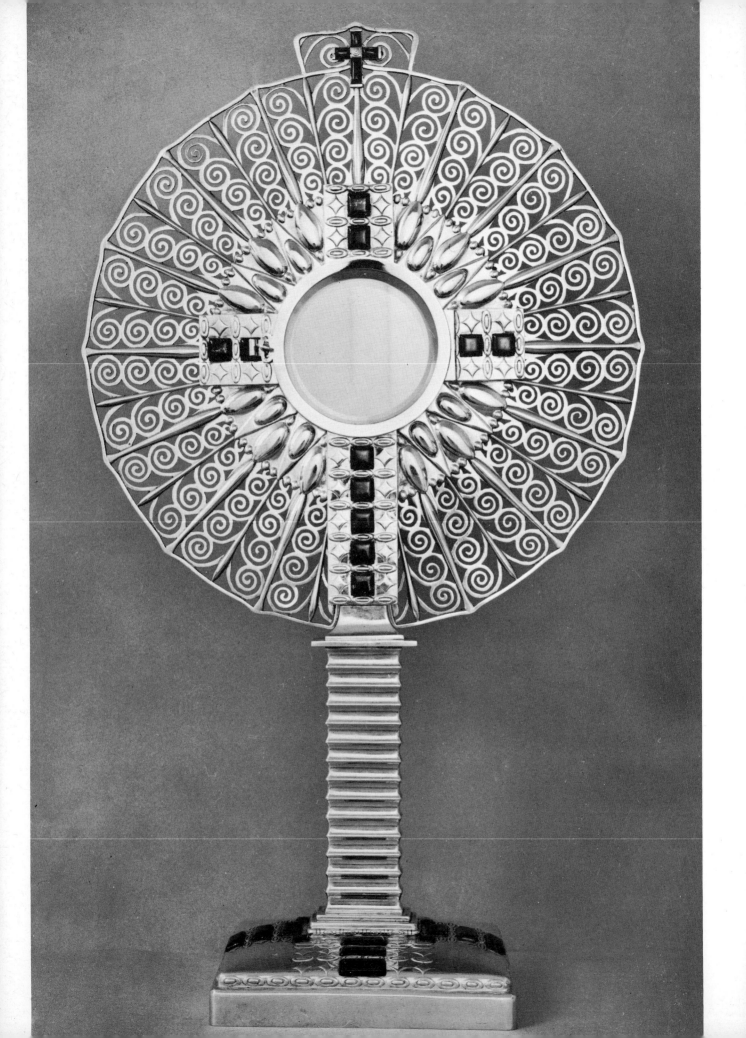

tendencies *à la* Peche at the Munich exhibition of 1922 as well as at the Paris International Exhibition in 1925 led to a violent dispute in which Adolf Loos and Julius Klinger opposed the Wiener Werkstätte. The Loos party's initiative was not aimed at combating Josef Hoffmann, but actually turned against the "feminine" trend which during the Peche period of the Wiener Werkstätte after 1915 exerted a supreme influence on part of its production.'[6]

Opposite:
Otto Wagner
Monstrance 1906
Gold and semi-precious stones, in Steinhof church, 50 cm./20 in. high
Photo Ritter

This deliberate turning inwards to the sweet side of the Viennese character, its sugariness and frivolity, brought with it the inevitable failure of the movement, because this hedonistic effeminacy was too modest to last. This was a case of 'pleasure at the helm; regardless of the sweeping whirlwind sway'. No advanced movement can proceed forwards for ever: by the end of the Austrian empire the Werkstätte had lost its impetus, and in the hectic twenties felt the heady flush of fever.

In the field of theatrical design, the great innovator was Alfred Roller (1864-1935), one of the very few people whom Mahler held in awe. He studied at the Academy of Fine Arts and was one of those brought to the School of Applied Arts by Myrbach. He was president of the Secession from 1901-2, edited *Ver Sacrum* for two years, and resigned with the Klimt group in 1905. Roller was chief designer at the Vienna opera house from 1903-9 and again after 1918. He collaborated mostly with Mahler, who was in charge of the opera from 1897 to 1907, and later Reinhardt, and designed both for the Burgtheater in Salzburg, and in Germany and the United States.

The great collaboration started with the epoch-making *Tristan* of 1903, which used red and orange for the drinking of the love potion in Act I. The love duet of Act II was in violet. This was commented upon as Mahler's 'music in light' and Roller's 'painting in light' but also criticized as too dark – a criticism of opera design which was to be heard by no means for the last time.[7] This was followed in 1904 by Mahler's version of *Fidelio* with the third Leonora overture after Act II, and a grimly realistic portrayal of the emergence of prisoners from a dark hole. In 1905 came *Rheingold* with spectacular cloud effects and no rams for Fricka. For the *Don Giovanni* of 12 December 1905, to commemorate the 150th anniversary of Mozart's birth, Roller introduced the so-called 'Roller towers' for the first time, permanent static features that served for various scenes. Since then, the permanent set has been much abused, not only in opera. His last collaboration with Mahler was *Iphigenia in Aulis* on 18 March 1907, in which the action took place in front of a curtain until just before the end when it parted to show the harbour of Aulis. Part of the campaign against Mahler was concentrated on the dimness of Roller's stage effects. Roller left soon after Mahler's resignation and only returned with the appointment of Richard Strauss in 1918. In 1911 he had designed for Strauss the now famous sets and costumes for the first performance of *Der Rosenkavalier* in Dresden and, four months later, in Vienna. His costumes have been followed more or less in every subsequent production. Roller did not design the world première of *Ariadne* in 1916, but he did do that of *Die Frau öhne Schatten* on 10 October 1919 and Pfitzner's *Palestrina* in the first Vienna performance earlier in the same year. In the Clemens Krauss era of 1929-34 he did the *Ring* as well as many other designs.

Twenty years after Roller's death one of the premières at the re-opening of the opera house in 1955 was *Rosenkavalier* with his scenery. Having started as an experimenter his designs became traditional, and his innovations are still being felt today.

99

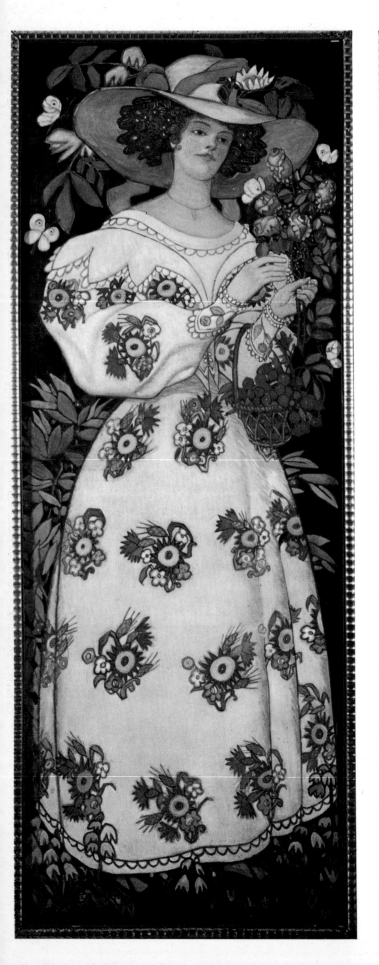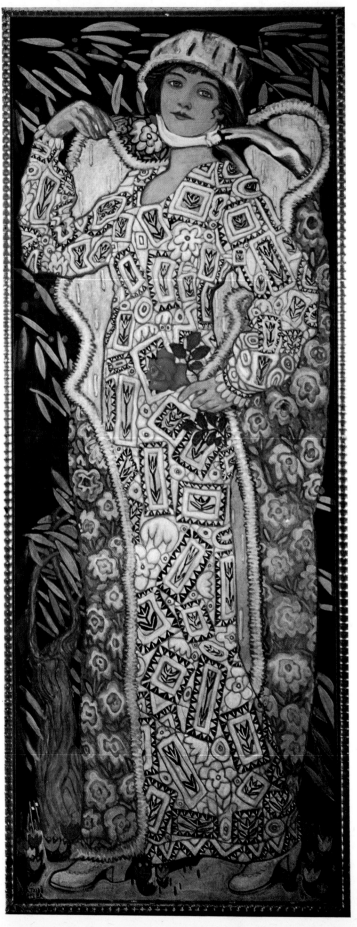

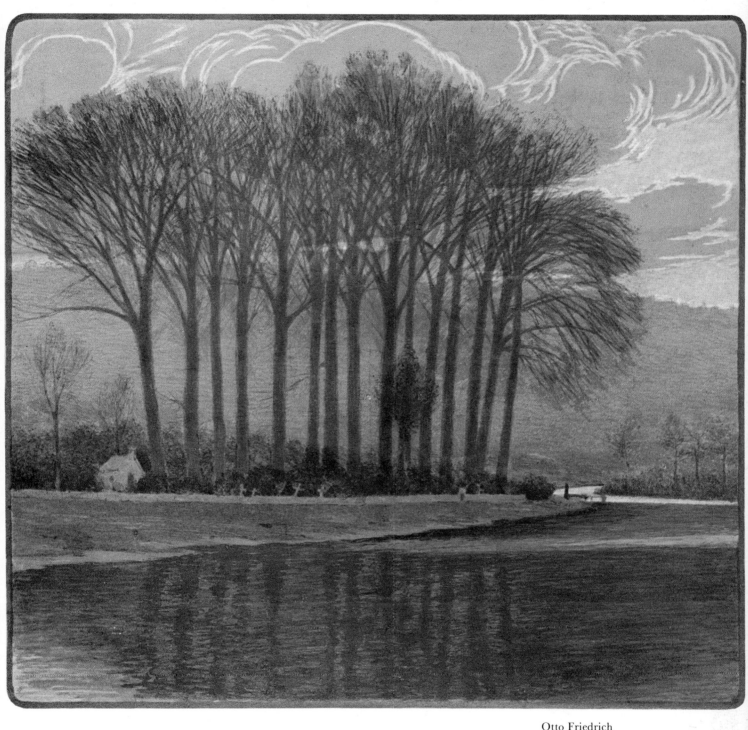

Otto Friedrich
Landscape c. 1908
Coloured lithograph,
31 × 34.5 cm./12 × 13½ in.
Artist's trial proof, possibly intended
for Secession portfolio of 1908,
with pencil sketches on reverse
Author's collection, photo author

Berthold Löffler
Two Decorative Panels 1913
Signed and dated, 210 × 80 cm./
83 × 31 in. including original frames
(probably designed by the artist)
Österreichische Museum für
Angewandte Kunst, photo
Galerie Pabst

PAINTING
AND THE BREAK WITH
HISTORICISM

Kolo Moser
Venus in the Grotto 1930
75 × 63 cm./29 × 25 in.
Private collection, photo Galerie Pabst

Franz Matsch
The Four Continents 1902
Signed, pastel on board, 51 × 85 cm./
20 × 33 in. maximum in original frame
Design for decoration in Palais Dumba
Galerie Pabst, photo Galerie Pabst

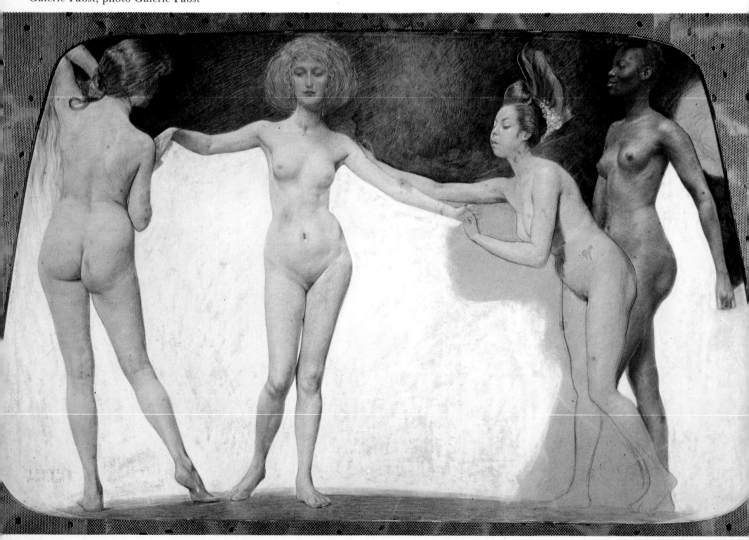

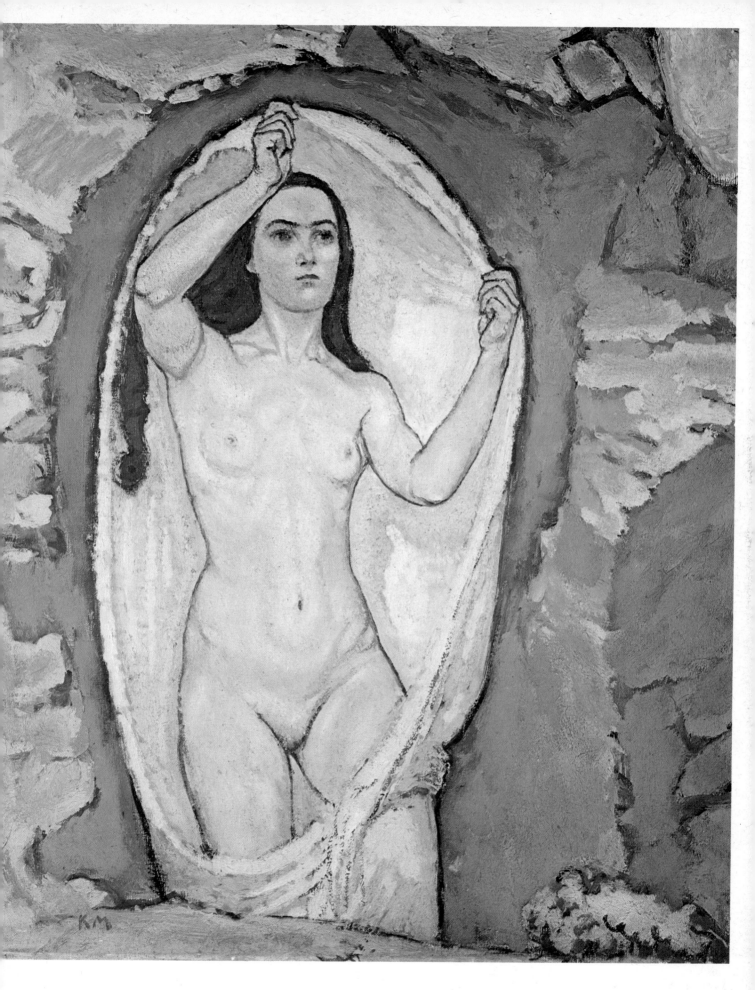

Künstlerhaus, Secession, Kunstschau and Hagenbund

Rudolf von Alt
Makart's Studio 1895
Watercolour, 69.5 × 100.4 cm./
27 × 40 in.
Historisches Museum der Stadt
Wien, photo Museum

If we are to understand why in 1897 nineteen artists formed the Vienna Secession, we must attempt to reconstruct the artistic atmosphere in that year. It was a situation as conservative and daunting as confronted the young architects walking along the Ringstrasse, and has direct parallels. Each year the Emperor opened the exhibitions of the Künstlerhaus, a society of architects, artists and sculptors founded in 1861 under the initiative of Siccardsburg from two smaller bodies, the Albrecht Dürer and *Eintracht* or Harmony groups. The new society was recruited mainly from the artists of the Ringstrasse, and soon became the bastion of the artistic establishment, housed in imposing but uninteresting buildings built between 1865-8. Under the presidency of Hans Makart (1940-84) the society achieved its greatest popularity.

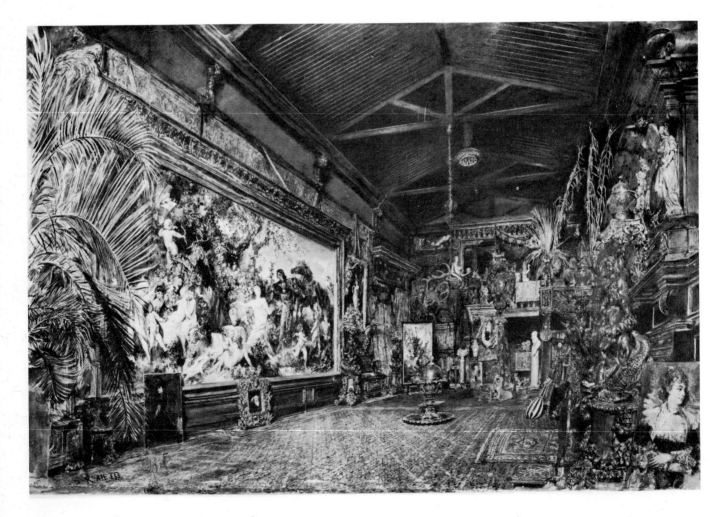

Makart's name is preserved in the phrase *Makart-Bukett*, a stiff arrangement of dried flowers and feathers, which exemplifies his rich and glutinous style. A pupil of Piloty in Munich, he was slightly influenced by Couture, certainly as to scale, and by Delacroix. He wished to re-create the world of Rubens, Titian and Veronese, and showed both by the sumptuousness of his studio with its hangings, armour and carpets, and his private receptions that the artist was to be considered a cultural prince in the affluent, and still very much aristocratic, Viennese society. To ensure a rich texture to his paintings, he used an asphalt base–which has damaged his works in the long run–and also added metal dust to his pigment.

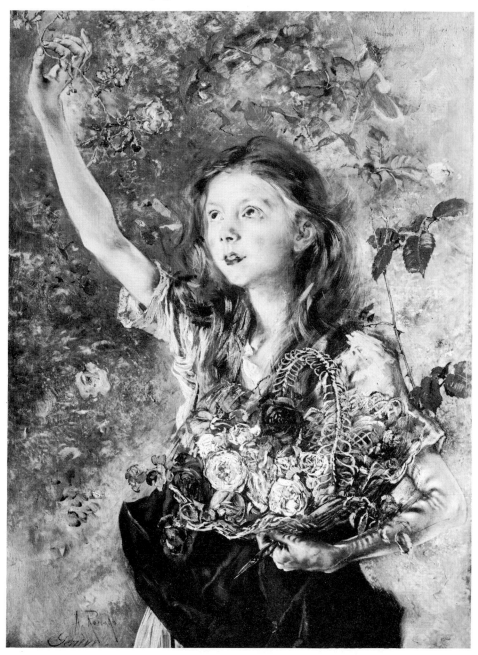

Anton Romako
Girl Picking Roses c. 1883
Signed, 89 × 66 cm./35 × 26 in.
Österreichische Galerie,
photo Museum

107

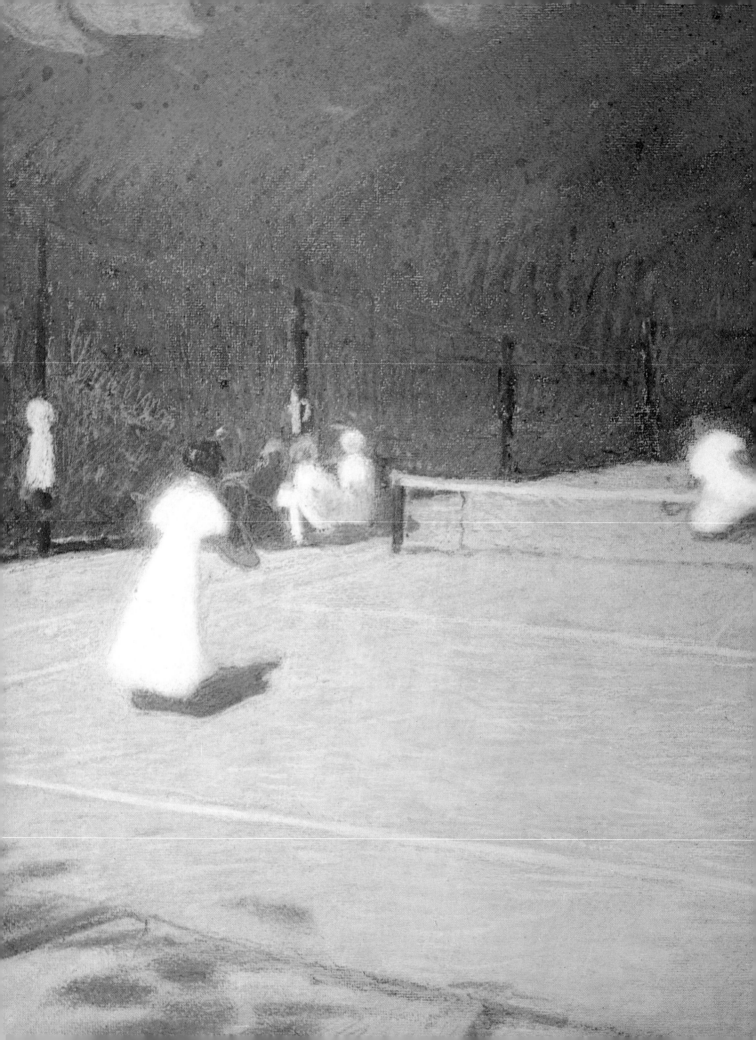

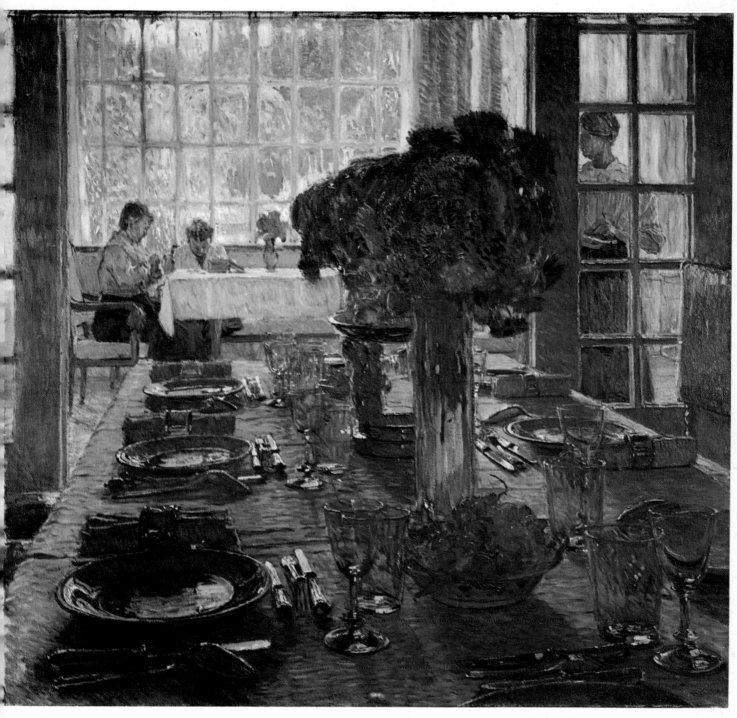

Carl Moll
The Breakfast Table c. 1906
86 × 93 cm./34 × 37 in.
Germanisches National Museum,
Nuremberg, photo Museum

Ludwig Graf
Tennis Party in Gossensass
(detail, see page 128)

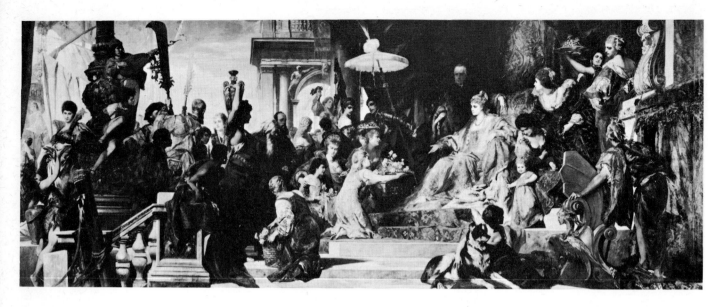

Hans Makart
Venice Honours Caterina Cornaro 1872-3
4 × 10.6 m./13 × 33 ft.
Österreichische Galerie,
photo Museum

Of course, not all artists were in the Künstlerhaus, for example Anton Romako (1832-89), the precise opposite of Makart by nature, and who considered himself professionally to be Makart's rival. The son of a joiner, he studied in Munich and then lived in Rome. There he married another expatriate, the daughter of a German architect, who, after bearing him two girls ran away with a man to Constantinople. He visited London and Geneva and in his last years returned to Vienna where he died in obscurity, his fresco sketches for the Rathaus refused and his life broken by the simultaneous suicides of his daughters and a young doctor from Orvieto. It has been suggested that he killed himself. He is best remembered for the romantic-heroic scenes of Tegetthoff on the bridge of his flagship at Lissa (c. 1880), for views of the Gasteiner Tal, and for portraits, sometimes of Italian fisher boys and peasant children. He painted in pale colours with a thin line and with indications, especially in his later works, that he was depressive. Indeed, if his work were shown nowadays, the influence of drugs would be suggested.[1]

Makart was much more successful. He organized the fancy-dress parade for the imperial silver wedding in 1879, and his monument by Tilgner in the Stadtpark of 1898 portrays him wearing his Renaissance costume, a cross between a stage Bluebeard and Charles V, whom he admired. From the 1870s onwards the fantastic carnival costume parties or *Gschnasfeste* were centred on him and his inspiration. The famous Italian Masked Festival was outdone by the Venetian Carnival, in which gondolas ran on wheels and attractive gondolieri helped the ladies in and out of their craft in the middle of the 'Canal Grande'. This was a highly successful period for the Künstlerhaus, since in one week 23,000 visitors saw Makart's *Entry of the Emperor Charles V into Antwerp*, and 50,000 visitors saw the Hungarian Mihály Múnkacsy's *Christ before Pilate*. Múnkacsy was born in 1846 and died after four years in an asylum near Bonn in 1900. In two months in 1881 95,000 people visited the Russian Vasili Wereschtschagin's cycle from the Russo-Turkish war, and again in 1897 he showed his famous series of Napoleon's Russian campaign. In 1873 Makart's colossal *Venice Honours Caterina Cornaro* (4 × 10.6 m.) took in 38,000 florins in entrance money and for various reasons was never seen again in Vienna until

1972. Makart died in the middle of painting his cycle of *The Four Seasons*, and planning a ceiling for the Kunsthistorisches Museum on the theme of 'the triumph of light'. Instead the ceiling was painted by Múnkacsy on the subject of *The Apotheosis of Art* with the already completed lunettes by Makart and spandrels by Klimt and his brother Ernst. In the Natural History Museum opposite, Hans Canon completed a large ceiling *The Life Cycle*. Klimt and Franz Matsch had already completed the ceilings of the Burgtheater in which Makart's pupil, Eduard Charlemont (1848-1906), was also involved in decorations for the foyer. The German Max Klinger's (1857-1920) multi-media triptych with a plaster sculpture border *The Judgment of Paris* (3.20 × 7.20 m.) of 1885-7 was presented to the state in 1901, while his *Christ in Olympus*, an even larger work (5.50×9.70 m.) painted in 1897, was the centre piece of the third Secession exhibition in 1898. He was very much taken up by the Secession and his multi-coloured marble, *Seated Beethoven*, was the centre-piece of the famous fourteenth Secession exhibition of 1902. Not all German artists were as successful. For example, Anselm Feuerbach (1829-80), who followed Makart as a professor of the Academy from 1873-6, had died neg-lected and all but forgotten in Venice before his *Fall of the Titans* was placed in position in the central hall of the Academy.

The Künstlerhaus and its membership stood for opulence and grandeur. An account of the achievements of a number of artists who are more or less ignored at the present time would be tedious indeed. Suffice it to say that like the historicist architects whose works we have examined the artists were likely to be history painters and monumental portrait sculptors. For a helpful indication of what their attitudes were, one can note the kind of foreign artist who was acceptable to them. In 1894, the International Exhibition had

Max Klinger
The Judgment of Paris 1885
Signed and dated, oils on wood and plaster, 3.2 × 7.2 m./10½ × 23½ ft. including frame
Kunsthistorisches Museum, photo Museum

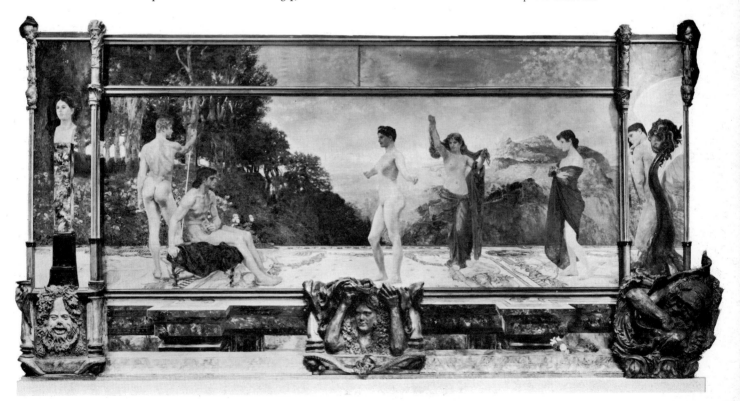

111

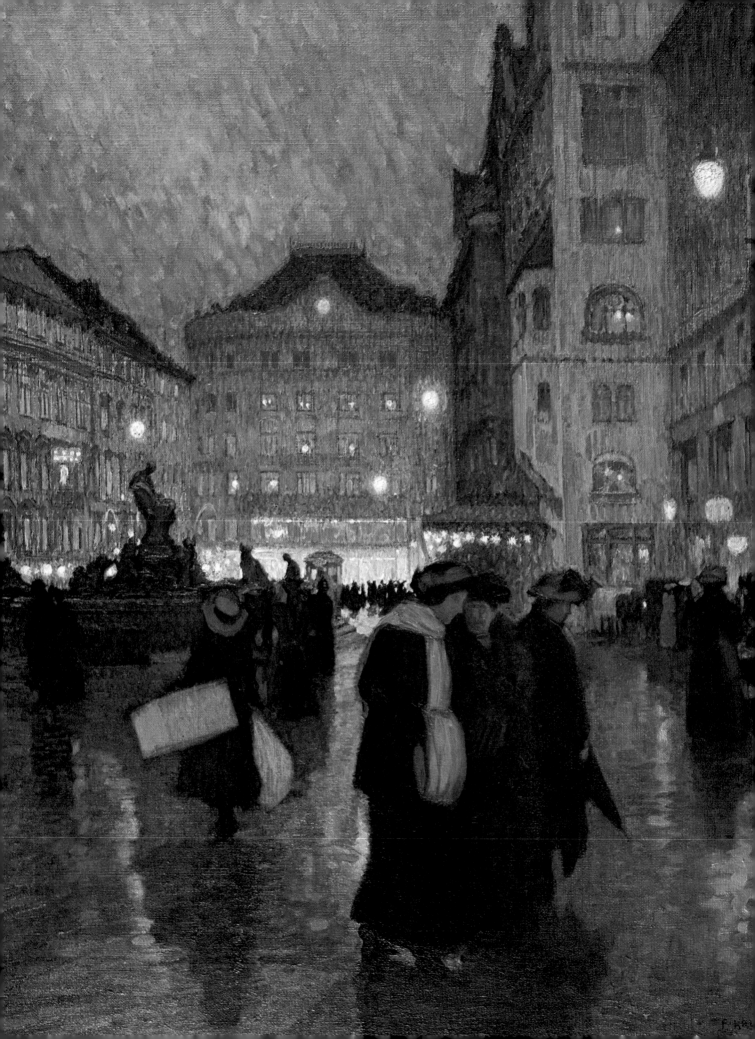

works by Alma-Tadema, Josef Israels, H.W.B. Davis, Sir Frederick Leighton, William Orchardson, Alfred Parsons and James Shannon. French contributors included Puvis de Chavannes, Alfred Sisley and Jean-Paul Laurens, and from Germany there was Max Liebermann. Later in the same year, an exhibition of 297 works from the Munich Sezession included Adolf Hölzel, Leopold von Kalckreuth, Franz von Stuck, Hans Thoma and Fritz von Uhde. At the Imperial Jubilee Exhibition in 1898 prizes were given to Solomon J. Solomon, Edwin Austin Abbey, Onslow Ford, Ilja Repin, Auguste Rodin, and a lesser prize to Claude Monet. In this exhibition which was, as it were, too late for the rebels, and which spread across the street to the rooms of the Musikverein by means of a specially built bridge, there were five works by Rodin including *Le Penseur*, bronzes by August Gaul, a sculpture by Klinger, paintings by Böcklin, who was made an honorary member, Adolph Menzel, the Düsseldorf Achenbachs, Trübner, Lenbach, Segantini and Fantin-Latour.[2]

In this atmosphere, what has been described as a palace revolution had been brewing since the Munich Exhibition of 1894. The final break, as far as it concerned the Künstlerhaus, came at an extraordinary general meeting on 22 May 1897. The dissidents, besides being discontented with the conservatism and lack of imagination in what was exhibited from abroad, were as concerned, if not more so, with the continued ill-treatment by the jury of Theodor von Hörmann (1840-95), a modest but excellent impressionistic *plein-air* land and townscape painter. He had fought as an officer at the battles of Custozza and Königgrätz, and then, in 1886, had gone to Paris where he

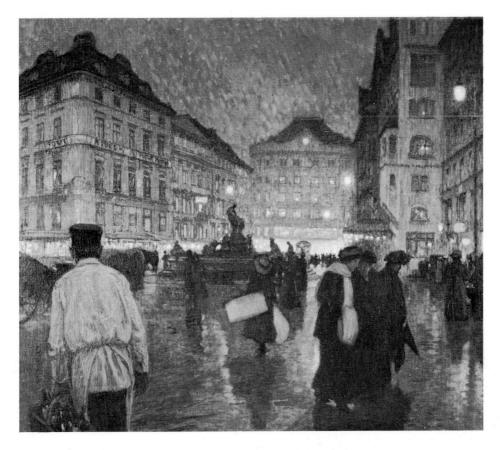

Ferdinand Kruis
Evening at the Neue Markt 1914
72 × 84 cm./28 × 33 in.
Historisches Museum der Stadt Wien,
photo Museum

studied painting under Raphael Collin. Having worked in Brittany and Barbizon, his work was light and naturally enough very French, so that he was even accused of painting with a toothbrush.[3] The critic Ludwig Hevesi (1842-1910) has described the efforts to get Hörmann hung in the Künstlerhaus.[4] Hevesi was very much on the side of the younger artists, and was to be responsible for the Secession's motto, placed over Olbrich's entrance: 'To every age its art, to art its freedom.' He became the Secession's first annalist with his book, *Eight Years of the Secession*, published in 1906. Four years later he committed suicide. Hörmann had exhibited with success in Paris, but the same pictures were refused by the Künstlerhaus jury, until finally, on a minor occasion, a Christmas exhibition, he was allowed to show thirty-six of sixty-five submitted. His friends wanted him to have a gold medal but this was refused. He believed so firmly in painting for his winter landscapes in the snow that he worked huddled like an eskimo, but eventually caught a chill doing this and died in 1895. On 26 March 1898, the anniversary of their leaving the Künstlerhaus, members of the Secession gathered at his grave to lay a wreath. In 1899, an exhibition was held in the Secession followed by an auction, and a fund for purchasing works of modern art was founded in his memory.[5]

In many ways the Hörmann case was the sand in the oyster for the Secession, but when Josef Engelhart (1864-1941), a well-to-do painter who had also been to Paris, returned to Vienna in 1893 with a watercolour *The Cherry-picker* depicting a nude under a tree, it was refused.[6] This was yet another irritation. In 1890 Gustav Klimt had been awarded the *Kaiserpreis* of 400 ducats for his painting of the interior of the Burgtheater, but in 1893, after he had been unanimously proposed for a professorship in history painting at the Academy, he was turned down for another due to direct intervention at the highest level, probably that of Archduke Franz Ferdinand.[7] On the other hand, in the same year, both Matsch and Klimt were put forward for the commission to paint a ceiling in the assembly hall of the university, and in September this was confirmed. What became of the commission belongs to the history of Klimt's development.

The feeling of unrest was in no way purely Austrian, because the Viennese artists were following in the wake of the rest of Europe. The Munich Sezession had been founded in 1892 by Stuck and his friends, followed next year by Berlin, which even had a new Sezession in 1906. In Vienna, from 1876 on, there had been a club of artists called the 'Haagen-Gesellschaft' who met at a *Gasthaus*. In the nearby Café Sperl, the 'Siebenerclub' had met from 1895. Then, between May and September 1897, Alt, Bacher, Bernatzik, Engelhart, Hellmer, Jettel, Klimt, Kraemer, Kurzweil, Lenz, Mayreder, Moll, Moser, Myrbach, Nowak, Ottenfeld, Olbrich, Pochwalksky, Roller, Sigmundt, Strasser, Stöhr and Tichy all left the Künstlerhaus. When, in 1898, Wagner followed them the revolution had come about.[8] Apart from the venerable watercolourist Rudolf von Alt (1812-1905), all the artists belonged to the younger generation.

The Society of Austrian artists, or Vienna Secession, had been formed *within* the Künstlerhaus in March 1897, and by April Klimt was writing as its president. On 21 June the first general meeting had been held, at which the idea both of a magazine and a building were first ventilated. In January 1898 the first number of *Ver Sacrum* appeared, running until 1903. The foundation stone for the house was laid on 28 April 1898. Apart from the income from the first extremely successful exhibition in March 1898 held in rented premises, the Mautner and Wittgenstein families both contributed to the costs of Olbrich's

114

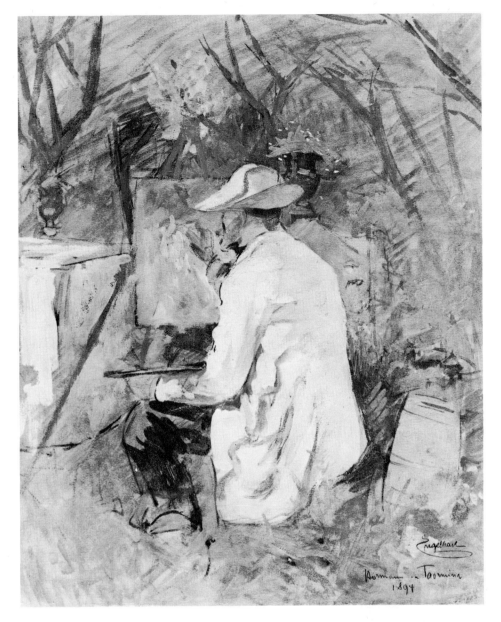

Josef Engelhart
*Theodor Hörmann Painting in
Taormina* 1894
Signed, tempera on card,
49.5 × 59.8 cm./19 × 23 in.
Österreichische Galerie, photo
Museum

building. An article in *The Studio* signed W.S. reported: 'The first exhibition
of the *Verein Bildender Künstler Österreichs* came like a revelation to those who
would not believe that modern art could ever make progress in this slow-
going city. Now it is a fact.' This was what the Secession was about, and *The
Studio* went on: 'Engelhart, Gustav Klimt or Wilhelm List (a young Austrian
artist who studied in Paris) and other members of the *Vereinigung* are convinced
of the fact that a frame should be designed in harmony with the picture.'
That, too, was in the spirit of the times.

Between the majority of the artists and the disparaged but rehabilitated
Hörmann, the topographical watercolourist Rudolf von Alt, honorary president until his death in 1905, who, by the brightness of his colouring, had been

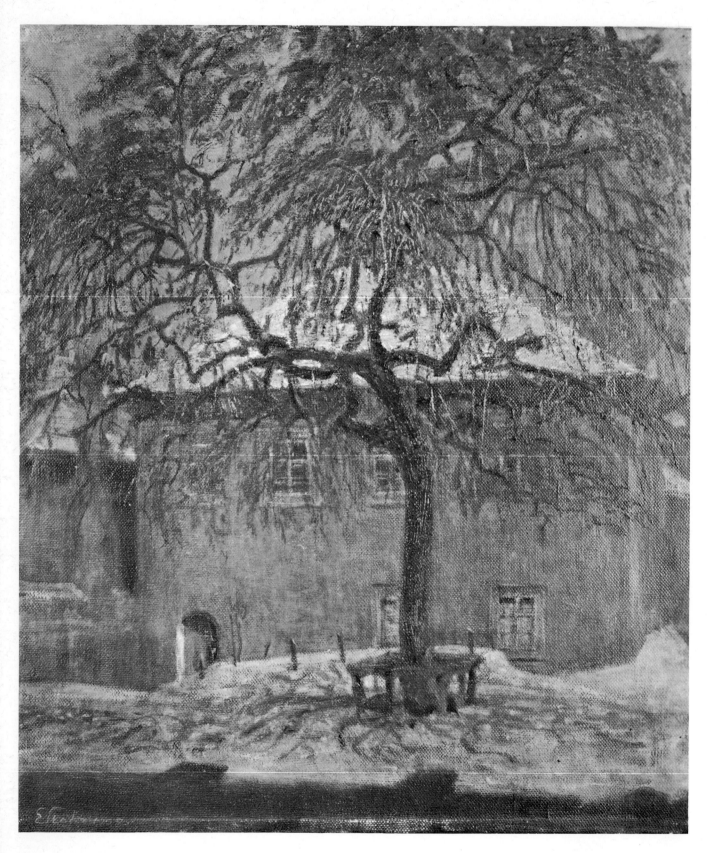

suspected of dangerous elements of impressionism, and Engelhart, whose stay in France did not leave him without a strong French streak in him, there is a tremendous gap. For the remainder it was not the French influence, but rather the kiss of a sacred springtime – the *Ver Sacrum* no less – of *Jugendstil* that had awakened them from sleep. In 1893 the nineteen-year-old Hofmannsthal had written:

> 'In Vienna art has no market. Here . . . even the most lively go to ground through a complete lack of competition and encouragement . . . People must be able to see pictures again – pictures and not hand-made oleographs; they must remember that painting is a magic writing that, with spots of colour instead of words, gives us an inner vision of the world, the puzzling, insubstantial, wonderful world around us. It is not a mere exercise of a skill, but has something to do with thinking, dreaming, and poetry, and nothing in common with making pretty pipebowls, tasteful hairdressers' dummies and similar objects, which are only indirectly connected with art . . . The art of colours must have the same hold on the spirit as the art of sounds.'[9]

An artistic movement is not made up of one single action. It is difficult to pronounce exactly how the change came about, because behind the related facts, there may have been other more significant and less obvious factors. Meetings at the salon of Bertha Zuckerkandl may have sparked off the action, as Hevesi reports. Alma Mahler-Werfel in *Mein Leben* said in 1960 that the first 'catacomb meetings' took place in her stepfather Carl Moll's new house, the villa built by Hoffmann. Certainly, according to Engelhart's memoirs, it was the sociably acceptable Moll who collected the necessary funds so that the new society could be a reality. According to Hevesi writing in the

Opposite:
Ernst Stöhr
Sexton's House at Melk 1905
52 × 46 cm./20 × 18 in.
Österreichische Galerie,
photo Museum

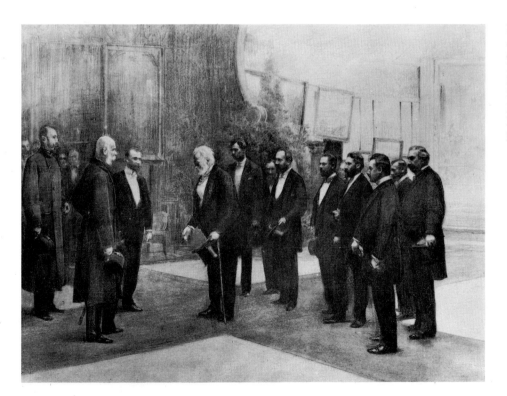

Rudolf Bacher
Franz Joseph I visiting the first Secession exhibition at the Gartenbau, 5 April 1898
Left to right: Klimt, Alt, Engelhart, Friedrich, Moll, Hoelzel, Tichy, Moser, Olbrich, Jettmar, Jettel
Pencil, 34.5 × 45.6 cm./14 × 18 in.
Historisches Museum der Stadt Wien, photo Museum

Studio special volume, *The Art Revival in Austria* in 1906, Moll 'was the very leaven of the new movement, Minister of Fine Arts without portfolio'.

Apart from the exhibitions connected with applied arts, in which Hoffmann was a guiding light, two more were of the greatest significance. The fourteenth (April to June 1902) at which Klimt's Beethoven frieze surrounded Klinger's *Seated Beethoven*, was momentous. Equally important for Austria and its influence on Klimt himself, must have been the sixteenth (January 1903), assembled by Wilhelm Bernatzik (1853-1906), who had been a pupil of Leon Bonnat in Paris. Called 'The Development of Impressionism in Painting and Sculpture', it included Renoir's *La Loge*, Manet's *Bullfight* and *Eva Gonzales*, no less than seven Cézannes and the same number of Degas; Medardo Rosso and Rodin were amongst the sculptors. Monet's portrait of *The Chef M. Paul* was bought for the state, and the Secession presented van Gogh's *Plain at Auvers* to the Modern Gallery, one of the earliest official acquisitions of his work to have taken place. The presentation was important in itself, because it encouraged the opening of the Modern Gallery in the Lower Belvedere in 1903, where it survived in that form until 1916. Another acquisition was Segantini's *The Wicked Mothers* (also called *The Child Murderers*). Alma-Tadema's *Fredegonde*, bought by Prince Liechtenstein from the 1894 exhibition at the Künstlerhaus for 15,000 gulden has been bequeathed to the gallery (but is now hidden in the depots of the Kunsthistorisches Museum).

The seventeenth exhibition, held in the spring of 1903, was a conspectus of secessionist work. There were vignettes to the catalogue by Ferdinand Andri (1871-1956), a strong portrayer of peasant life, by Adolf Böhm (1881-1927), the pointillist painter, Hoffmann, Rudolf Jettmar (1869–1939), a fine engraver, the Bohemian Emil Orlik (1870-1932), a painter and designer who lived for years in Japan, leaving to teach at the Kunstgewerbemuseum in Berlin where he died, and Leopold Stolba (1863-1929), a draughtsman with a clear *Jugendstil* line, and an important collaborator on *Ver Sacrum*. The poster was by Max Kurzweil (1867-1916) who had spent two years from 1892 onwards at the Academie Julian in Paris. He divided his time between winters in Vienna and summer in Concarneau, in Brittany, and married the daughter of its deputy mayor. His Vienna flat was decorated by Hoffmann. At the beginning of the First World War he had to leave his wife behind in France. He was called up, eventually becoming a war-artist, but in 1916, he committed suicide by shooting himself with his pupil and admirer Helga Heger, in the tradition of the Archduke Rudolf. Although far from famous in his lifetime, he was 'rediscovered' in an exhibition in 1965. Kurzweil never managed to balance his academic Viennese background with his French inclinations towards artists like Vuillard, Bonnard and even Marquet. An eclectic element persists in all his work except in his clearly thought out graphics, for instance the beautiful woodcut in five colours *Der Polster* (1903) of his wife Marthe sitting on a divan with her arms resting on a cushion.[10] He sent twenty oils from Concarneau to the 1903 exhibition. There were also representative works by Carl Moll, another artist in the centre of the *Jugendstil*, with whom Kurzweil was to be associated again in a collective exhibition at the Galerie Miethke in 1911.

Moll was a pupil of Jakob Emil Schindler, a *plein-air* naturalist landscape painter, whose daughter, the famous Alma Mahler, lived in his villa after her father's death and Moll's marriage to her mother. (She married in turn Mahler, Walter Gropius and Franz Werfel, and was loved and often portrayed by Kokoschka.) At the end of his life, Moll was considered by her to have been

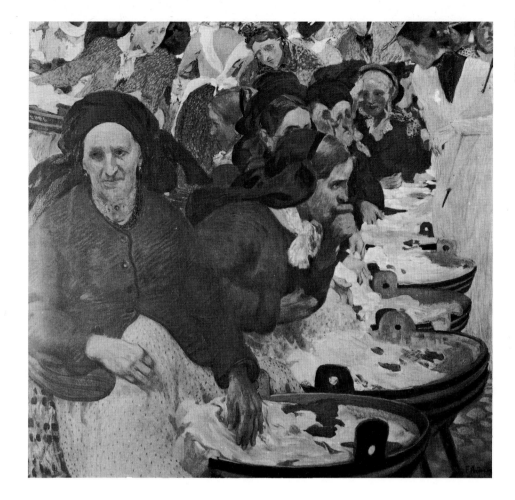

Ferdinand Andri
The Butterwomen 1902
Signed, 113 × 120 cm./44 × 47 in.
Österreichische Galerie, photo
Museum

a terrible Nazi, and when the Russians finally entered Vienna he felt that life
was no longer worth living, so he killed himself together with his daughter
(Alma Mahler's half-sister) and son-in-law, a notorious, patriot-hanging judge.
Although Alma Mahler hated her stepfather, yet according to her memoirs,
which are not absolutely reliable, he was responsible for three important
things in her own and Austria's cultural life. It was Moll who commissioned the
famous bust of Mahler, letting Mahler think that Rodin wanted to do the head
anyway; incidentally, it was Moll also who took Mahler's death mask. Then,
in the winter of 1912, Moll said to Alma, 'There is a gifted young fellow,
if I were you I would let him paint you.' This was her first meeting with
Kokoschka. Later, Moll annoyed her by presenting a series of her father's
landscapes to the gallery of Modern Art. In her memoirs, she dismisses him in
a few words, 'The eternal student of my father, Carl Moll, went from one
doctrine to another; to the end of his life he often sought out the most hetero-
geneous doctrines – to the detriment of his small talent.' Moll deserves better
than this, and it is strange that he has not been accorded at least the courtesy
of something beyond a doctoral thesis. On the selection committee of the
Kunstschau in 1908 he was certainly one of the earliest to encourage Kokoschka
by giving him the chance of appearing in public. Kokoschka subsequently

became one of Moll's friends, painting his portrait in about 1913. Also, between 1903 and 1908, Moll painted a series of fine interiors of the second villa 10 Woltergrasse in the nineteenth district of Vienna, built for him by Hoffmann in 1901. They include a view from the terrace (1903), a self-portrait in his studio (1906), showing a van Gogh portrait of his mother and Georges Minne's large sculpture *The Kneeling Boy*, *The Breakfast Table* of the same year, and two other views in his house, which show his wife. The predominant colour in them is blue, and they are painted with a strippled and scumbled technique and the parallel strokes characteristic of the time (List's *Female Portrait in Black and White* (1904) and Richard Gerstl's early portrait of Arnold Schönberg have this same technique). Moll's brushwork is left-handed with an upper left to bottom right diagonal stroke. It may well be that this strong brushwork was taken from Segantini, who probably influenced other artists, as we shall shortly see in discussing Böhm. Born in Avio, north of Lake Garda, Segantini was, to the Austrians, a South Tirolean, but well known through exhibiting in Vienna. Werner Hofmann describes Moll's style in this way:

'The historians of the turn of the century in Vienna praise the "practical idealism" of his talent for organization, which emerged especially in the preparation of exhibitions. As a painter he has conveyed something of the

Max Kurzweil
Sketch for 'The Cushion' 1902
Ink and bodycolour on blue,
30.5 × 38 cm./12 × 15 in.
Wiener Secession, photo Secession

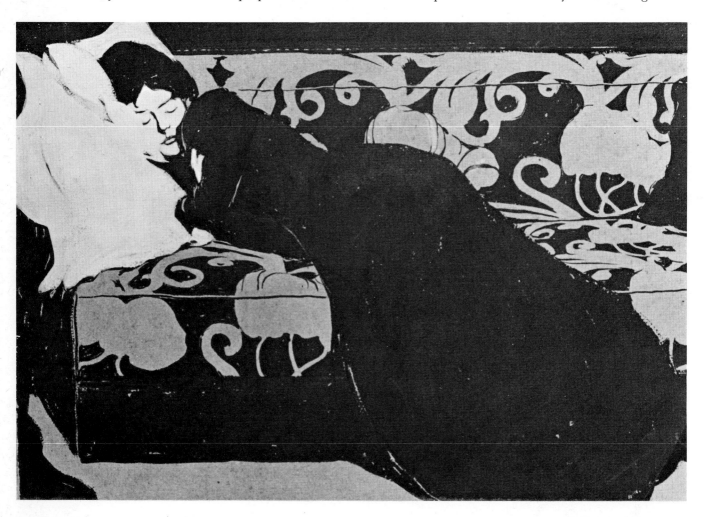

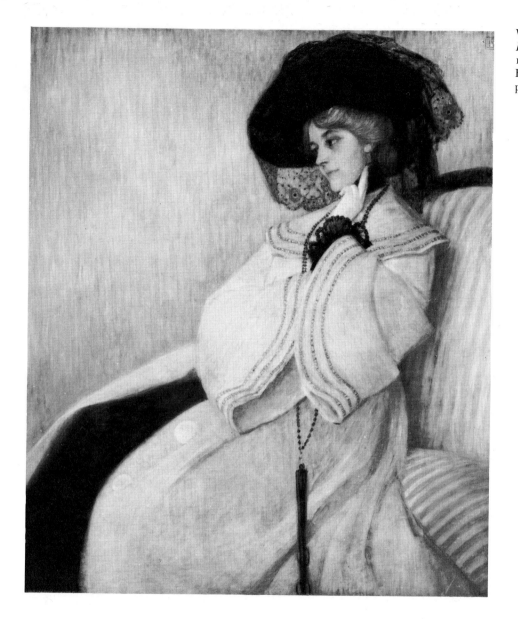

Wilhelm List
Female Portrait in Black and White 1904
135 × 119 cm./53 × 47 in.
Historisches Museum der Stadt Wien,
photo Museum

lack of pretension in the bright interiors which Hoffmann designed in his villas at the time. The picturesque weight of historicism has disappeared. Uprights and horizontal lines predominate, bright colours are shown in sunlight. The square format and the carefully considered brush strokes increase the impression of friendly tidyness. It is no abstract or decorative surface geometry, which surrounds these people, but a three-dimensional straightforward clarity. These are rooms which lead out into the open air. In his *Breakfast Table* (it is not perhaps a luncheon table?) Moll weights the cold, sparkling smoothness of the glasses, plates and cutlery with the sun-drenched curtain of light of the background. It is an atmosphere in which coolness and warmth are balanced. Here the 'sacred' springtime is divested of its literary pathos and becomes the appropriate season of a cultivated way of life. Moll is master of a factual, sensible, and restrained post-impressionism, which produces at one and the same time a scene of everyday life, and a symbol of harmonious tranquility.'[11]

But in addition, these interiors, almost severe in their blues and greens, are an extremely valuable evocation of what Hoffmann's interiors were like to live in. The geometrical squared effect is significant since Hoffmann's own designs were dictated to a considerable extent by his always drawing on squared paper.

To return to the exhibition of 1903, there was a cabinet of eleven landscapes by Alfred Roller, who had painted them as a calendar from his studio window. A further cabinet was devoted to genre scenes by Engelhart. Though affluent, he lived in a popular district where he easily found models to come into his studio from the street. He was a fine draughtsman, and when he returned from France after the 1890s his charming scenes of Viennese dance-halls and ball-rooms displayed something of the light colouring of Toulouse-Lautrec, whom he had met in Paris. As he grew older Engelhart lost this lightness of touch, but continued to portray Viennese low life and street fairs, circus people, waiters and actors. He was president of the Secession twice, first in 1899, and again, after the Klimt breakaway, in 1910, and travelled to Germany, France, Belgium and England on behalf of the Secession to collect works and foreign members. His perceptive descriptions of meetings with Klinger and Fernand Khnopff should be more widely known. He recalls taking Khnopff with Hermann Bahr to the Wurstelprater, where the Belgian painter was so horrified by the Croatian girls dancing with soldiers that he ran out holding a handkerchief to his nose – to the great delight of Bahr. Engelhart also describes the mystic atmosphere of Khnopff's Brussels villa in the Avenue des Courses and how that effete artist appeared at the top of the stairs in a magic circle of marble beside a single vase with a single flower on the floor, and protected by a footman and a metal barrier from unworthy intruders. Engelhart visited Boldini in Paris with Bernatzik, and asked if they could meet Whistler, whose portrait Boldini was painting. At last the American came in,

> 'a doll-like, delicate little man, with nervous movements, in a grey morning coat and trousers, and a grey top hat in his right hand. In his left he carried a stick as thin as a needle. His grey hair was curled into locks with the tongs, and his moustache brushed up. I was almost astonished not to discover the peacocks' feathers that the master was supposed to wear in his hair. His slender legs ended in black silk socks, and he wore thin pumps with delicate spats which revealed his chilblains. His cheeks and eyebrows were made-up and as he came towards us with his monocle in his eye, I had for some seconds the awful feeling that one of E. T. A. Hoffmann's gruesome figures was provoking us.'

Engelhart tried to arouse Whistler's interest in the Secession, by giving him a copy of the statutes and naming some of the Viennese and foreign members. ' " Is Degas one of them? You must have Degas. You can't do without him – there is nobody in painting besides Degas and myself." ' At this Boldini began to laugh quietly. In fact, works by Degas were exhibited by the Secession, and Whistler became a corresponding member as did Boldini.[12]

Engelhart cannot in all honesty be described as an artist of the *Jugendstil* but rather one of French influence, an influence which directly affected Adolf Böhm and Franz Jaschke (1879-1910) both of whom had more than a little pointillism

122

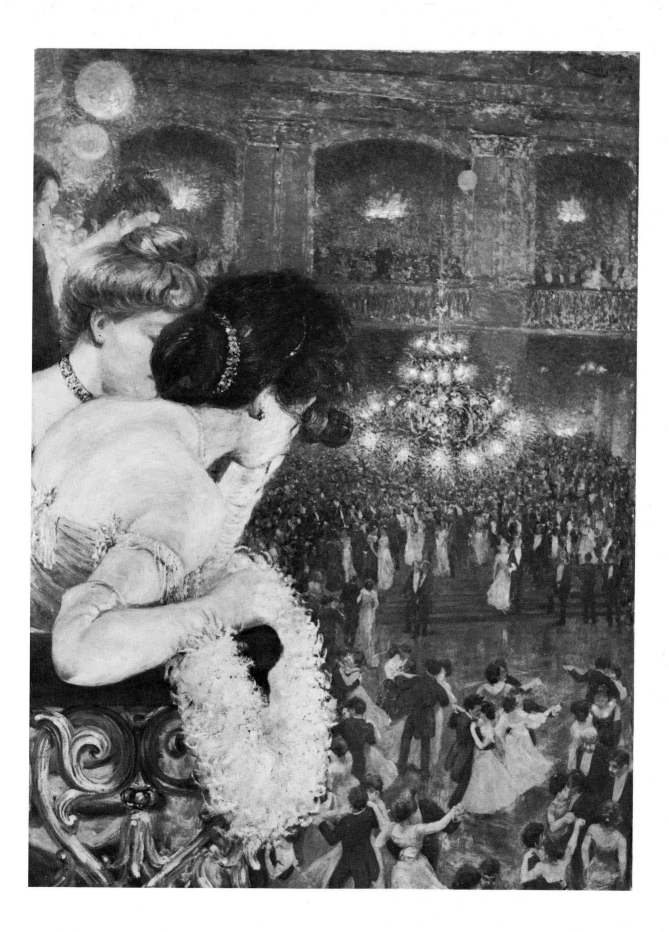

in their work, though Segantini must also be behind their spots of paints.

Also in 1903 the Secession held an important collective exhibition of the works of Klimt as a demonstration on his behalf in connection with the scandal of the University cycle. In the eleventh exhibition, in 1904, there were works by the Swiss Ferdinand Hodler, who also designed the poster. A friend of Klimt's he bought his *Judith* and exerted some influence on Austrian artists. However twenty works in the same show by Edvard Munch were of greater significance, and influence, having a marked effect not only on Gerstl but also on Kokoschka.

The twenty-first exhibition in 1904 was devoted to Albert Besnard and the German Wilhelm Trübner, whose still-life work was not unlike that of the Austrian Carl Schuch who had died the year before. The twenty-second show of 1905 (with a poster by Plečnik) was devoted to sculpture, including works by Bourdelle Hildebrand and Mestrovič, and, among the Austrians, works by Hellmer and Anton Hanak.

Franz Jaschke
The Danube Canal, Vienna, Winter 1903
Signed, 83 × 113.5 cm./33 × 45 in.
Österreichische Galerie,
photo Museum

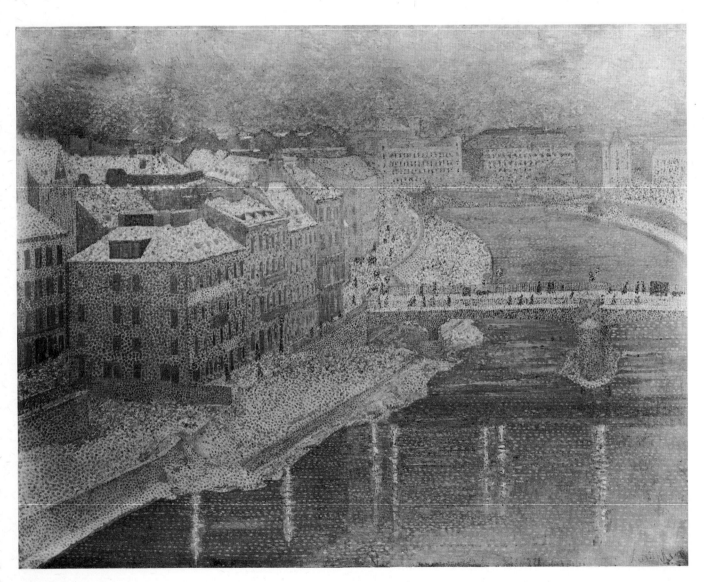

As recently as 1972, the Secession was again torn by a conflict between commercialism and principles. The first break occurred in 1905: when the owner of the Miethke Gallery had died, a new backer, the jeweller Paul Bacher, had been found on condition that Carl Moll should become artistic adviser (which in the event he did), since, owing to him, there had been shows at Miethke's of Gauguin, van Gogh and Goya, as well as works by Romako and Schuch after their deaths. But Bacher also insisted that the gallery should be run within the Secession. Even Engelhart was against this, because this open commercialism was exactly the kind of objection they had made against the Künstlerhaus. A vote was taken and the Klimt group, which included eighteen members, broke away. They were Josef Auchentaller, Wilhelm Bernatzik, Adolf Böhm, Adolf Hölzel, Josef Hoffmann, Felician Freiherr von Myrbach, Hans Schwaiger, Franz Jäger, Gustav Klimt, Max Kurzweil, Wilhelm List, Richard Luksch, Koloman Moser, Franz Metzner, Carl Moll, Emil Orlik, Alfred Roller and Otto Wagner. With the exception of two or three at the most the work of all these artists is still of considerable importance.

When the Secession was first founded it had been agreed that the society should exist in the first instance for ten years. The Secession continues still, but this split removed much of the first impetus and enthusiasm after only eight years. That impulse was only regained in the forty-ninth exhibition held in March 1918, for which Schiele did a poster of himself sitting at a table with other artists, and sold twenty of his works – a great personal success. A number of other contributors to the show were to become prominent in the twenties, though none of them were members, including Anton Faistauer, Alfred Kubin and Albert Paris Gütersloh. This exhibition, although it occurred in the moral depression occasioned by the end of the war, opened the way to the twenties.

After the split came two important events, namely the Kunstschau exhibitions of 1908 and 1909. They offered a public view of the young Schiele and Kokoschka, who had also been shown publicly by a lesser, but not uninteresting, breakaway group, the Hagenbund, active between 1900 and 1938. The Kunstschau exhibitions and the Hagenbund both deserve investigating in more detail.

The Kunstschau exhibitions of 1908 and 1909 should be considered as one manifestation. Klimt's role was of the greatest importance, he being president and making the opening speech. In 1947, Edith Hoffmann wrote of the Kunstschau that it was the 'apotheosis of Klimt, and gave birth to the art of expressionism in Vienna. *Art Nouveau* was seen here at its height – and on the point of passing beyond its zenith.'[13] Peter Altenberg called the Klimt room of the 1908 show the 'Gustav Klimt Church of Modern Art'. Hevesi wrote: 'The world has become magnificent again. For the first time since Makart . . . that Viennese nuance . . . is a feeling that can be sensed. People are beginning to open their hearts to Klimt. How much longer before he will be called "our Klimt"?'[14] Klimt was either ecstatically acclaimed or equally hated, the negative views of the liberal Karl Kraus and the advanced Adolf Loos being shared by the conservative Eduard Pötzl. Werner Hofmann expresses dismay that the state should have given a subvention of 30,000 kronen to the Kunstschau, that Josef Hoffmann should have shown a design for an imperial pavilion, and that Kolo Moser should have shown postage stamps for Bosnia-Herzegovina in the very year when the provinces were to be annexed, and only ten years before the disaster at Sarajevo,[15] yet this is hindsight in an extreme form. While the Klimt group were hardly the establishment, they would have been astonished at the idea of giving a politically engaged artistic demonstration.

After the breakaway of 1905 the Klimt group had no home or gallery to exhibit their work. Since 1908 was yet another Imperial Jubilee, they used it as an excuse for a grand exhibition, and looked round for a home for it. Next to the Vienna ice-rink was a piece of ground, where there had once been a cavalry barracks, and which was reserved for the site of the Konzerthaus to be opened in 1913. On this site Josef Hoffmann created a series of exhibition pavilions with fifty-four rooms in all, and alongside them built his inexpensive 'country house'. The garden was by Alfred Roller and the architect Emil Hoppe designed a small concrete court. In the first and more comprehensive exhibition of 1908, all fields of art from ecclesiastical art and theatre design (there was an open-air theatre) to playing cards and tombs were included. One room was devoted entirely to posters, and outside the pavilion there was sculpture by Franz Metzner. Roller showed designs for Hofmannsthal's *Ödipus und die Sphinx* as performed by Max Reinhardt's Deutsches Theater in Berlin, as well as for Mozart and Wagner operas, and there were designs by Orlik for *Die Räuber*, also for Reinhardt. Böhm organized a room devoted to art for children. A garden gate by the architect Karl Maria Kerndle was described in the catalogue as an attempt to use reinforced concrete artistically. Moser's mosaic and window designs for Wagner's Steinhof church were in the church art section. The Werkstätte exhibited, amongst other objects, the extraordinary silver casket made by Czeschka for the Emperor's visit to the Skoda works in 1906 which showed the battleships *Zenta* and *Babenberg* with *repoussé* work by Klimt's brother Georg. In the gardens there were ceramics by Powolny and others.

The second exhibition, which was a complement to the first, had foreign contributors, including works by Cuno Amiet, three sculptures by Ernst Barlach, three paintings by Bonnard, one by Maurice Denis, one by Gauguin, no less than eleven by van Gogh, two by Matisse, sketches for Ibsen's *Ghosts* by Munch, twelve works by Jan Toorop, four by Felix Vallotton, two landscapes by Vlaminck, and two paintings by Vuillard. There was also a display of German and British applied art. In 1908, there were posters for the exhibition by Löffler, and, more astonishingly, by the twenty-two year old Kokoschka. In one room, Kokoschka had his first public show, some designs for tapestries called *Die Traumtragenden* (the dream bearers), which he had refused to submit to the jury, and which were bought by the Werkstätte but are now lost. There was a sculpture of a girl's head, and also book illustrations, probably designs for *Die träumenden Knaben*, which was published that year with a dedication by Klimt. In the second part in 1909 were new works by Kokoschka, including his portrait of the actor Reinhold, the 'white animal killer', and another sculpture, probably his own self-portrait. It was in the open-air theatre that Kokoschka's *The Murderer, Hope of Woman* was performed with a resulting scandal. Kokoschka has described his being saved by the help of Adolf Loos and a handful of faithful followers from being battered to death. Although Joseph Lux in *Deutsche Kunst und Dekoration* described Kokoschka as a 'Rimbaud' the more general attitude to him was that of the heir to the throne, Franz Ferdinand, who on first seeing a picture by Kokoschka uttered the now notorious remark, 'They ought to break every bone in that fellow's body.'[16]

Klimt showed sixteen paintings and a number of drawings in 1908. Apart from *The Kiss* there were the *Three Ages of Man*, the portraits of Frau Fritza von Riedler, Adele Bloch-Bauer, and Margaret Wittgenstein-Stonborough, and the provocative *Danaë*. In the 1909 show there were his *Judith II* also called *Salome*, and the two versions of *Hoffnung*, a pregnant woman in profile, of which one was draped. He had not shown the nude variant since it was painted in 1903. The latter's first owner was Fritz Wärndorfer, who thought it best to keep it in a shrine protected by doors.

In the second show there were four works by Egon Schiele, including portraits of the painters Hans Massmann and Anton Peschka, both seated in profile, with their arms stretched out on the arm-rests of their chairs.[17]

Werner Hofmann cannot accept Lux's description of the Kunstschau as 'a house of life', because of its optimism in the face of considerable social poverty at the time, and because it failed to foreshadow the coming disaster of 1914-18. Yet Bertha Zuckerkandl recalled sitting in the café of the Kunstschau with Hevesi and Richard Muther discussing how to counter the press attacks, which implies that it was not the positive success its sponsors would have wished for it.[18] Hofmann may consider the Kunstschau to have been an anachronism, yet it was still an artistic manifesto for contemporary supporters. This is, I think, the right view. All that Hoffmann, Klimt and Moll believed poured out in an agglomeration of *Jugendstil* and the Werkstätte. Loos considered it frivolous and for that reason tried to save Kokoschka from the contamination of employment by the Werkstätte by getting him commissions outside that body. It is

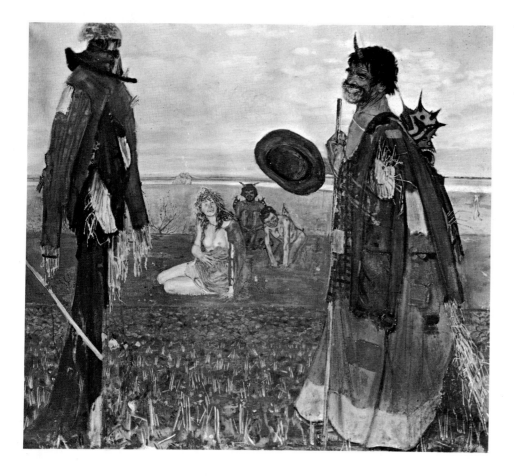

Vlastimil Hofmann
The Scarecrow 1900
Signed, 125 × 146 cm./49 × 57 in.
Österreichische Galerie,
photo Museum

127

true that the photographs of the Kunstschau buildings demonstrate how much of the immediately modern ideas had congealed in Hoffmann's execution, but nevertheless with the inclusion of Kokoschka and Schiele it did show the way into the future.

Similarly, the Hagenbund, though a minor aspect of artistic life in Vienna, was important because it supported another group of artists who, in turn, were not afraid to include and further the two younger talents. The Hagenbund had its origins in the Café Sperl group of artists who produced a portfolio of prints shown in the Albertina in 1905. When the first break with the Künstler-haus took place in 1897, there were still a number of moderately progressive artists who were excluded from the Secession. Therefore the *Künstlerbund Hagen* was first constituted on 3 February 1900. They then included Albin Egger-Lienz (1868-1926), the independent expressionist East Tirolean who took his name from his home town, a strong painter who like Stanley Spencer decorated a war-memorial chapel. Ultimately, he only exhibited as a guest. Josef Urban (1875-1933), the architect and graphic artist, was the most important of the group. He designed their exhibition buildings in the Zedlitz-gasse by transforming a market hall. He left for America in 1911, having been

Ludwig Graf
Tennis Party in Gossensass 1908
Signed and dated, chalk with white on card, 45 × 63 cm./ 18 × 25 in.
Österreichische Galerie, photo Museum

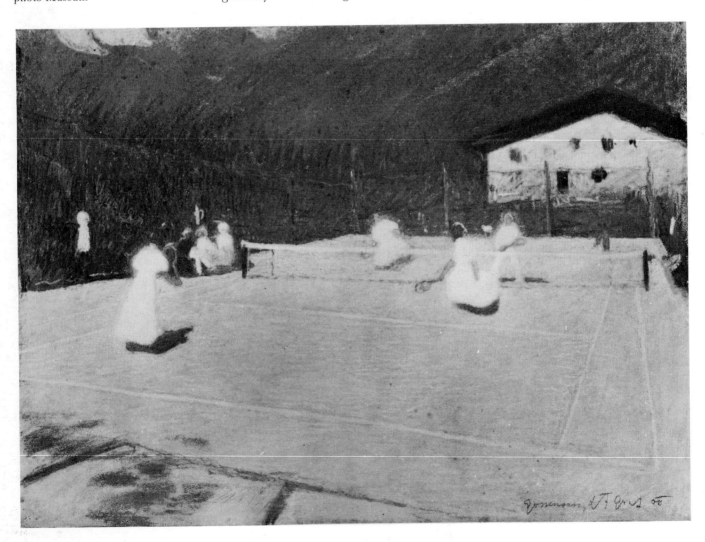

president in 1906. The other members ranged from Ludwig Ferdinand Graf (1868-1932), a *Jugendstil* painter of considerable charm and appeal, to the sculptor, Georg Ehrlich (1897-1966), an associate of the Royal Academy until his death. Heinrich Lefler (1863-1919) best remembered as a graphic artist was the first president of the group and brother-in-law of Urban. He was in charge of a painting class at the Academy, when he saw Gerstl's *The Sisters* in the studio which the young artist shared with Viktor Hammer, and since Gerstl had just left the general class of Griepenkerl, Lefler asked him to join his own class. Later he infuriated Gerstl by participating in the Imperial Jubilee of 1908, but this and the other consequences of 1908 belong to Gerstl's own story. Kokoschka, on the other hand, did costume designs for the procession for his professor Löffler, including the delightful peasant boy on an ox. Both Löffler and Powolny were members and showed ceramics in the early exhibitions. Oscar Laske (1874-1951), a pupil of Otto Wagner, who did colourful lithographs of scenes in Istanbul and north Africa with a gift for indicating bustle and crowds, joined in 1907, becoming a member of the Secession just before his death.

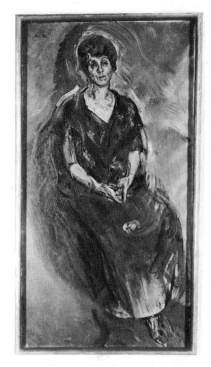

Anton Kolig
Bertha Zuckerkandl 1915
150 × 81 cm./59 × 32 in.
Historisches Museum der Stadt Wien,
photo Museum

With a group of friends, including Faistauer, Gütersloh, Peschka, Böhler and Wiegele, Schiele formed a group 'Neukunst' soon after leaving the Academy which showed at the Pisko Gallery in about 1909. In January 1911 this group were shown together at the Hagenbund, the members that exhibited being Gütersloh, Kokoschka, Anton Kolig, Laske, Georg Merkel, Schiele and Wiegele. Some of Kokoschka's works of this period remain amongst his most important, such as the portraits of Karl Kraus, Adolf Loos and his wife Bessie, Peter Altenberg and the exclusive tailor Ebenstein. There are also the wonderful portraits of the son of Oskar Reichel, one of his earliest collectors. In the next spring show of 1912 Schiele's pictures caused another shock. Already in 1910 he was writing to Peschka, 'I would like to get away from Vienna as soon as possible. How ugly everything there is. Everybody is jealous of me and underhanded. There is falsehood in the eyes of former colleagues. Vienna is full of shadow, a black city.'[19] Quite apart from Schiele, the rest of the group provoked an outcry, but Arthur Roessler's judgments read strangly now. In 1911 he wrote, 'In order to be sure of a trump card the youngest asked Kokoschka to be their guest. He came and filled two rooms with his lemurs covered in a broth of milky pus, blood and sweat, thickened with ointment. I thought before that Kokoschka was artistically impotent. I no longer do this as I saw proofs that he has gifts as a painter.'[20] Next year Schiele was described by one critic as 'perverse' which annoyed Roessler who was a supporter of his painting.

The Zedlitzhalle was closed in 1912 until after the war, probably due to the opposition by Archduke Franz Ferdinand, but the society lived on with vicissitudes until 1938, when together with the Secession it became suspect to the Nazis through its independence and disappeared.

The artistic movements and exhibitions of 1894-1918 have shown the background in which the four most important artists confronted the public and their colleagues. The canvas on which to depict Klimt, Schiele, Gerstl and Kokoschka is, so to speak, primed.

Gustav Klimt, Leader of the Revolt

A painter can start as a rebel and end in extreme respectability and wealth. Such was Millais, an obvious example of an artist whose style changed radically. On the other hand some artists have reputable beginnings, but their later life and ultimate achievement is surrounded with controversy. This was the case with Gustav Klimt. During his lifetime, he remained isolated in Austria in spite of exhibitions abroad, only a handful of works finding their way into foreign collections.[1] He did win gold medals for his great *Philosophy* (1900) at the World Exhibition in Paris, and for *The Three Ages* (1908) in Rome. Both *Philosophy* and *Pallas Athena* were reproduced by heliogravure by a London firm, no doubt in connection with their exhibition in Paris, but without any great results as far as Klimt's international reputation was concerned.

Klimt's artistic personality is not as easily pinned down as a corpse of some brilliant moth or butterfly in a showcase. It will help our understanding of him if, before any formal discussion of his work, we can establish the reasons for the fundamental change that came over him between about 1892 and 1895, and appreciate the cause of the 'fault' in his character that urged him towards such strong eroticism. The influence of other artists on him in single works, and the views of three contemporaries are fundamental to our understanding of this change.

Klimt started his career as a decorative painter on a grand scale, not only influenced by Makart, but in his early works even being confused with that showy artist.[2] As such, he was employed by the Empress Elisabeth in 1885, working as a team together with his brother Ernst and Franz Matsch on the ceilings of her bedroom, salon and study in the absurd but delightful Villa Hermes near Schönbrunn, in the Lainzer Tiergarten. (It was built for the Empress by Hasenauer in 1883, with plenty of cast-iron verandas and terraces in a sort of asymetric Deauville-Scarborough style.) However one wonders whether the Empress even knew Klimt's name at the time.

For Semper and Hasenauer's Burgtheater, the team were again employed on the grand staircases between 1886 and 1888, for which they had to paint a history of the stage. Klimt's ceilings were *The Chariot of Thespis*, which leant heavily on Alma-Tadema and Frederick Leighton, *Shakespeare's Theatre*, for which he used costume photographs of his brother Georg and other relations, and the splendid *Theatre in Taormina*, again very like Alma-Tadema, and for which we might suppose he had visited Sicily, though there is no evidence for this.

He was next employed on another public commission, the staircase of the Kunsthistorisches Museum, which would have been carried out by Makart had he not died. For this he painted on a stucco background, all within one year between 1890 and 1891, figures symbolizing art through the ages from Egypt to the Cinquecento. Klimt himself considered his eight spandrels and two figures between columns as an important point in his development, as indeed they are. They foreshadow his idea of ideal beauty in woman and even his extremely idiosyncratic designs in dresses and drapery. The most interesting is one of the two minor figures between columns, the girl from Tanagra, who represents the second stage of Greek art. Klimt slipped in a very modern young Viennese in a chic dress leaning forward towards a sprig of laurel. With her hair piled forward on her brow, and falling round her shoulders so that at first glance it looks like a boa of feathers, she suggests Mucha, although that artist was all but unknown in Vienna. After working as a scenery painter, the young artist was a founder member of the Secession from 1897-1901. Klimt underwent a tremendous change, his own dark night of the soul, which happened to him before the first visit to Ravenna in 1903. The revolt of 1897 was symptomatic of this malaise, and much more of a climacteric than the Kunstschau exhibition of 1908. In 1887 he had visited Paris, in 1888 Venice, Trieste and Munich. In 1892, both his father and his brother Ernst died. In the beginning of that year the two Klimts and Matsch had moved their studio to the Josefstadt, but by 1894, Gustav's brother gone, the studio began to break up and forced Klimt into independence. (Matsch continued his career by working for the Empress at the Achilleon in Corfu, and becoming the Emperor's favourite portraitist.) Consequently, although the first and second Secession exhibitions in 1897 and 1898 were still overloaded with palm trees, garlands and laurels—in spite of or because of Olbrich—yet the involuntary protest at the heavy hand of imperial Austria was important to Klimt, and therefore far more significant than what he and his group might or might not have done in 1908.

If Klimt (and others with him) felt a strong dissatisfaction with the state of their immediate world this was expressed in the change in Klimt in the decade before the Ravenna visit, and the beginnings of his great 'gold' period. Beyond this sacred springtime, there was a sense in all branches of art that now was the time to demystify the subject. The straightforward sexuality of Klimt's work from now on, that open-mindedness which he passed on to Schiele, stem from his confrontations with the fetters of censorship. The alterations which were demanded to his very first Secession poster are typical. On the right Pallas Athena, symbol of 'To every age its art, and to every art its freedom', stood protected by a shield. Above her and apparently behind a wall the naked Theseus wrestled with the Minotaur, whose nakedness was partly masked by a bush of tangled hair and his own swirling tail. To appease the censors Klimt was obliged to cover Theseus' sex organs with the stem of a tree which suddenly grew up parallel to the goddess' spear. Nor can the trauma of the scandal concerning the commission with Matsch for the ceiling to Vienna University's main hall be ignored. In 1899 Klimt was finishing his *Schubert at the Piano* for the over-door of the Palais Dumba music-room, the first indication of a softness in treatment, but in the next year he painted *Nuda Veritas* with a quotation from Schiller inscribed above the nude figure: 'You cannot please everyone by your deeds and your art—do it right for the few. To please the crowd is bad.' Klimt showed it in the fourth Secession exhibition in 1899 as *The Naked Truth*, and it entered the collection of Hermann Bahr. When in March 1900 he showed *Philosophy* the first of the pictures for the university ceiling in the Secession, there was an outcry. He now began to feel the bonds of a moral censorship, and was to become more and more openly aggressive, for example in the pregnant woman of *Hoffnung I* of 1903 (although he did not exhibit it then), his *Danaë* of 1907-8 shown in the Kunstschau, and the illustrations to an edition of Verlaine's *Femmes* and to Lucian's 'hetaira dialogues' in 1907. In both these German publications, it is true that drawings rather

131

than deliberately commissioned material were used, yet not for nothing could a distinguished English art-historian remark in front of Klimt – and Schiele – at the Royal Academy Secession exhibition of 1971, that he had never seen such a display of pubic hair before.

Nebehay believes with other commentators that the death of Klimt's father and that of his brother in the same year had an extreme effect. The deaths were a terrible break, 'making a caesura in his creative work'. Klimt was very attached to Ernst, who had been married to Helene Flöge for fifteen months, and there was a daughter by the marriage of whom Klimt became the guardian. The Flöge sisters owned an extremely smart dressmakers' establishment in the Casa Piccola on the Mariahilferstrasse. The interior was decorated by the Werkstätte with collages by Kolo Moser. Before this occurred, Klimt had become attached to the younger sister Emilie, who was to be his mistress, and for whom he called when he was dying, 'Emilie must come.' Hans Tietze, who knew them well, wrote in 1919, immediately after Klimt's death, that there was a contradiction in Klimt's life.

[His] 'primaeval power affected people, especially women, and one sensed a strong earthy essence in his presence. But there was an interior flaw, which damaged his complete surrender to life. For many years he was tied to a woman by the closest ties, but could never bring himself to a complete acceptance. One feels that the erotic neurasthenia that vibrates in many of his most deeply felt drawings, is filled with his most profound and painful experience. Klimt was never able to dare to take the responsibility of his happiness, and only crowned the woman whom he loved for years with the privilege of looking after him in the pain of his dying.'

As Nebehay points out, living together in imperial Vienna and in the way they did needed considerable courage on Emilie's part. Klimt designed clothes for Emilie Flöge and for the Casa Piccola shop. The portrait of her which he painted in 1902, and which he showed in his collection at the Secession in 1903 is one of his finest. From photographs it seems to be a good likeness, but neither of them liked it and it was sold to the Historical Museum of the City of Vienna in 1908. It was the only formal portrait he did of her, and it was also the first of his portraits with a decorative background.[4]

All great artists borrow. The influences on Klimt range from the early formalism of Sir Lawrence Alma-Tadema and Sir Frederick Leighton in the period of his palmcourt or first neo-antique period, to the loosening influences of Khnopff and, in particular, the Dutchman Jan Toorop. Toorop had several works in the seventh Secession exhibition in 1900. The bouffant hair-dos and the angular gestures of the long thin arms which probably stem from the shadow puppets that were part of Toorop's own Javanese background, are often used by Klimt, particularly in the naked 'hostile powers' of the Beethoven frieze. Nebehay reminds us that Klimt's lakeside and water effects would have been impossible without some knowledge of Monet, even if filtered through Theo van Rysselberghe. The Belgian's appearance in the third Secession exhibition of 1899 was certainly decisive. The Secession itself acquired his *Nude Girl at her Toilet*, and no less than eighteen works were bought, one purchaser being Hevesi.[5]

In 1891, Klimt was invited to the formal opening of the Imperial Kunsthistorisches Museum (on which occasion, being a mere civilian, he would have had to appear in evening dress at half past ten in the morning), and there he

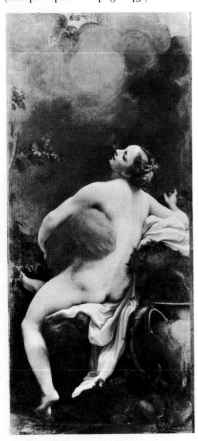

Correggio (d. 1534)
Jupiter and Io
163.5 × 74 cm./64 × 29 in.
Kunsthistorisches Museum,
photo Museum
(compare plate on page 145.)

132

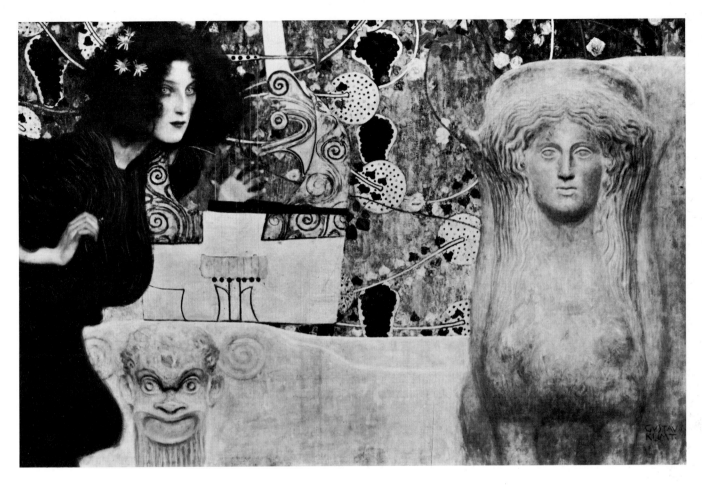

Gustav Klimt
Music II 1898, destroyed 1945
150 × 200 cm./59 × 79 in.
Photo Austrian National Library

probably would have seen Correggio's *Jupiter and Io* in its new setting. Later in 1895, when he painted *Love* he used the pose of the Correggio in reverse with the girl's head thrown back to the left, and with the lover now moustached. Instead of oak leaves in the clouds above Correggio's disembodied pair there are leering heads, and the leaves are replaced by roses in the golden panels to the right and left. Roses were the symbols of love, illusion, poetry, the mystery of life, and especially of maidenhood in the language of the *fin de siècle*.[6] For the first time Klimt suspended figures in space symbolizing the ages of man and death, a method of composition he was to repeat in some of his greatest works.[7] Moreover, he follows Correggio's underplayed palette of pale greys and mauves, just as he later used the pinks of Correggio's *Ganymede and the Eagle* in the same manner for *Schubert at the Piano* (1899) or the portrait of Sonia Knips of three years later, in 1898.

Simultaneously with *Love*, Klimt was entering on his own more deliberate second antique style with *Music I*. The symbolic *Pallas Athena*, protectress of the new Secession, is taken directly from Franz von Stuck's poster for the Munich Sezession of 1897. She carries a spear in the left hand, and wears fish-scale armour, while a miniature Nike figure balanced on a globe is held in the right palm. All are from Stuck except for the helmet, but Stuck's version is more Germanic and Wagnerian, Klimt's more authentically Greek. Klimt was to copy Stuck again in his *Water Serpents II* of 1904-7, this time *Die Sünde*

133

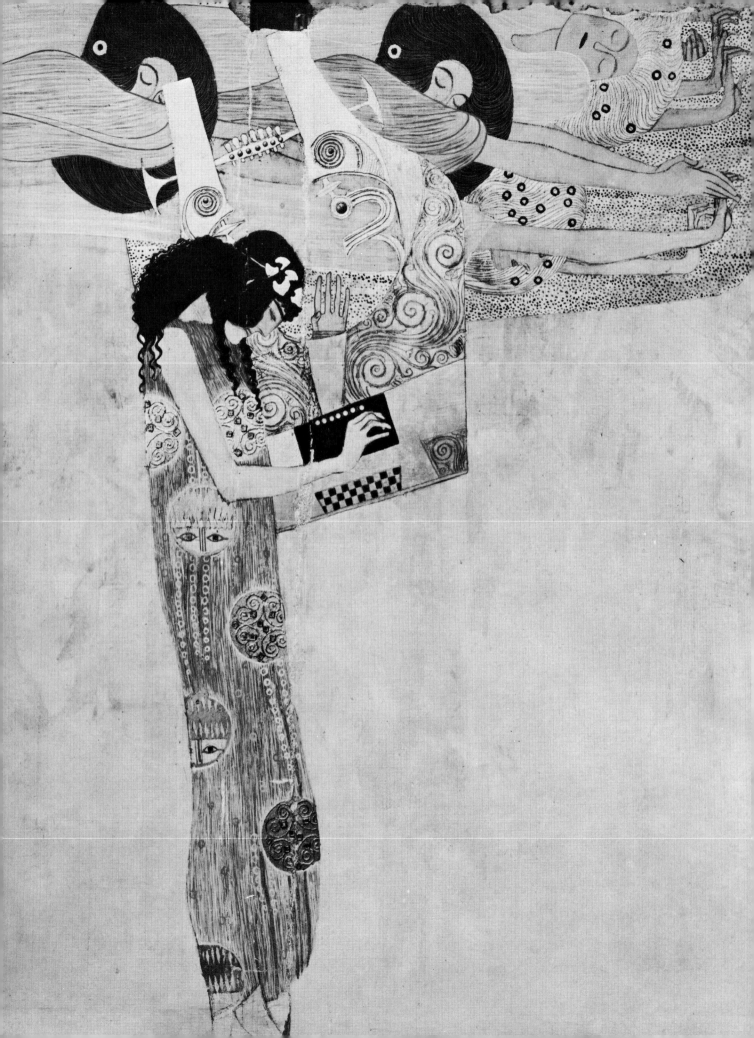

(The sin) which had been reproduced in *Ver Sacrum* in 1902, and shown in the first Secession exhibition of 1898. Nebehay makes a nice comparison with a further development of the pose by the young Schiele in his *Märchenwelt* (World of the fairy tale) of 1908, and points out three further borrowings by Klimt.[8] At the twelfth exhibition of the Secession in 1901 Hodler had secured a personal and indeed international success, and in an interview in 1905, Hodler remarked on Klimt's 'liking for repetitions'. In that exhibition Hodler had shown *Spring*, a frieze of women with upstretched hands, which Klimt had taken straight into his Beethoven frieze next year. For the Stoclet frieze in the great 'gold' period of Klimt's art, I have already mentioned a connection with S. Apollinaire in Classe, and Jaroslav Leschko has shown the relation between the spirals of the baptistery walls in Ravenna and the similar double spiral branches in the *Tree of Life* for the Stoclet frieze.[9] At the same time, 1907-8, Klimt was working on *The Kiss* which, as Nebehay has shown, was taken from Margaret Macdonald's coloured gesso decorations for the music room in the house of Klimt's patron, Wärndorfer. The original collage oil and tempera design of *The Opera of the Winds* and *The Opera of the Sea* by her husband and herself has both the three-quarter-length figures and, even more important, the flowered dress and upturned head of the girl who appears in *The Kiss*.[10] Finally *Leda* of 1917 is taken from an identical pose in a similarly situated heroine on Shiele's *Danaë* of 1909. Arthur Roessler has recorded Klimt's visit to Schiele's studio in Schönbrunn and saying after a long silence, 'I envy you the expression you have put into the two faces on your canvas.' Years later when Schiele suggested that they might exchange drawings Klimt asked why, adding, 'You draw better than I do anyway.'[11] In the end, Schiele was to draw Klimt on his deathbed.

Alma Mahler as an old woman wrote of Klimt:

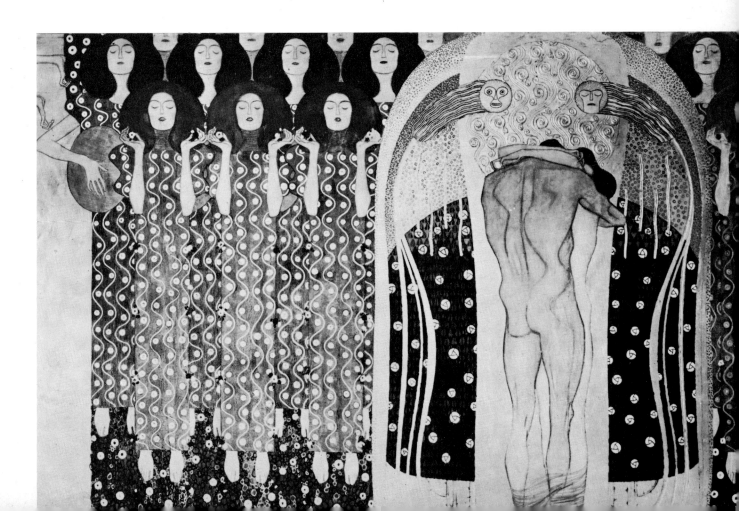

Gustav Klimt
Expectation 1905-9
Design for Stoclet frieze, mixed media
on paper, c. 190 × 100 cm./75 × 40 in.
Österreichisches Museum für
Angewandte Kunst, photo Museum

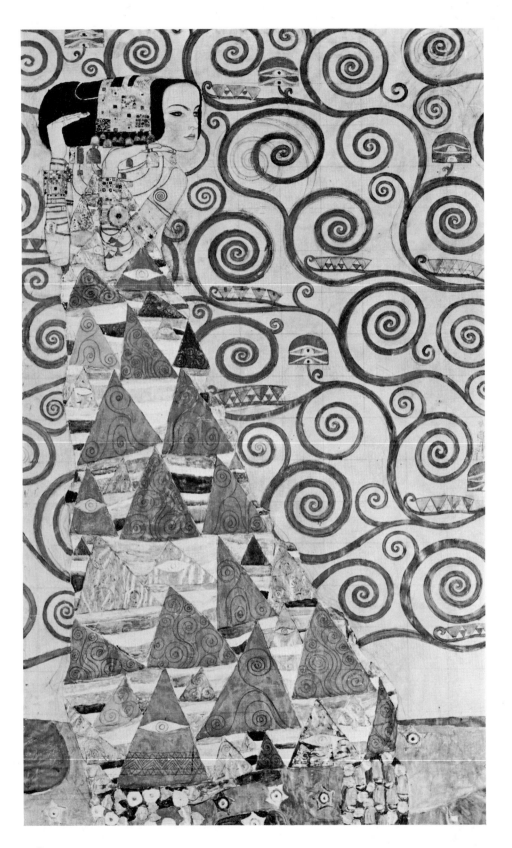

'I owed him many tears and my awakening . . . I was deaf to all his persuasions and requests to visit him in his studio. He often saw me later and said "Your magic never ceases to work upon me, it is even stronger." I shuddered when I saw him, and this remained a strange kind of betrothal for many years – as I recalled what he had asked me and demanded of me years before.

'Many years later he himself said that we had sought each other for a lifetime, and had never found each other in reality. He played with human feelings as a hobby. But as a man, he was all that I then sought – mistakenly.

'Meanwhile his art took crooked paths. He fell for the Byzantine idea of the Wiener Werkstätte, a society of applied artists, to which well known foreign and Austrian interior decorators and architects belonged. They achieved great things in their way, but Klimt was led astray by them – in the same way that happened to Fernand Khnopff and Jan Toorop.

'But their way was quite otherwise predestined, and their detour did not hurt them. Klimt's pictures, which had started off in a grand manner, he covered with tinsel rubbish, and his artistic vision sank in gold mosaics and ornaments. He had no one around him except worthless women – and that was why he sought me out, because he felt that I might help him . . . Gustav Klimt came to me as the first great love of my life, but I was an unwitting child sunk deep in music and far from the world.'[12]

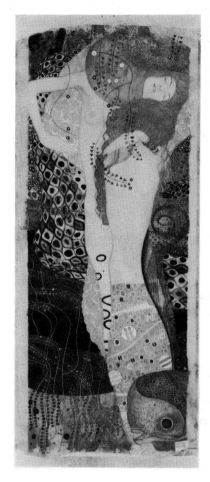

Gustav Klimt
Water Serpents I 1904
Mixed media on parchment
Signed, 50 × 20 cm./20 × 8 in.
Österreichische Galerie,
photo Museum

Enough from this romantic but nevertheless highly important witness. Writing in the 1950s, only ten years before her, Engelhart has this to say:

'Klimt's best quality was his taste. He was able to convey his artistic wishes in colour and content through his masterly and exceptional draughtsmanship. People try to say that his talent is not permanent since his colouring was taken from Persian, Chinese and above all oriental influences, and the controversy which his works roused in many of his artistic colleagues is possibly due to this unusual element.

'His first works, which he carried out together with Matsch for the Burgtheater, were extremely elegant but possibly more down to earth. *Music* and *Schubert* in the Dumba Palais showed a transition. He then tried completely new territory with his ceiling paintings for the university, over which passionate disagreements broke out until they were finally turned down by the university. Yet would they have been in any way effective at the great height, one wonders? Far too delicate and too dark in their colouring, their composition was not designed for monumental effect, and they would have been better suited for small wall panels or as book decorations.

'Klimt was a simple fellow, who was only motivated by decorative, painterly, and colourful subjects. He must often have laughed when critics saw deep philosophical problems secretly introduced into his works, and of which he had certainly never thought. All in all, he was a very gifted and influential painter, whose creations were, in spite of their peculiarity, a milestone in the art of the old Austria.'[13]

This is a practical judgment by a sober and steady artist, and Engelhart's remark about the vast height of the huge university ceiling is perfectly valid.

When Klimt died, Alma Mahler wrote in her diary: 'His education was slight. He came from the most modest background. But he always kept in his

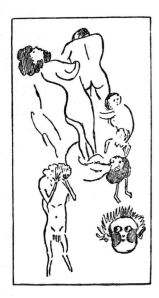

Eduard Pötzl
*Caricature of Klimt's University
Paintings* c. 1907
From *Heuriges* vol. 14,
3.7 × 7 cm./1½ × 2¾ in.

coat pocket a *Divine Comedy* and a *Faust*.'[14] It would be tempting to seek the influence of Freud in his thinking, but Klimt probably never even heard of him. The philosopher Otto Weininger, who committed suicide in 1903 in the year that his important *Geschlecht und Charackter* was published, is far more likely to have been known to Klimt. His book on the psychology and metaphysics of sex, and the psychology of genius, and his theory on the psychic and physical bi-sexuality of the human, was much more in Klimt's line, and it immediately won considerable acclaim. So far as is known the only books that Klimt ever bought or had in his library were on art and art criticism, including some on erotic Japanese art. If for Werner Hofmann, Hofmannsthal is even ahead of Freud in his ideas about painting in 1893,[15] we may be sure with Engelhart that whatever else Klimt did, he painted unconsciously. Most of the symbols he used were in the current repertory, for instance the dandelion clocks in the two versions of *Music* or the knight in armour in the *Longing for Happiness* section of the Beethoven frieze. At the end of his life in 1917, Klimt wrote a poem with the lines, 'The water lily by the lake is in flower, she feels melancholy for a handsome man.' An anthropomorphic idea, even if meant on this occasion as a joke, which may be compared with his use of sunflowers as a transmutation of the female figure.[16] It would be valuable to know where Klimt got his complicated programme for the Beethoven frieze, such as the giant Typhon and the three gorgons, and more complex themes ('The arts lead us to the kingdom of the ideal' and so on).[17] Two of Klimt's symbols, however, are entirely original to him: the black Typhon himself with his full-face grimace and inset mother of pearl teeth, and even more imaginative, the octopus of evil about to engulf the bowed naked prisoner—a strange foreboding of the emaciated, concentration camp figure in *Jurisprudence*, which Klimt started in 1903. Snakes and fishes were often among Klimt's accessories in his scenes of naked women. Klimt was a natural artist, even if with a morbid vision, and had a childish sense of humour which emerges in two or three caricaturing self-portraits, and the enchanting description of him throwing paper hats down from the windows of Emilie Flöge's elegant dress-shop onto the heads of the Viennese sitting at the café tables below.[18]

Gustav Klimt was born on 14 July 1862 in a small house on the Linzerstrasse, then a countryfied Vienna suburb. His father, whose family came from northern Bohemia, was an engraver. Of the seven children Gustav was the eldest son, his painter brother Ernst being two years younger (1864-92), while Georg (1867-1931) was a gifted metal sculptor. The family suffered great poverty especially in the bank crisis year of 1873, when they lacked bread, let alone presents at Christmas. From 1876 Klimt studied at the Kunstgewerbeschule, where his principal teacher until the professor's death in 1881 was Ferdinand Laufberger, designer of the Minerva fountain between his school and the Museum of Applied Arts, and which may even have been in Klimt's mind when he painted *Pallas Athena*. Through Laufberger, the Klimt brothers and Matsch were employed at the Kunsthistorisches Museum, helping him with his sgraffito decoration. In 1883 Klimt finished his studies. In 1894 he was commissioned to produce designs for the university ceiling, and he and Matsch presented their designs in 1896. Next year Klimt left the Künstlerhaus. In 1898, the year of the first Secession exhibition, the university commission was confirmed. In 1899, Klimt completed the decorations for the music room in the Palais Dumba. In 1900, Klimt exhibited the unfinished *Philosophy* at the

Opposite:
Gustav Klimt
Jurisprudence 1903-7, destroyed 1945
430 × 300 cm./14 × 10 ft.
Photo Austrian National Library

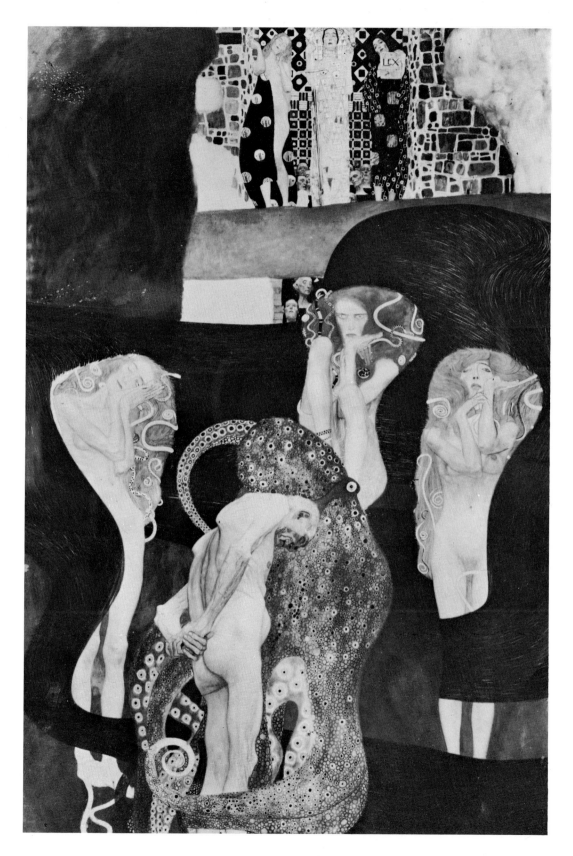

Gustav Klimt
Adele Bloch-Bauer I 1907
138 × 138 cm./54 × 54 in.
Österreichische Galerie,
photo Museum

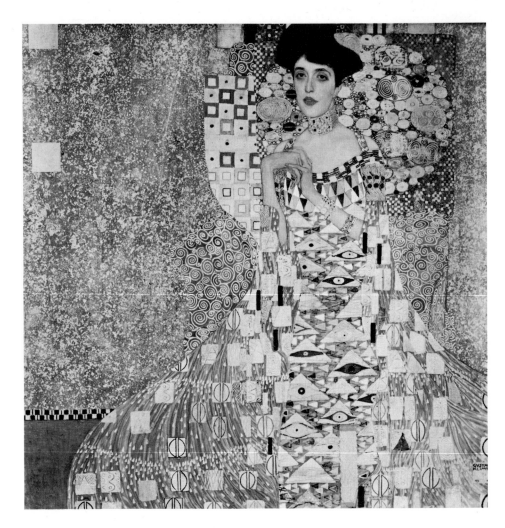

Secession. Even the sketches had been so much criticized in committee that Klimt had nearly withdrawn. Of the sketch for *Medicine* the committee had said, 'Above all the wish was expressed that the figure in the middle character-izing suffering Humanity should have an attitude less inclined towards contro-versy and obscene jokes, and possibly be replaced by that of a youth.' This was nothing to the attacks on *Philosophy* in the press. 'He has taken a humorous approach,' or, 'A sickly, nervous, and flat-breasted elegance, chic and coquetrie turning towards the boundless fantastic.' Eleven professors signed a petition against the picture, and this was followed by another eighty-seven signatures. The ministry behaved admirably in rejecting the criticisms, even if, having commissioned what they thought would be an academic Klimt, they now found that he had turned into a salamander. Pötzl produced a very funny caricature, but Klimt in revenge won a prize in Paris, though the anti-semitic Jew, Karl Kraus, wrote that the Parisians had complained of the *gout juif* in the works exhibited from the Secession. When *Medicine* was shown next year the authorities tried to confiscate the number of *Ver Sacrum* containing sketches for it but the court ruled that the designs were for a public commission. A question was asked in parliament and Bahr defended Klimt in a lecture, which was enough to make Kraus change his line of attack from Klimt to

Bahr and the Secession itself. In 1903 the unfinished *Jurisprudence* was shown in Klimt's collective exhibition at the Secession. The committee looked at the Faculty pictures and accepted them, this time criticizing Matsch, but, and this was a terrible reservation, they suggested that Klimt's pictures should go to the modern gallery and not to the university. Finally in 1905 Klimt wrote to the Minister of Education withdrawing his pictures and returning the fees. In this year too he and his friends broke away from the Secession, and the year after Hoffmann asked him to collaborate on the Palais Stoclet. (The corners of the ceiling are still bare.) While Matsch's *Theology* hangs in the dean of theology's room, Klimt's faculty paintings were burnt in Schloss Immendorf by order of a German officer, together with thirteen other works, in 1945 – a desperate scorched earth moment in the twilight of the gods.[19]

There was more to the faculty pictures than Kraus's quip that *Medicine* was a picture of the 'chaotic muddle of infirm bodies symbolizing conditions in the general hospital'. Klimt had emerged wounded by his brother's death, and showed in his figures that each discipline has its dark side. For instance, justice is cruel and envelops the accused in an amorphous mass, while health and knowledge have dark mysteries and uncertainties. In his unconscious symbolism he showed that truth is far from reassuring or certain. So it was not

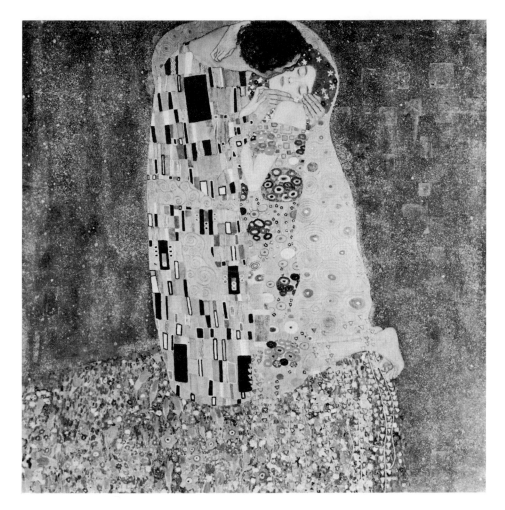

Gustav Klimt
The Kiss 1907-8
Signed, 180 × 180 cm./71 × 71 in.
Österreichische Galerie,
photo Museum

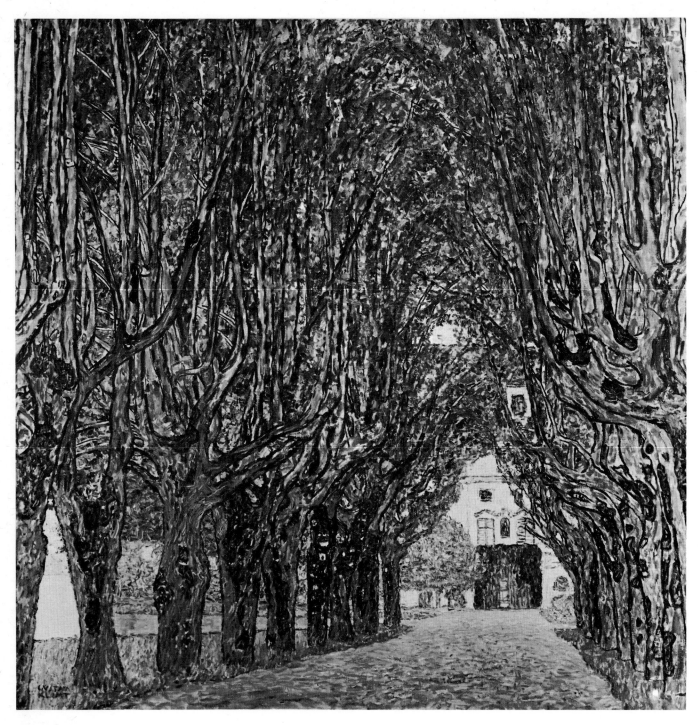

Gustav Klimt
Avenue at Schloss Kammer 1912
110 × 110 cm./43 × 43 in.
Österreichische Galerie,
photo Museum

142

their modernity that gave offence to the university and conservative critics, but the hint of unpleasant truths behind the façade of respectability. Even in reproductions this message of insecurity is still what most disturbs.

In the midst of these complications, whose effect on an even moderately sensitive person must be obvious, Klimt painted the Beethoven frieze *tout d'un coup* in 1902 for the Klinger exhibition, working in a fresco technique. It is a resumé of his ideas, the kissing couple naked, his memories of the Toorop and Hodler girls, and old worn-out symbols like the knight in armour (which he repeated riding a horse in a canvas which belonged to Karl Wittgenstein), but it also contains his extraordinary invention of the fat, middle-aged half-nude amongst the 'evil spirits', as frightening as the god Typhon with his hideous black face, furry arms and tail of coiling fur, that was to be used immediately afterwards in *Jurisprudence*. These are terrifying images, and it is hardly a surprise to hear that the art-collector and patron, Graf Karl Lanckoronski, shouted out·'*Scheusslich!*' (hideous) in front of them, because the Beethoven frieze is not friendly, even if it is great like the composer it honours.

In 1906, Klimt travelled to Brussels and London in connection with the Stoclet frieze and the Imperial Austrian exhibition, and next year completed the faculty pictures, exhibiting them in Vienna and Berlin. *The Kiss* was the most important of his pictures at the Kunstschau of 1908. In 1909 work on the Stoclet frieze began in the Werkstätte, and he went to Paris and Madrid. He was shown at the Venice Biennale of 1910, and next year won the prize in Rome. 1914 saw him again in Brussels. During the war he became an honorary member of the Vienna and Munich Academies of Art. Finally, on 11 January 1918 he had a stroke which turned to pneumonia, and he died on 6 February. He had been a fencer, a light athlete and a wrestler, rowed and sailed, and above all liked to walk early in the morning. His first landscapes date from 1898 after the 'caesura', but the first painting of this kind in his own characteristic style was *Big Poplars I* of 1900. Two years afterwards he started the lake water studies on Attersee, which employ impressionist brushwork. He returned to retrogressive views of beech woods about 1903, but after the Ravenna visit he burst into colour and jewel-like meadows and sun flowers. From 1910 he painted a great series of views round Schloss Kammer on Attersee, which are all but expressionist records of actual scenes, and finally in 1913 after a stay on Lake Garda, his views of Cassone and the marvellous 'Malcesine', only to be compared with the lowering, oppressive townscape in Gastein of the year before he died.

Just as his landscapes became more idiomatic and identifiable, so the portraits developed together with his own style. Although after a series of men's heads in about 1896 he never painted another man, his women went through the same metamorphosis as his imaginative painting, at first more jewelled with decorative backgrounds (which did not always please the sitters), but evolving towards a very Viennese melancholy with oriental elements in the surroundings. Anton Faistauer, who painted the decorations in the Salzburg Festspielhaus removed by the Nazis in 1938, summed up Klimt in 1923 by contrasting him with Schiele:

'If Klimt was the portraitist of high financiers and decorated their salons with panels sparkling in gold and silver, and bright landscapes flowing with silver, Schiele could be called the painter of the proletariat. Both painters, typical city-dwellers, divided between them the poles of social

Opposite:
Gustav Klimt
Love 1895
Signed and dated, 60 × 44 cm./
23 × 17 in.
Historisches Museum der Stadt Wien,
photo Museum

structure. Klimt attached himself to the light, shallow and dissolute rich jewry of the city centre, becoming their painter, while Schiele took on the suburbs with their tragic faces of hunger, their hatred and grimaces. In their representation of women, their social conscience separated them. Both sought the demi-monde, Schiele in the outer districts, Klimt inside the Ringstrasse. They both carefully avoided the middle classes, and thereby both appeared uncomfortable, eccentric and perverse. Klimt was able to catch the blasé attitude, arrogance and pride of his types in detail, rather better than Schiele the outlines of his. For neither was the human being of any significance, people were more or less figurines, with Klimt a complex and subtle play of nerves, in Schiele a dark dreary crowd.'[20]

In the chemistry of this creative moment of time, Klimt was the reagent without whom the rest cannot be imagined. For, without Klimt, most Austrian of them all, this whole movement would not have coalesced. He carried the others with him to the Secession and out and forward again. For Kokoschka and Schiele he was a spiritual leader. That Gerstl refused to exhibit with him was not a denial of Klimt but rather a reluctance to be compared with him. Klimt is not only the strongest artistic personality in this galaxy, but like the greatest artists he always progressed through mutations in his style until the war that robbed him of a wider recognition and death that prematurely ended his life. Without Klimt the spring would not have been so blessed.

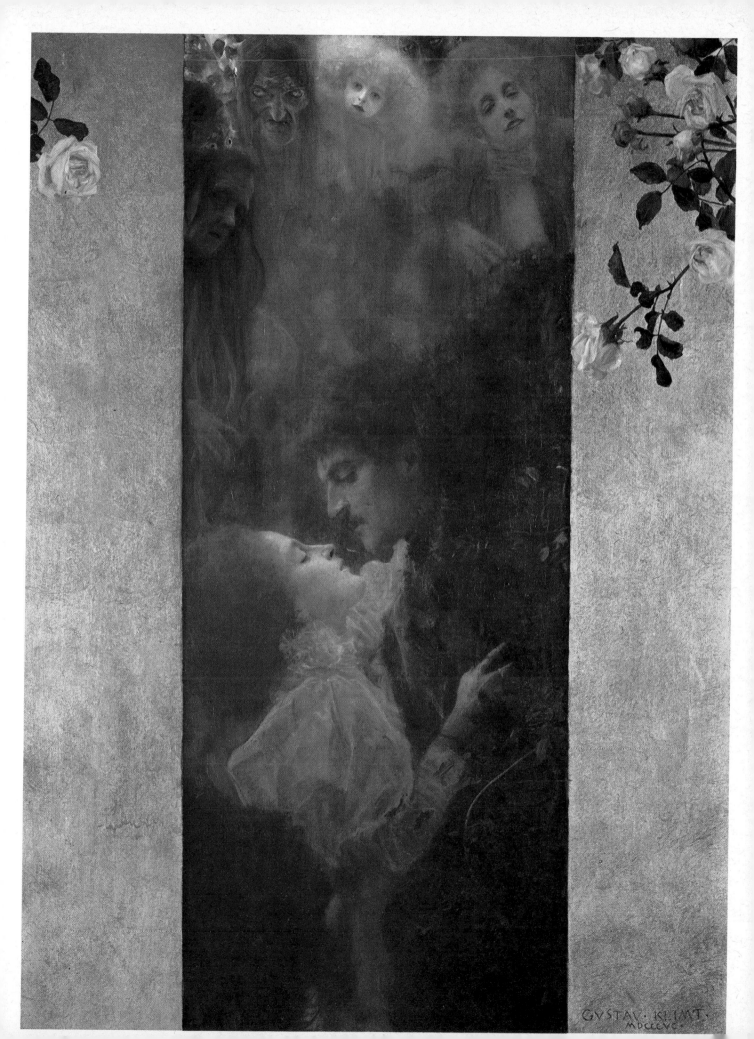

Egon Schiele, the Self-seer

'In every case of love the man loves only himself. He needs nothing so urgently, he desires nothing more warmly than to be nothing more nor less than himself . . . He projects his ideal of an absolutely worthwhile being, which he cannot keep isolated within himself, onto another human being, and this and nothing else is the meaning when he loves this being.'

This is not Schiele analysing himself, but Otto Weininger writing on *Sex and Character* in 1903. Schiele was obsessed with himself, and no single artist can have drawn himself so often. His recurrent themes are his head and body, the women he loved, formal portraits of men and boys, blindness, dead trees, dead towns, and death itself. More than Klimt he was in love with easeful death, almost as though he sensed that his life was to be a short one. In it he produced an extraordinary full oeuvre of about 360 paintings, of which some 60 are lost, and many watercolours and drawings.

In an essay on expressionism Hermann Bahr wrote in 1916, 'There had never been a period so shaken with horror, with so much grimness of death and the silence of the grave. Never had man been so unimportant, nor so anxious. Never was pleasure so distant and freedom so dead.'[1] This was one aspect of expressionism, but the other, in which real colour was replaced by an imagined formal scale, and in which the outline was in some ways more important than the surface and surroundings, is mentioned by Albert Paris Gütersloh in 1912 in an essay on Schiele. 'Colours suddenly have meaning: red is action, blue the dying off of a rotating movement, yellow the conjunctive, negative, finally the sign of insanity.'[2] One thinks of the bizarre profiles outlined in blues and purple, of the self-portraits in oranges, or mustard, with nipples, navel and sexual organs picked out in red, when Schiele deliberately presents the subject for the contour and its more than substantial significance. Gerstl, who was painting at the same time, was to daub over and blue his outlines, and Kokoschka to break up his lines in what Werner Hofmann describes as 'a masochistic frenzy'. These two expressionists expressed themselves in their own way, but Schiele, like Klimt, never left the protective security of a clear outline.

In 1964 Gütersloh devoted almost the entire epilogue in the most complete anthology of all the arts of the period to Schiele:

'Egon Schiele was exceptionally good-looking, and had nothing artistic about him: no long hair, no beard even a day old, his nails were never uncared for, and even in his poorest period his coat was not threadbare. He was—and this is no recollection embellished by time—an elegant young man, whose good manners strangely were, at least at that time and for those times, quite at variance with his supposedly bad manner of painting. But one sees that real revolutionaries are like the Jesuits, "one does not notice what they want at once." '[3]

The fastidious Schiele could never have worn the kaftans affected by Bahr or Klimt. He was very much a member of the middle class.

Born on 12 June 1890 the youngest of four children, the other three being sisters, Elvire who died young, Melanie and Gertrud, his father was the station master of Tulln, twenty miles from Vienna in Lower Austria, and died very protractedly after a long agony in 1905, an inhibiting example for his son, by then fifteen years old. The boy became the ward of his uncle, a railway inspector, who was reluctant to let him take up painting. In so far as the railway can be said to have had any effect on the artist, it is worth mentioning that the sunflowers along the tracks, turning with the sun, were painted by Schiele early in about 1908 and again in 1911, 1914 and 1917. Even here, he saw in the fading flowers a symbol of mortality.

He was very close with his sisters. He painted Melanie twice in 1907 and 1908, and after his death she owned the long mirror in which he so often studied himself. His sister Gerta married Anton Peschka the painter, and he painted her twice in 1908 and 1909. He painted his mother twice, and later two marvellous portraits of his wife, one in a striped dress (1915), and the crouching figure in a blue dress (1918). There is an early, Lautrec-like portrait of Bertha von Wiktorin smoking a cigarette (1907), and one portrait of his favourite model Walli Neuzil (1912). In the midst of his career he only painted three formal portraits, Fräulein Rainer the sister of the 'Rainer boy', Arthur Roessler's wife in 1912 and Fräulein Beer in 1914, but it is true that Schiele had been beaten to the easel by Klimt, who had already painted all the smart, modern-minded society women likely to want an advanced likeness. In any case, Schiele liked girls for his models, even new-fledged ones, who would kick up their skirts, scratch or comb themselves, and who were surprised to find, as Gütersloh puts it, that no more harm was going to come from the artist than from a nude photographer, only interested in catching them relaxed and off their guard. His line was as fluid and clear as Klimt's, but unlike Klimt, his models give the air of not having been hurt by their small world. That the world was small, unreasonable and cruel, was brought home to Schiele first in Krumau the romantic little town on the Moldau, in the deepest Bohemian provinces which he visited twice, in 1911 and 1913. In spite of being warned to be careful by friends and well-wishers, like railway inspector Heinrich Benesch and the collector Carl Reininghaus, he was arrested for immorality and seduction in April 1912 during a stay in the tiny town of Neulengbach near his home town on the main line to Vienna. The complaint was not so much that he had very young girls posing for him, but that he kept nude drawings on his walls and showed these to them. At first Schiele thought that he was being arrested for debt, and after twenty-four days in remand he was found not guilty of the main charge, but given three days in prison for 'the distribution of indecent drawings'. The young judge, who himself collected the work of an obscure, sensual, Jesuit artist, solemnly burnt a drawing from Schiele's bedroom wall in the flame of the symbolic candle on the bench.

In prison, Schiele painted first in spittle, and then, when he was allowed watercolours, twelve drawings of his cell, himself lying on his bed, oranges, handkerchiefs and an escapist Trieste fishing boat of which he had dreamed. On one drawing of two chairs hung with a cloth, and brightened into expressionist blues and green he inscribed in capital letters, 'ART CANNOT BE MODERN IT IS PRIMEVALLY ETERNAL (*UREWIG*)'. He kept a poignant diary completed after his release, in the last entry of which he wrote:

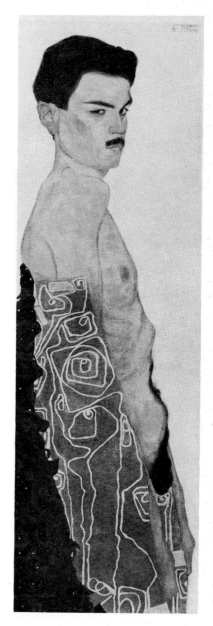

Egon Schiele
Self-portrait 1909
Signed and dated upper right,
110.5 × 36 cm./43 × 14 in.
Photo Courtesy of Marlborough Fine Art (London) Ltd

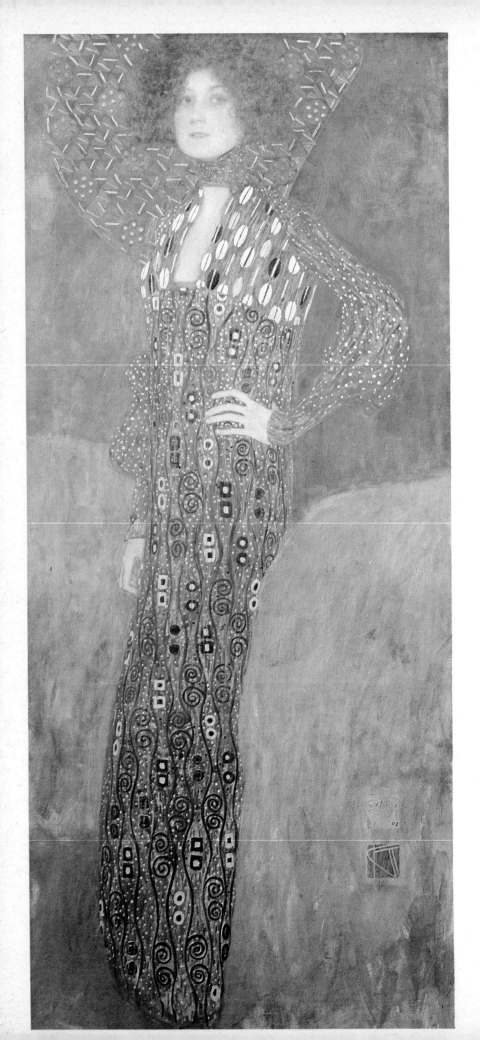

Left:
Gustav Klimt
Emilie Flöge 1902
181 × 84 cm./71 × 33 in.
Historisches Museum der Stadt Wien,
photo Museum

Right:
Gustav Klimt
Water Serpents I
(detail, see page 137)

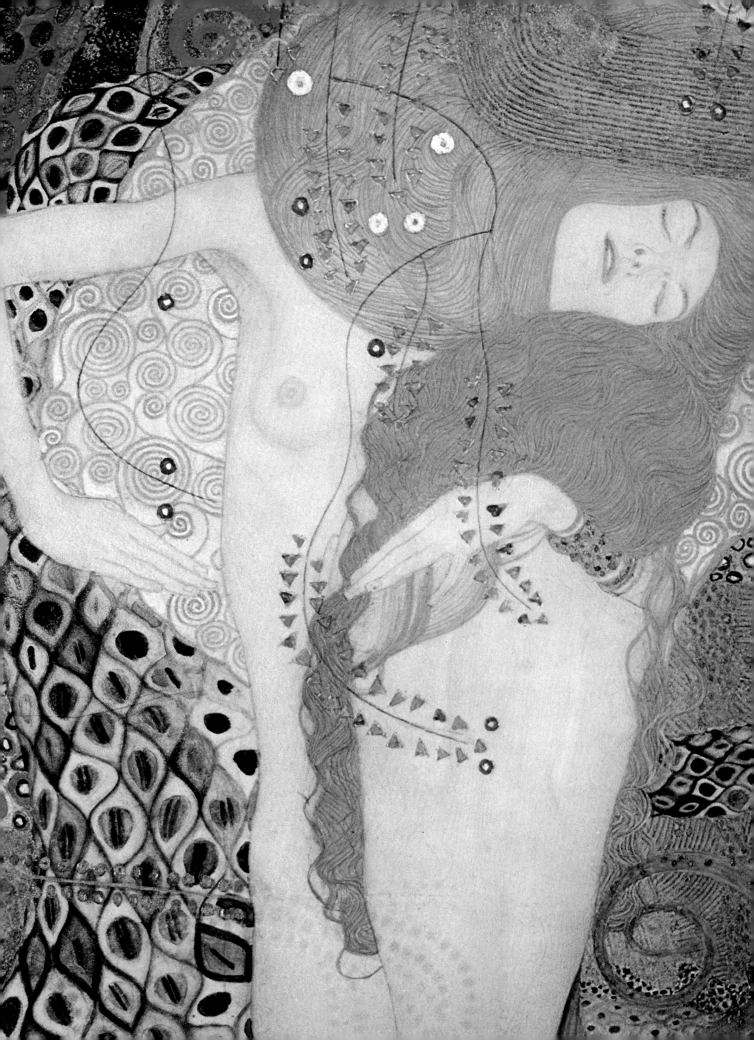

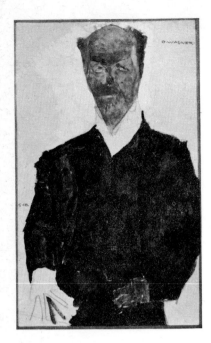

Egon Schiele
Otto Wagner 1910
Watercolour, 42.5 × 26 cm./17 × 10 in.
Historisches Museum der Stadt Wien,
photo Museum

'Auto-da-fe! Savonarola! Inquisition! Middle Ages! Castration! Hypocrisy!' Although he was justified to a great extent in this outburst and he made the wounding discovery that the artist may be ahead of society, yet he is still a part of it. The self-portraits immediately before and after his imprisonment showed how much the episode had hurt him, and for five months afterwards Schiele completed no major work.[4] The injury to his artistic pride, and which he had to some extent provoked was one aspect of this episode, the other was the damage to his image of 'respectability'.

In 1906, the year after his father's death, he was accepted for the Academy and worked under Professor Christian Griepenkerl, a professor of the old Ringstrasse school, with whom Schiele naturally did not get on. By the age of seventeen he was living on his own. In 1907 he painted his uncle twice, some views at Klosterneuburg where he had been to school, and the first scenes from Trieste, which he visited with his sister Gerta, and the Klimt-like *Märchenwelt*. By 1909, he had painted over eighty-five works. He met Klimt for the first time in 1907. In 1909 he left the Academy and joined the *Neukunst-gruppe* with his colleagues Peschka and Faistauer. There he met Gütersloh and Hans Böhler, a sensitive self-taught artist (1884-1911), and, as a group, they showed at the Pisko gallery. In the same year, he started to work for the Werkstätte, though Hoffmann had rejected the portrait of Poldi Lodzinsky (1908) intended as a design for a glass window in the Palais Stoclet, a work which is nevertheless important, for its angular, tortured hands with pronounced joints, a neutral background, and the frontal view which he was to make so much his own. Between 1909 and 1911 he wrote a series of prose poems, and in 1910 he met the writer Arthur Roessler at the Pisko gallery. Importantly for Schiele, Roessler introduced him to the collector Reininghaus, who became one of his best supporters. In his house Schiele was able to study his collection of Hodler, whose landscapes certainly influenced Schiele. Of Reininghaus and others he painted large portraits, and he was also allowed to start a head of Otto Wagner, who unfortunately lost interest and came to less and less sittings. Yet Schiele managed to catch the great architect in a strongly characteristic study. Wagner at least bought, via Hoffmann, a watercolour of a nude girl from Schiele. In the autumn of 1910 he also met Heinrich Benesch for the first time. In 1911 Schiele exhibited at the Miethke gallery, and in May rented a small garden house in his mother's birthplace, Krumau, where he lived with his model Walli Neuzil. Because of this promiscuity and the first complaints of his using little girls as models he had to leave by August. He then joined the Munich 'Sema' group and in 1912 his self-portrait lithograph appeared in their portfolio. In that year too, he exhibited in Budapest. After his spiritual defeat in Neulengbach of the early summer, he travelled to Carinthia and Tirol, then moved in with his mother, with whom he did not always get on because he felt she had abandoned him, which explains, according to Breicha,[5] his many paintings of a dead or blind mother. At the end of June he joined the painter Erwin 'Mime' von Osen in his studio. Osen posed for him nude in typical Schiele attitudes, and stole his paint and some drawings. At the end of the year Schiele went on further journeys to Munich, Bregenz and Zürich, and moved to the studio in the thirteenth district which he kept until just before he died. He still exhibited with the Hagenbund and in Cologne. Perhaps more important for his future he was invited to the industrialist Baron August Lederer's house in Györ in Hungary for Christmas and New Year. There he painted the wooden bridge over an arm of the Danube whose abstract geometry appealed to him as had similar bridges in the South of France to van Gogh. There also, one of the sons, Erich, became his pupil, even if it was a tactful form of helping financially, and he painted his portrait. Serena Lederer had been painted by Klimt in 1899, and Klimt was to paint the daughter Baronin Elizabeth Backhoven-Echt in 1914, but the young Schiele was not to have any luck with rich female models.

In 1913 Schiele travelled and exhibited all over Germany. He joined the Berlin magazine *Die Aktion* for which he drew two typical self-portraits, the

Egon Schiele
Heinrich and Otto Benesch 1913
Neue Galerie der Stadt Linz,
photo Museum

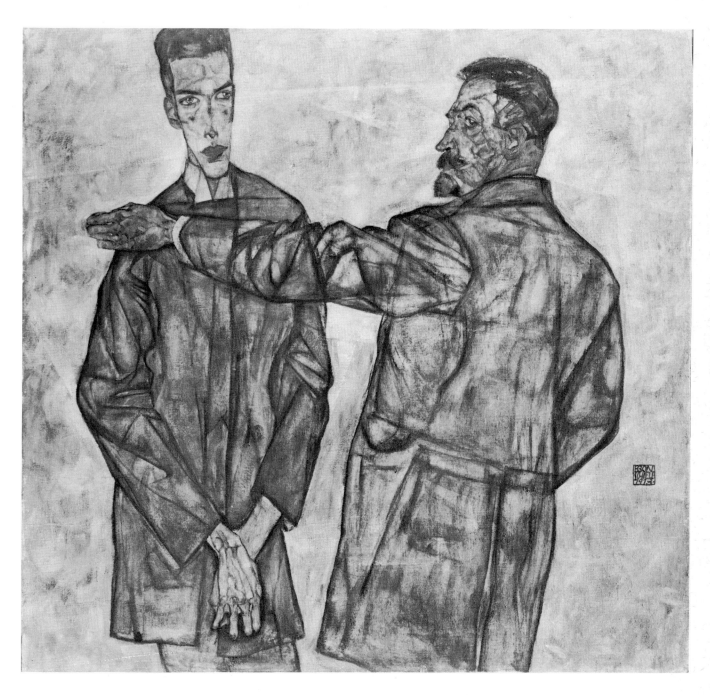

151

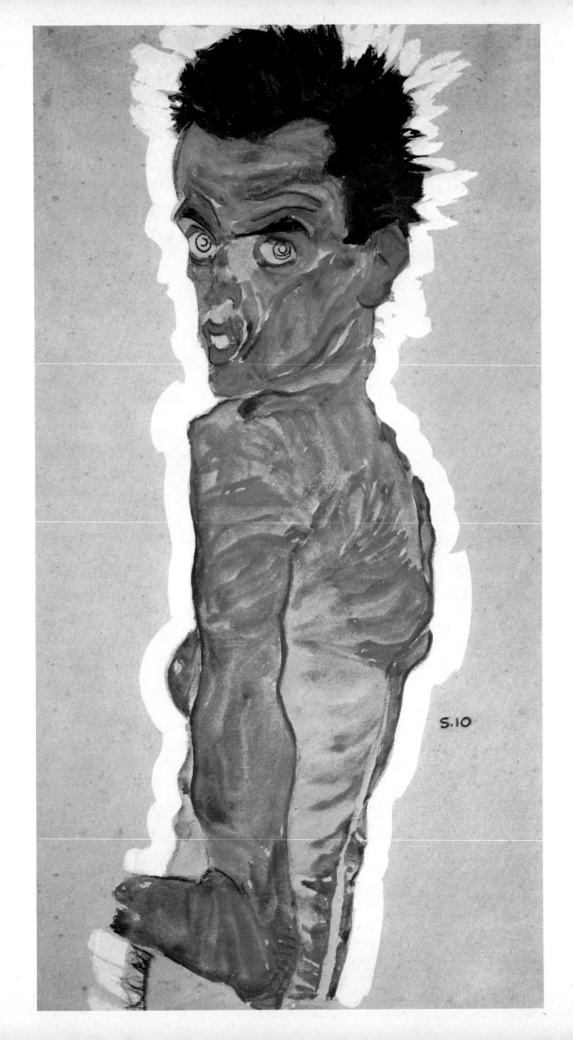

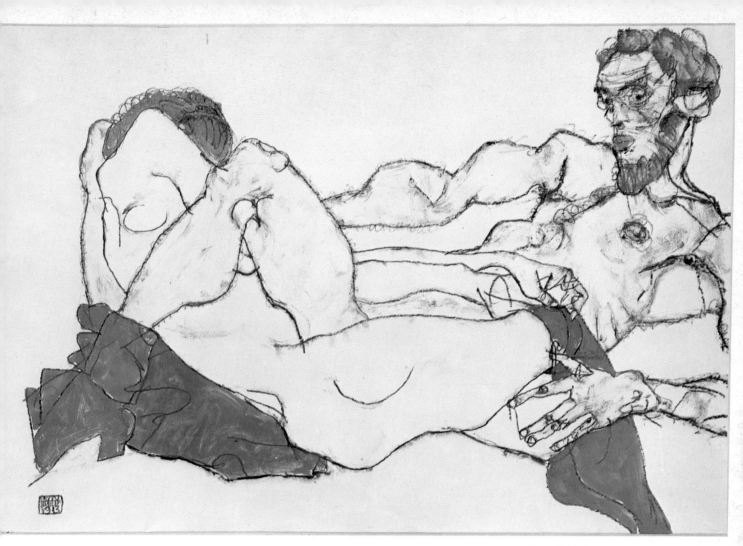

Egon Schiele
Man and Woman 1913
31.5 × 40 cm./12½ × 16 in.
Albertina, photo Museum

Egon Schiele
Self-portrait 1910
Gouache on brown paper,
57 × 37 cm./22 × 14 in.
Collection Dr Rüdiger Engerth

second of which was reproduced on the front page in 1916. In 1914 Schiele wrote an article entitled 'Art – the New Artist', and later for the front page did a portrait from a photograph of Charles Peguy who had been killed on the enemy side at the beginning of the war. In 1916 he published the small woodcut of *Three Men Bathing* in the magazine.

All in all, 1914 was an important year for Schiele, even if it started with a set-back. For in January Carl Reininghaus had organized a competition with an exhibition at the Pisko Gallery, for which Schiele entered an unfinished and unsuitable work against the advice of Heinrich Benesch, and the prize was won by Anton Faistauer, with Gütersloh as the runner-up. It should be mentioned that Reininghaus bought the painting to console Schiele. The year was more successful in other ways however. In the spring he learnt engraving and woodcut from Robert Philippi, and posed for a series of photographs by the photographer Johann Anton Trčka. Being photographed obviously

Egon Schiele
Death and the Maiden 1915
Signed, 150 × 180 cm./59 × 71 in.
Österreichische Galerie,
photo Museum

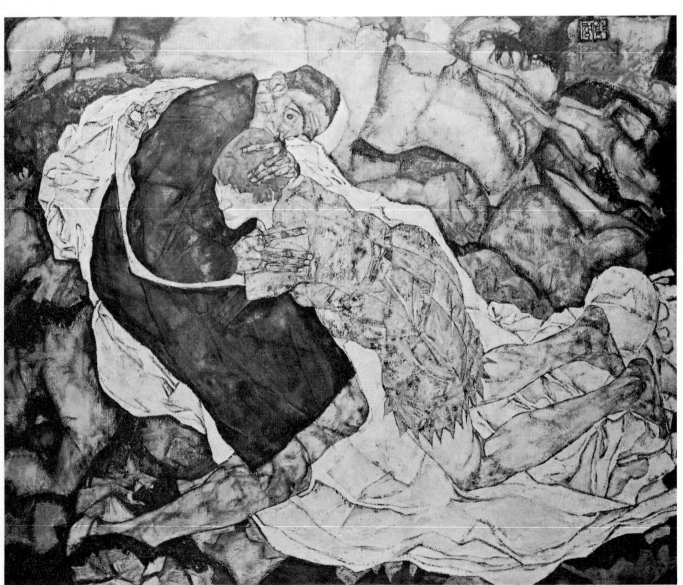

154

appealed to Schiele, as he pulled faces and opened his hands in a V with his head above them as in one of his own self-portraits. Schiele then took on Hans Böhler's cousin Heinrich as a pupil, and exhibited in Rome, Cologne, Brussels and Paris before the outbreak of the war. In December he had a collective show in the Arnot Gallery in Vienna. He exhibited sixteen canvasses, as well as drawings, and Otto Benesch, the eighteen year old son of the railway inspector, and future Rembrandt scholar and director of the Albertina, wrote a preface for the catalogue. Schiele also designed a poster of himself as St Sebastian, the martyr artist being shot through with arrows. At the beginning of the war which was to destroy Austria-Hungary, the choice of the soldier saint as a symbol was bizarre, but the complex young narcissist was certainly referring to himself as the loser in Reininghaus's competition and his moral defeat at Neulengbach. It was in 1914 too, that he met the two sisters, Adele and Edith Harms, who lived opposite his studio in Hietzinger Hauptstrasse. Attracted by both of them, he suggested they should go to the cinema with him and Walli which they did, and he invited both to go on excursions to Laxenburg and Mödling near Vienna.

In the next year he had drawings and watercolours on show in the Kunsthaus in Zürich. He married Edith in June while remaining more than closely attached to Adele, but was called up four days later to Prague. Edith went with him and they stayed in the Hotel Paris, which still exists. After a month's training in Bohemia, he returned to Vienna, where he was assigned to guard duties and did a number of heads of Russian prisoners. He managed to obtain permission to sleep at home, and even to wear civilian clothes. In 1916 he continued to exhibit in Berlin, Dresden and Munich. In 1917, he was posted to the rations headquarters in Mariahilferstrasse, where an art-dealer Karl Grünwald was an officer, and he was able to travel to Munich and the Tirol, and on to Bolzano and Trento. He planned a new group of artists, the *Kunsthalle*, to include Arnold Schönberg, Klimt, Hoffmann, the sculptor Anton Hanak, the poet Peter Altenberg, as well as his brother-in-law Anton Peschka. Nothing came of the idea, but in October Richard Lanyi published a portfolio of twelve photogravure reproductions of drawings. Schiele also collaborated in a new magazine *Der Anbruch*, whose contributors included the artist Alfred Kubin and, as writers, Bertha Zuckerkandl and Felix Braun. In the twenties it was to carry reviews of the Vienna music school and Schönberg. In the third number Schiele wrote of the dead Klimt as 'an artist of unbelievable perfection – a man of rare profundity whose work is sacred'.

The big exhibition of his works in the nineteenth Secession exhibition in March 1918 brought him considerable success and numerous commissions to paint members of the intellectual and commercial élite. He was able to move his studio, and in July and August travelled to Hungary, to the Ossiachersee in Carinthia, and to Lower Austria. Then, on 28 October, his wife Edith, who was expecting a baby, died of Spanish influenza in the studio gardenhouse, Schiele caught it and died in her parents' house on 31 October 1918. He was just twenty-eight.[6]

Apart from the innumerable references to himself in his drawings, at least fifteen paintings are direct self-portraits, and in many of his imaginative paintings the subject is really himself. There are parallels with Dürer's self-portraits in which the artist points to his own handsomeness and virility, but these are modest compared with Schiele's obsession with his own attractiveness.

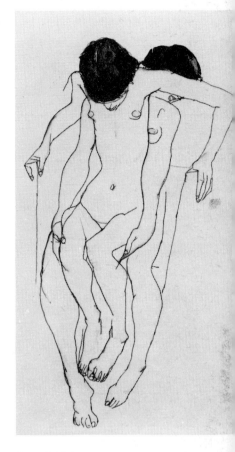

Egon Schiele
The Friends 1915
Pen on paper, 52 × 35 cm./20 × 14 in.
Collection Dr Rüdiger Engerth,
photo author

155

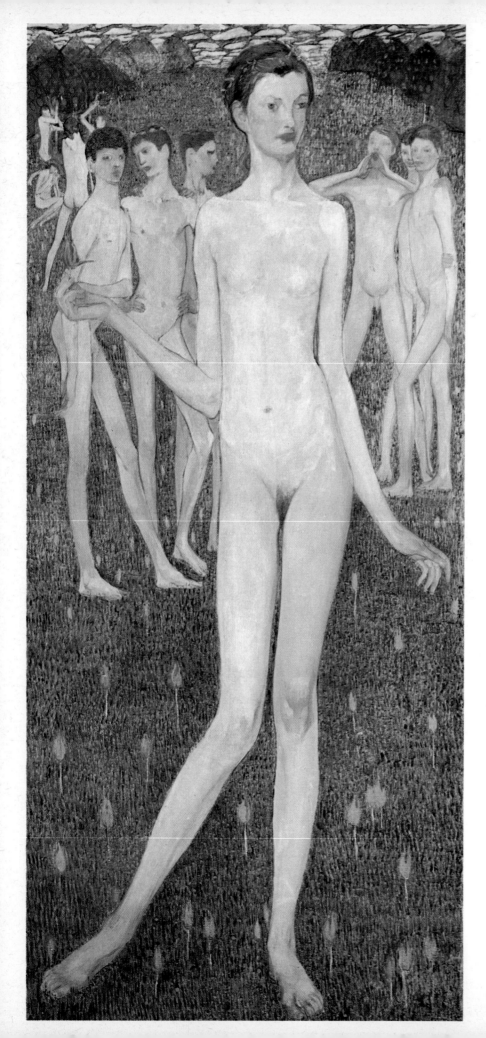

Left:
Elena Luksch-Makowskaja
Adolescentia 1903
Signed with initials, 172 × 97 cm./
67 × 38 in.
Österreichische Galerie,
photo Museum

Right:
Ferdinand Andri
Butterwoman 1907
Coloured lithograph for *Ver Sacrum*,
15.5 × 16 cm./6 × 6¼ in.
Galerie Pabst, photo Galerie Pabst

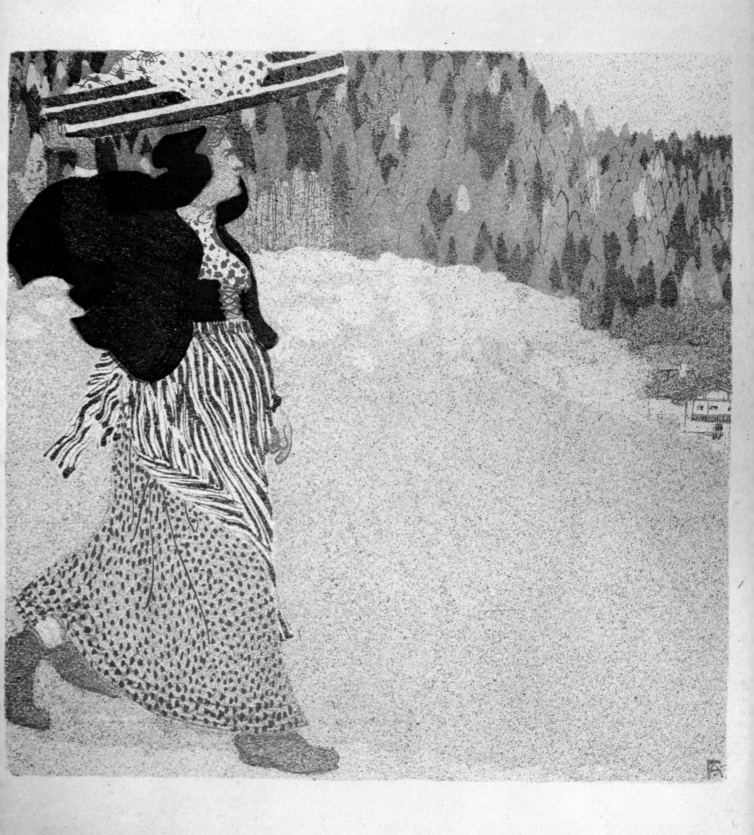

Even the act of producing works for sale seemed to him a giving away of a part of himself. His prose poem in a letter to Arthur Roessler in Juanuary 1911 shows his subjective attitude, 'Buy!—Not pictures, not products, not work, pictures? Out of me, not by me, selling myself?' The verb *erkaufen* which he uses has the sense of selling one's soul. Perhaps the most obvious proof of his equivocal attitude is the fact that he was the subject of four out of five posters that he produced. In his first poster for the *Neukunstgruppe* in December 1909, he is standing with his knuckles anxiously pressed together. In 1910 he did a poster for a lecture on 'Shaw or Iron' by Egon Friedell with his so-called 'Red Head' grimacing. In 1914, he did the St Sebastian for his show at the Arnot Gallery, and for the great collective show at the Secession he depicted the jury with himself sitting at the head of the table, for which there was an oil sketch.[7] The first two catalogued paintings are self-portraits done while still at school.[8] Apart from one self-portrait of 1910, which shows a 'dead city' behind him, the most revealing documents are the two self-portraits

Egon Schiele
View of Krumau 1916
110.5 × 141 cm./43 × 55 in.
Neue Galerie der Stadt Linz,
photo Museum

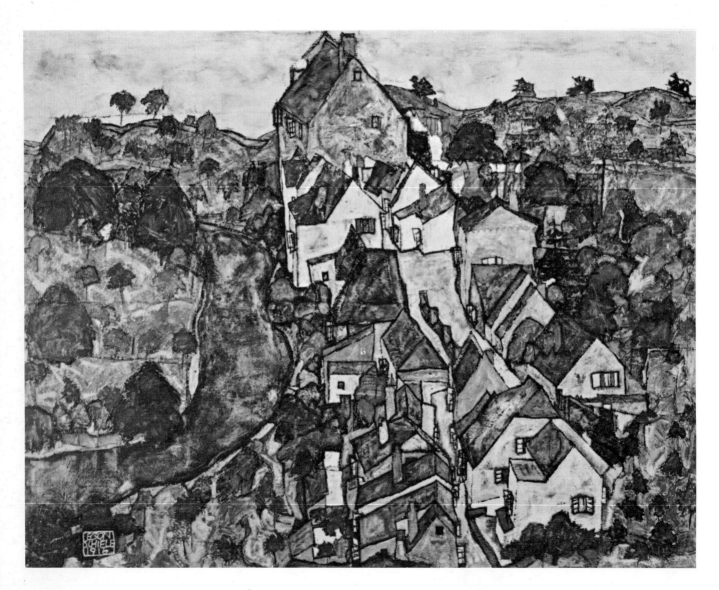

of 1910 and 1911, in which a crouching *Doppelgänger* peers from behind the self-portrait's shoulder. The first shows the artist naked with a draped figure behind. In the other both figures are dark and cut off at half-length the one behind being Death, with a skull for head. His own title for the work is *Die Selbstseer*, or 'self-seers'. Here is the self-love suggested by Weininger that is Schiele's artistic testament, here he shows himself to be his best friend, the person whom he most trusts. An important drawing of 1910 shows the artist sketching the back of a nude girl in a toque and stockings seen in a mirror, the same long mirror in front of which he was photographed in 1915, the mirror which his sister Melanie possessed after his death. It can be compared with the double photograph probably done in 1914, possibly by Trčka, or another which shows a further stage in Schiele's idea of himself – with eyes shut he grimaces between his spread fingers, as in a drawing with closed and dead eyes of the same year. His gestures with the expressionist hands, the exaggerated eyelids, and the very many naked pictures and drawings of himself with unflattering hair on his body and under his arms no doubt served to prove his virility. Probably no other artist drew himself with his hand on his penis as he did. This picture of himself is as cold and unromantic as his drawing of more objective subjects, his nude models and young girls. The series of oil sketches of about 1910 which he sold to Reininghaus include some of himself that are as brutal and as 'naked' as the drawings of new-born babies of the same period.[9] His hand is clear, as he sometimes used a hard pencil, especially around 1910, and if his line is not as fluid as that of the immensely volatile Klimt, it is unmistakable. Instead of Klimt's uncanny facility, Schiele had an extravagant angularity, made more alien by his use of abstract colour, an expressionist trait which he remained faithful to even in his late drawings of Russian prisoners in violent emerald and violet.

A further theme of Schiele's is the couple embracing or sitting beside each other, sometimes in the apparent despair of existential life, more often in the hopeless situation of the cardinal and the nun, or death and the man or girl, and death and the blind mother. The contortions are nowhere so erotic as in the fully clothed loving couple of 1914. The blindness theme is seen even in his double portrait of himself and Klimt, *The Hermits* of 1912, where the older man kneeling behind Schiele is blind.

Over his townscapes lie emptiness and desolation. The series of views of Krumau between 1910 and 1912 are usually subtitled *The Dead City*, although Schiele speaks of a warmth and spring in writing of his towns. Nothing moves in them, they are the scenery in which his hopeless human theatre is played out. Against this scenery are the death-wishes enacted – the confrontation between death and the maiden, between the priest of death and the mother, and most important of all between himself as a monk and a girl with red, made-up lips staring not into her lover's eye, but into that of the onlooker. Towards the end of his life Schiele painted couples and even three figures alongside each other, no longer tormented by hopeless love, as though he himself had found a kind of satisfaction. It is perhaps important to record that Schiele did not wish to confine himself to these tight compositions. As far back as 1910 he had painted a decoration for an international hunting exhibition. Otto Benesch has described a large composition of about twelve figures dressed as monks including the Benesch father and son, and Klimt. There were also nude females seen from the back. The work which was not completed for the Reininghaus exhibition was also to have been a large work, but all that Schiele completed was the

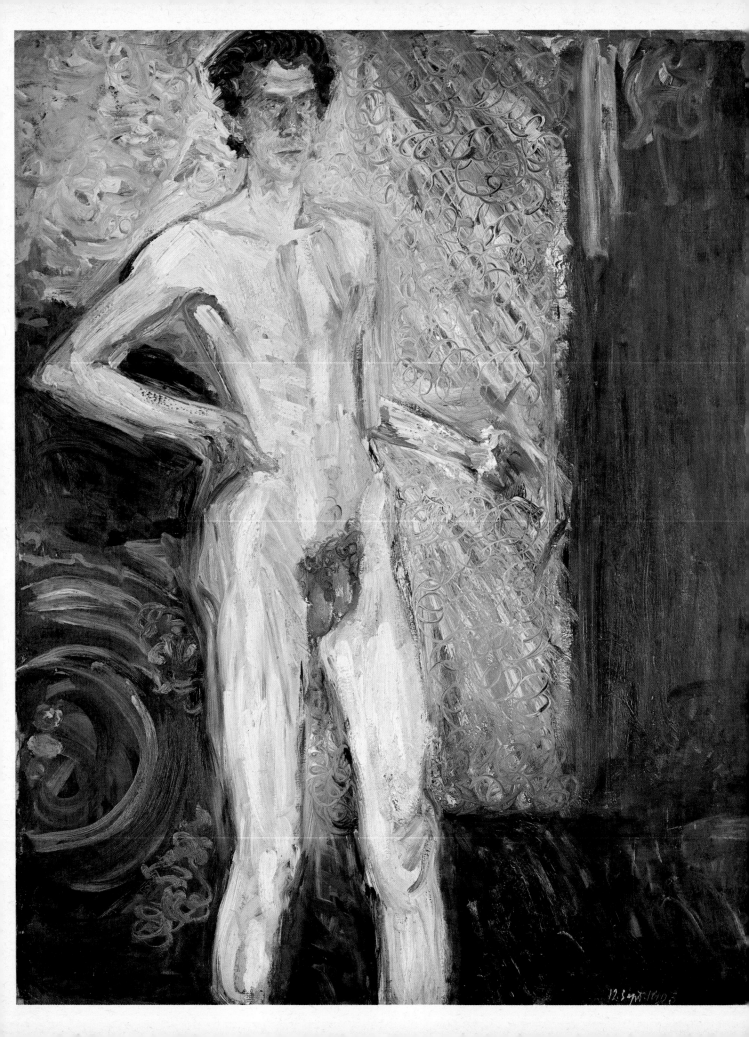

12. Sept 1903

section called the *Meeting*, including a self-portrait half covered by a shirt or towel. There were to be six blind figures to the right. Schiele had himself photographed in front of it dressed much more smartly than in the picture.

After he died a few exhibitions of his work were held up to 1930. The Viennese did not consider him important enough to save, and a number of works emigrated to America with their owners. Some were left behind in India by Fritz Lang, the film director and originally painter, who called himself a pupil of Schiele's, and there are some works as far afield as Brasil. The first Viennese exhibition after the war was in 1945 with Klimt and Kokoschka, who is on record as saying 'Schiele always had lots of girls round him, that was his bad luck. Klimt also drew women mostly but he was a *real* artist.'[10] Yet Schiele will continue to rise in estimation, not through his cold views of towns, nor his chestnut trees with the leaves dropping in an eternal autumn, but by his portrayal of frail and yet expectant love, and even by the precise eroticism of his nudes.

Opposite:
Richard Gerstl
Full-length Self-portrait dated
12 September 1908
141 × 109 cm./55 × 42 in.
Dr Rudolf Leopold, Vienna,
photo owner

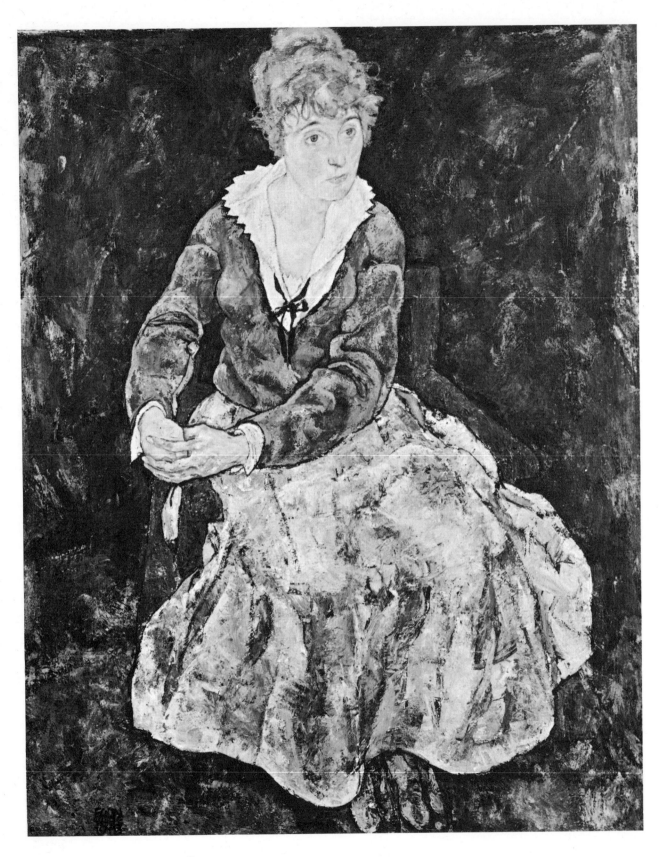

162

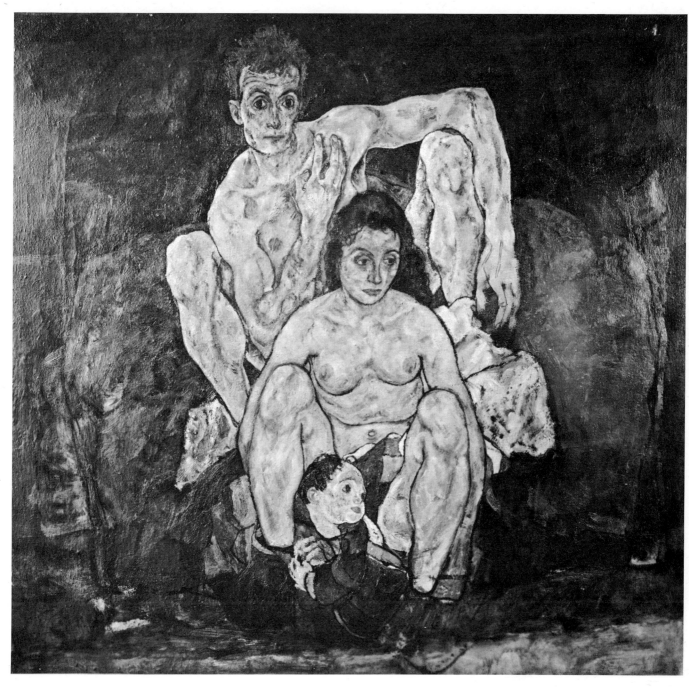

Egon Schiele
The Family 1918
149.7 × 160 cm./59 × 63 in.
Österreichische Galerie,
photo Museum

Egon Schiele
The Artist's Wife Sitting 1918
Signed, 139.5 × 109.2 cm./55 × 43 in.
Österreichische Galerie,
photo Museum

Richard Gerstl, the Angry Young Painter

On his rediscovery in the autumn of 1931, twenty-three years after his death, Richard Gerstl was called 'an Austrian van Gogh' and a genius. In exhibitions he was brought before the public at the Venice Biennale in 1932 and again in 1956, and he is well represented in the Österreichische Galerie. As lonely and insecure as Schiele he burnt himself out in a bare four and a half years of painting. He was born on 14 September 1883 and hanged himself, aged only twenty-five, on 7 November 1908.

His father, a well-to-do Jewish man of money, came to Vienna from Neutra in Hungary (now Nitra in Slovakia), and his mother was Bohemian. He had two elder brothers August, and Alois, of whom he did a distinguished portrait in uniform. Due to his father's whims, the family moved their apartments seven times in Gerstl's short life, within the respectable eight and ninth districts, in itself a disturbing factor. Educated at the excellent catholic Piaristengymnasium, he proved to be a difficult pupil, and left for a private school. While his father only just tolerated his artistic leanings, he was encouraged by his mother, and at the age of fifteen he entered the Academy under Griepenkerl who had painted the curtain and frescoes in the auditorium of the opera, and a frieze in the Parliament, and under whom Schiele had been a student. He broke away in 1901. He spent two summers in 1900 and 1901 with the Hungarian painter Simon Holosy at his summer school in Nagy Banya. Having rented a room on the Hohe Warte, he learnt Italian and Spanish, attended concerts and the opera where he became a passionate adherent of Mahler, and met both Schönberg, and Schönberg's teacher, later Gerstl's brother-in-law, Alexander von Zemlinsky, the composer and opera conductor. Zemlinsky was to be the subject of one of Gerstl's most penetrating portraits in 1908, and was also painted by Schönberg. In 1904, he took up painting with Griepenkerl again, but after two terms he appears to have been dismissed for unsatisfactory work. He shared a studio with Viktor Hammer (born in Vienna in 1882 and died in Aurora, New York in 1968) and it was here that Lefler saw the portrait of the Fey sisters, which is now in the Österreichische Galerie. Gerstl agreed to go back to the Academy provided that he was allowed a separate studio. Fellow students included Franz Wacik, one of the more interesting graphic artists of the Secession, and Anton Kolig, the sensuous painter from Moravia who died in Nötsch in Carinthia (1886-1950).

Gerstl painted Arnold Schönberg and his wife, Anton Webern's cousin, Professor Ernst Diez, in a morning coat and striped trousers, and Alban Berg's sister, Smaragda. He became more and more attracted by music and even thought of accepting a job as a music critic, but retired to a sanatorium near Baden with a nervous stomach complaint. He spent the summers of 1907 and 1908 at Gmunden on the Traunsee with the Schönbergs, and taught the composer who had begun to paint. Schönberg did some ninety works including drawings, about a third being done between 1908-10. He was sufficiently important for Kandinsky and Gütersloh to write about him as a painter in 1912.

In 1907, Klimt showed the Faculty pictures at the Miethke Gallery. Gerstl was offered an exhibition there but refused unless all works by Klimt were removed. He annoyed his professor Lefler who was involved in the 1908 Imperial Jubilee preparations. He was also in disgrace with the Schönberg circle because he had taken Mathilde Schönberg to his studio in the Liechtensteinstrasse, and when this exceedingly plain woman wanted to return to her husband, he killed himself.[1] Lefler tried to arrange an exhibition in the Hagenbund, but after this attempt failed the pictures were taken out of their frames until the autumn of 1931 when most of them were acquired by the Neue Galerie and shown together for the first time. About fifty works survive.

Suicide is a feature of Austrian intellectual life. Romako's daughters killed themselves for love and Schnitzler's daughter killed herself. Mahler's brother Otto shot himself at the age of twenty-two. Hofmannsthal's eldest son Franz shot himself two days before the poet's own death. The writer Adalbert Stifter, who had an incurable disease, cut his throat and died two days later in 1868, the year that van der Nüll committed suicide in disappointment over the public reception of the opera house. In 1905 Otto Weininger killed himself in his twenty-third year, and Hevesi followed him in 1910. Georg Trakl, an opium addict, took an overdose of drugs at the eastern front in the first year of the war, and Kurzweil shot himself and his mistress towards the end of it. In 1931 the sculptor Franz Barwig took his own life. Between 1938 and 1945, several people committed suicide as a result of the political situation. Egon Friedell threw himself from a window when the S.A. came for him. In 1942 Stefan Zweig killed himself in Brasil together with his second wife. Carl Moll killed himself with members of his family in 1945, and in the same year the poet Weinheber took an overdose of pills. This list is not given from any morbid sense of curiosity but to show that Gerstl's suicide, whether from despair or love, was by no means an isolated case. Without doubt, the Austrian atmosphere breeds a Slavonic and Magyar fatalism, and Vienna lies between the western and the eastern climate, and is liable to *Föhn* winds and the consequent depression it brings.

As a young man Gerstl is known to have admired the Velasquez paintings in the Vienna gallery. He probably also saw the impressionist exhibition at the Secession, held in his twentieth year, but he certainly visited the Munich show in 1904, which influenced his double portrait of the Fey sisters. They both wear long white dresses, and their Pontormo eyes look sunken and tired. What can they have thought of this portrait? It would be interesting to know if Gerstl had ever seen Rudolf Bacher's picture of two old women in black (1901). Van Gogh's exhibition in the Miethke Gallery of 1906 is reflected in the self-portrait of him laughing. The formal portrait of Schönberg sitting on a figured oriental divan with a diamond patterned wall-paper behind him, painted in 1906, has the scumbled brushwork of a Moll or the impressionists, while his second portrait of Mathilde Schönberg (1907-8) has the flowered dress of the *Jugendstil*, and the elongations of some of Klimt's formal portraits.

Gerstl's progress can be followed through his own self-portraits. The first one, which is life-size, shows himself half-naked at the age of nineteen standing modestly with his hands in front of a white sheet wound round his lower half. The background is an abstract Prussian blue space. He stares with his lower face marked by a thin long moustache. In the next self-portrait he stands fully dressed and respectable with his palette in his hand. The laughing self-portrait belongs to 1907. In the half-length portrait in front of a stove,

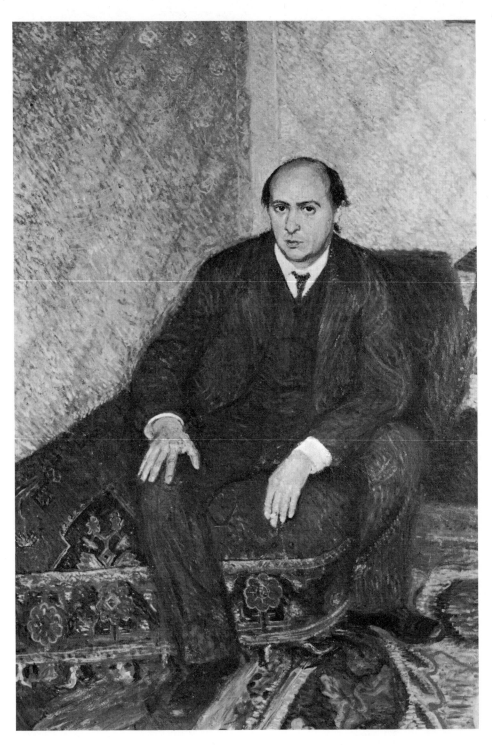

his line is already breaking up. Finally, for the month of September 1908, a few months before the end, he painted himself naked in front of the mirror, his body sketched in pink and mauve, his left hand on his hip and painting hand out of focus as it moves with the brush. The wall-paper is now a scrawl of scribbles and the furniture all but unrecognizable, hinted at in deep purples

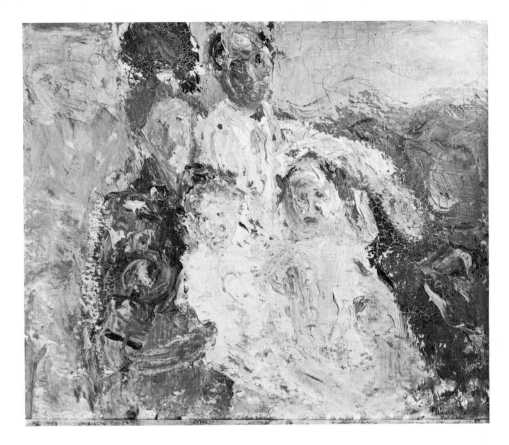

Richard Gerstl
The Schönberg Family 1908
Signed, 169 × 110 cm./66 × 43 in.
Museum des 20. Jahrhunderts,
photo Museum

and mauves. Breicha sees in this work not only the angry young man made tragically lonely and a martyr to his own passion, but the artist still able to evoke the hopelessness of his own situation in a unique moment of self-observation and sensitivity.

In his early portraits of his father and brother and Schönberg, there is still the hint of what had been learnt from observation. On the other hand in his landscapes he was soon to break away from line, with strong, thin brush strokes marking both the contour and the spaces, painted on an untidy surface in a manner far ahead of his time. This is the same treatment which he gives not so much to the friendly picture of Zemlinsky standing agreeably in a white suit and hat leaning on a stick in slight mauve shadow in front of sparkling lake water, but in his rougher handling of the Schönberg family. In one version they sit in a tight, oblong group with pale hints of blue, white and mauve on a sunlit green. In the other, figures emerge from a background of buttercup green. The person in a brown suit and bald head is Schönberg, another man wears a suit of blancmange pink, while Zemlinsky is barely hinted at in his white leghorn hat. Otherwise there are only figures and hands. This is nervous painting, uncertain but cerebral. It suggests that Gerstl wanted to progress beyond the statements about people and landscape that Corinth was to make only a few years after Gerstl's death.

Gerstl's painting is manly, brutal and unsatisfied. Its roughness and directness makes Gerstl in many ways the most modern of these Austrian artists. A painter who was fond, not of painters, but of musicians, Gerstl used paint as though he were trying to break through to the pure colour of abstraction.[2]

167

'The Tempest' and the Young Kokoschka

Oskar Kokoschka was born in Pöchlarn on 1 March 1886, but was brought up in Vienna. His father came from Prague, the last in a long line of goldsmiths and his mother, a Styrian, came from a family of imperial foresters. In 1904, when the young Kokoschka had passed his matriculation examination, at first he wanted to be a chemist. As a boy, he had spent his time at museums, being most attracted by the rich collections of the Ethnographical Museum especially those from the South Sea Islands, which included some discoveries from the Cook expeditions. A mask from New Mecklenburg with shells and shark teeth impressed him especially, and instances of masks in his painting are *Still-Life with a Mask* of about 1920, and the poster design for his play in the garden theatre of the Kunstschau of 1908 which is directly based on a primitive mask. However the only painter he admitted to having influenced him was Anton Romako, whose exhibition in 1905 he must have seen, as well as that by van Gogh in the year after.[1] Indeed his first Hungarian landscape, and his first portraits are filled with the dark essence of Romako,[2] and, even without his admission, the portraits up to that of Baron Victor von Dirsztay (1911) are unthinkable without Romako's melancholy. Further, Kokoschka probably visited the 1906 van Gogh exhibition, for the *Still Life with a Pineapple* (c. 1906) and the grimacing portrait of an old man, *Vater Hirsch* (1907), both owe a great deal to van Gogh. Again, the portrait of the insane Ritter von Janikowsky, whom Loos persuaded to sit for a portrait in 1909 is, by its pronounced ear, almost a pastiche of van Gogh.

From 1905 to 1909, Kokoschka had a scholarship at the School of Applied Arts in Vienna, first under Czeschka, then, from 1907, designing postcards and fans for the Werkstätte. He also collaborated in Hoffmann's Fledermaus cabaret, producing coloured metal figures for the shadow play *The Spotted Egg* for the opening. For the Kunstschau he did the tapestry design, *The Dream-Bearers*, of which nothing is now known except that it caused a great deal of laughter among the viewers, and he also exhibited his illustrated expressionist poems *The Dreaming Boys* done for the Werkstätte. These in turn were influenced by Schliemann's discoveries.[3] The fairy story dedicated 'in admiration' to Klimt is a broken poem of red fishes, processions from ships, 'I was the dancer of kings', erotic symbolism, and nameless beasts. It is all but unreadable today. However, the strong line and simple primary patches of colour in the illustrations have an alien charm.[4] This could not be said of the first performance in 1909 of his play, *Murderer, Hope of Women*. The twenty-two year old, in an attempt to show the thoughtlessness of our male-dominated society, based the play on the revolutionary idea that man is mortal and woman immortal, and that only the murderer tries to reverse the state of affairs. 'That is how I became the bogeyman of the bougeoisie.'[5] Significantly watered down to *Hope of Women, Murderer, Hope of Women*, together with *Sphinx and Man of Straw*, the play put on at the Art School in 1906, and *Play* of 1911, was published with the first essay on the artist, 'Dramas and Pictures' in *Der Sturm*. Later, in 1916,

Fritz Gurlitt published twelve lithograph illustrations to Kokoschka's poem *The Bound Columbus*. He also issued illustrations to a Bach cantata, and in 1917 eleven lithographs and a lithographic title page to the *Book of Job*.

Wingler has summed up Kokoschka's situation in 1908 like this: 'He is firstly a draughtsman, then, in addition, a poet. He was teaching himself to be a painter by slow stages. In order to become a painter he had to abandon the professional goal of his school, and give up the idea of a secure existence. He needed to get out into the world. Encouraged by Adolf Loos, he made the decision which decided his future.'[6] The best witness to this is Loos himself in an essay he wrote to introduce a collective exhibition at the Kunsthalle Mannheim in 1931:

'I met him in the year 1908, after he had designed the poster for the Vienna Kunstschau. I was told that he was an employee of the Werkstätte, and was occupied in painting fans, designing postcards and the like in the German style; this was art serving shopkeepers, and it was clear to me at once that this was the greatest sin against the Holy Ghost. I had Kokoschka sent for. He came. What was he doing now? He was modelling a bust (it was only finished in his brain). I bought it. What did it cost? A cigarette. Done, I never haggle. But we finally agreed on fifty kronen.

He had also done a life-size design for a tapestry for the Kunstschau, the clou of the exhibition, and the Viennese rushed in to laugh themselves silly over it. I would have loved to acquire it, but it belonged to the Werkstätte—it ended in the rubbish dump with the rubble of the exhibition.

I promised Kokoschka that he would have the same income if he left the Werkstätte, and I sought commissions for him. I sent him to my sick wife in Switzerland and asked Professor Forel, who lived near, to allow himself to be painted. I then took the completed picture to the museum authorities in Berne, and offered it for two hundred francs. Turned down. I sent it to an exhibition in the Künstlerhaus. Turned down. Then to the Klimt group for an exhibition in Rome. Turned down by the opposition. Only the Kunsthalle Mannheim dared to buy it.

Two hundred francs it cost—no one, no gallery wanted it.

When my house on the Michaelerplatz was built, my enthusiasm for Kokoschka was seen as a proof of my inferiority.

And today? We have both survived. For my sixtieth birthday, Kokoschka sent me a letter, which proves that the greatest creativity includes the greatest humanity.'[7]

So the young artist went to Switzerland with an advance of 400 francs given him by Ludwig von Ficker, the Innsbruck editor of *Der Brenner* whose portrait he did in January 1915. He stayed with the famous zoologist, Forel, who made it a condition of the sittings that he should not have to buy the portrait. As Kokoschka was leaving, he asked who Loos was. 'The most famous man in Vienna,' Kokoschka replied loyally.[8]

The kind of portrait which the long-faced, amiable, and somewhat naïve young artist had been painting before he met Loos is typified by the *Traumspieler* (trance actor) a portrait of Ernst Reinhold, the principal actor in *Murderer, Hope of Women*. It was completed by the autumn of 1908.[9] Certainly his first formal portrait, it was one of the most immediate and direct of his representations and foeshadowed all the many portraits he was to paint. While it was to a great extent a likeness of Reinhold, yet at the same time it has an icon-like,

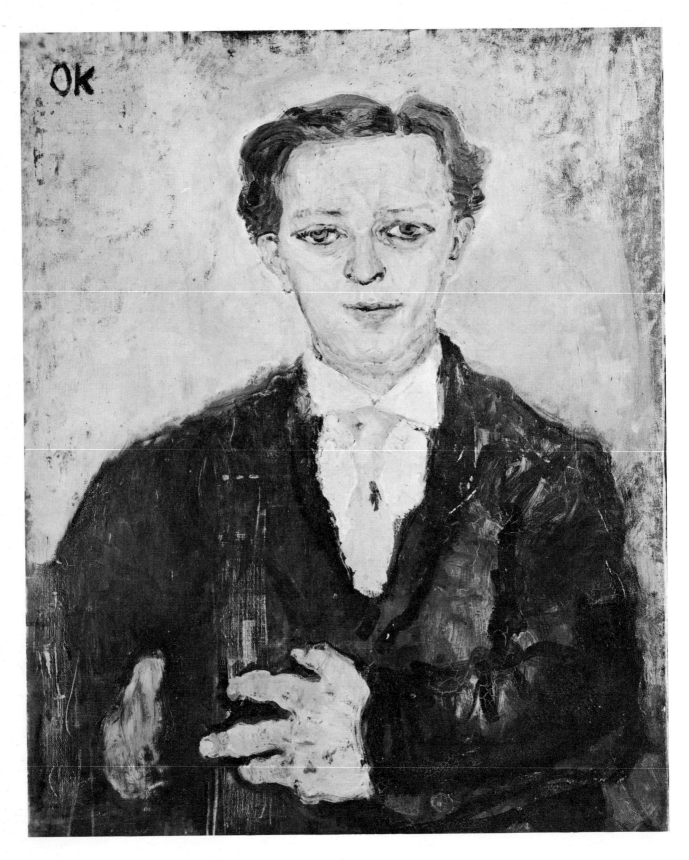

170

distant quality. The young Kokoschka had a capacity near to genius for feeling inside the sitter, for demystifying the subject, a process which was in the very spirit of the times. At the same time the alienating side of his analysis could put people off. In one of the first attempts to evaluate the early portraits Franz Grüner wrote in *Die Fackel* of February 1911 about the Hagenbund exhibition which had twenty-five works by Kokoschka and was his first representative show in Vienna:

> 'The people whom he represents look as if they had experienced serious illness, or several years in jail . . . as though they were suffering from repulsive physical and, of course, mental diseases . . . It need not be denied that the way in which Kokoschka attains the effect of his pictures is not the one that also leads to the beautification of his subjects: another goal is aimed at by other means.'

The portrait of the mentally afflicted Ritter von Janikowsky was in fact one of the works shown.

One of the first of the works commissioned thanks to Loos's benevolent interest was the portrait of the court tailor, Ebenstein, who not only sat for Kokoschka but dressed him and advised him on the anatomy of suits. This was closely followed by the first portrait of Karl Kraus, and the portrait of Loos himself on which the architect wrote the date 1909. Other sitters were Constantin Christomanos, reader to the Empress Elisabeth, and Peter Altenberg, whom Kokoschka painted to look like a tired Bismarck. It was at this point that Loos arranged for Kokoschka to go off to Switzerland. There he painted Bessie Loos, the architect's wife, at the end of 1909, and, at the beginning of 1910, Professor Forel, the Duchess of Rohan-Montesquieu, and the portrait of her husband.

On his return to Vienna, Kokoschka was introduced by Loos to Herwath Walden, the editor of *Der Sturm*, who carried him off to Berlin. Throughout 1910 he did a drawing for the title page nearly every week. In June he exhibited in the gallery of Paul Cassirer and did a sensitive and beautiful portrait of Cassirer's wife, the famous actress, Tilly Durieux. He also had his first exhibition in a museum at the Folkwang-Museum in Hagen, Westfalia.

From 1912 until he was severely wounded on the Russian front in 1915 the artist's life has elements of the gossip column and of farce, but the love affair with Alma Mahler produced his one unquestionably great work, *Die Windsbraut* (known in English as *The Tempest*). Undoubtedly, she was the greatest influence on him after his mother and Loos, and for ten years she appeared again and again in his work. Gustav Mahler had died in May of 1911, and she even married the German architect Walter Gropius in the autumn of 1915, but it only lasted a short time. According to her it was in the winter of 1912 that Carl Moll suggested to her that she should let herself be painted by a young genius. The young artist sat in a box with Alma Mahler at the opera to watch Diaghilev's Russian Ballet, an inexperienced young man with one of the best known hostesses of Vienna. She promised to marry him if he produced a masterpiece. He did so, but they never married. He first painted a rather ungenerous portrait of her with him in his new lighter style and clearer colouring. Another, for which the study is dated 16 June, annoyed the composer Hans Pfitzner. 'What a murder . . . these colours without meaning . . . this heartlessness . . . Where is your face?' This is the portrait with a Gioconda smile, despite the fact that Alma Mahler was no Mona Lisa.

Opposite:
Oskar Kokoschka
Der Traumspieler (Ernst Reinhold) 1908
84 × 65 cm./33 × 25 in.
Musées des Beaux Arts, Brussels,
photo Museum

Oskar Kokoschka
Adolf Loos 1909
Pen and indian ink
Photo Austrian National Library

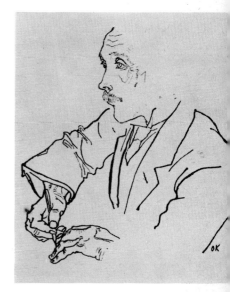

They travelled to the Tirol together and Venice and Naples. In August 1913 the Dolomites produced the important landscape *Tre Croci*, in restful blues and greens. On the other hand, the upheavals of the fir-trees and the mountains may symbolize their own stormy passage.

For her house on the Simmering, where well-to-do Viennese families and the Archduke Karl Ludwig had summer properties, Kokoschka painted a huge fresco over the fireplace, which was a continuation of the play of the fire below. He stood in a Hell surrounded by snakes and death while she pointed to Heaven in a ghostly light. In 1955, Alma Mahler wrote that it had been painted over and ruined.

When the war came, the artist was almost glad to volunteer. He joined the exclusive Imperial and Royal Dragonerregiment no. 15, partly to show his snobbish friends that he could be elegant in the blue and red uniform, partly

Oskar Kokoschka
Die Windsbraut (The Tempest) 1914
181 × 221 cm./71 × 87 in.
Offentliche Kunstsammlung, Basel,
photo Museum

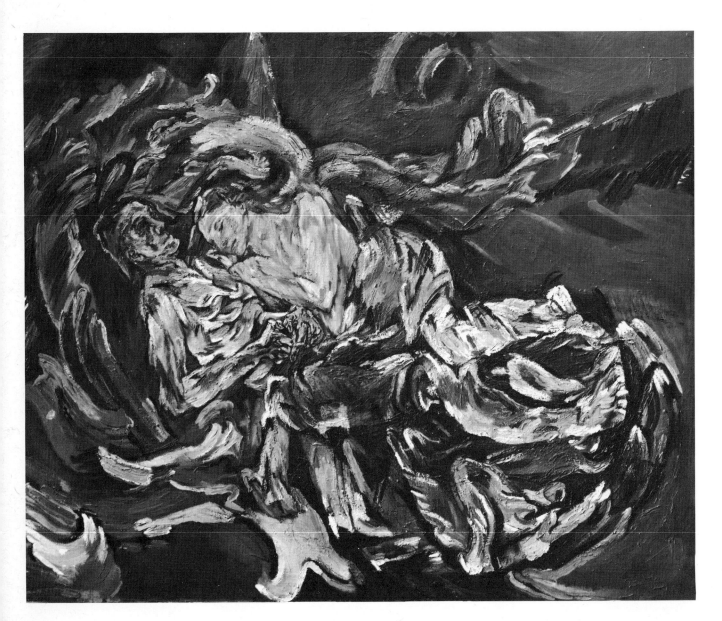

due to the insistence of Loos, who had him photographed like an actor from the Burgtheater. In a symbolic act of sacrifice and escape he had to sell *Die Windsbraut* to buy a horse. Before leaving for the war he gave Alma Mahler a series of six fans he had painted between Christmas 1912 and 1914 which she kept to the end of her life. Painted in watercolours on swan's skin, they show a self-portrait with Alma; a man and a woman in a boat and a woman riding; the *Windsbraut* theme and St George; the artist sleeping under a tree; two girls and a cow, and a woman with a sphinx; lastly, a woman with two children in a war-torn landscape, and a soldier and a cannon, a self-portrait of himself wounded. This last scene was prophetic, for at the beginning of September 1915 Kokoschka was shot in the head and bayoneted in the lung on the Galician front. (Convalescing in Vienna in 1916 he met Rilke and Hofmannsthal.) However, he never went back as a soldier. After being a war artist on the Isonzo front and because his lung would not heal he was withdrawn. He then went to Berlin as the guest of *Der Sturm*, visited a brain specialist in Stockholm and was lost to the Vienna scene for a time. From 1917 he settled in Dresden, and his thicker Rembrandtesque period began, with groups painted in low tones of grey-white and blue and green.

Alma Mahler had suffered for Kokoschka, especially when he wrote to her about being drilled. She never forgot him and when Klimt died she wrote: 'Oskar Kokoschka is by far the stronger of the two, and Klimt had great respect for his talent.' In the next line of her memoirs she mentions the name of Franz Werfel, the writer and, after Gropius, her next husband. She continued to keep in touch with the artist and mentions one or two painful and poignant meetings in Venice. She also recalls the life-size doll that Kokoschka had made in Dresden, with long blonde hair, and a face painted to look like herself – or so he described the lay-figure to her. 'The doll lay on the sofa. Kokoschka spoke to it for hours, carefully locking himself in first . . . At last, he had me where he had always wanted me: an obliging tool with no will under his thumb.'[10]

The period with Alma Mahler was very productive. He did a number of sensitive self-portraits, the best being at the age of twenty-six which is now only known from reproductions. One next year in 1913, shows him with his right hand on his chest. One in greens is like *Tre Croci* and *Die Windsbraut* of the same period, with his right hand raised to paint, and a sad one with an elongated face done on Christmas Eve 1914. There were also portraits of Egon Wellesz, the beautiful double portrait, *Spozalizio*, a woman with her husband behind her with his hands on her shoulders, the portrait of Carl Moll of 1913 or 1914, the head of Anton von Webern of 1914, and finally the portrait of Ficker painted, at the last moment as it were, in January 1915.

Yet nothing was as fine as the double portrait of himself with his mistress painted at the beginning of their friendship, in which the artist, tired and sensitive, looks to the onlooker for sympathy – *Die Windsbraut*. Painted in the spring of 1914, it was shown in Munich at the end of May. In the charcoal sketch the lovers lie side by side. In the finished work they lie in a boat in the same position, but the half-naked woman with her eyes closed, lies apparently above the artist, in the same dominant position which she had in the lost summer-house fresco. The scene is night-time and a half-clouded moon emerges from behind high mountains, while the little boat tosses on deep blue-purple waves. The man's figure has something of the resignation of Holbein's dead Christ with the feet turned in. It is probably the saddest depiction of modern love, and the story of the end of a stormy love has not been better told.

One more picture was to be almost as prophetic. *The Knight Errant* was painted at the beginning of 1915, just before Kokoschka joined up. A wounded soldier lies in his armour in a landscape foreshadowing the devastations of the Western front. One leg is crossed uselessly under the other. With his outstretched arms the soldier appeals to heaven.

Although Franz Ferdinand said that someone ought to break every bone in Kokoschka's body, he was only expressing something that Kokoschka, with the second sight characteristic of his family, felt himself and showed in his unhappy and disturbing painting. It was not for nothing that critics spoke of his X-ray mentality, or sense for dissection in portrayal. On the other hand, others have spoken of the humanity of his art. He is surely one of the most human artists, and near to the heart of earthbound man—at least in this great early period.

SCULPTURE

Monuments and Fountains

There had never been any lack of good sculpture in Vienna. In the Stephanskirche Anton Pilgram from Brno carved his great works, the pulpit with the heads of Church fathers and with his own portrait, seen again at the base of the stone organ loft (1513-15). The Augustinerkirche contains Canova's masterpiece, the white marble monument to Maria Christine of 1805. The Ringstrasse demanded its complement of sculpture. The most important complex was the monument to Maria Theresa completed to a programme by her tireless biographer, Alfred von Arneth, director of the House, Court and State Archive, and winner of the competition was the German Kaspar von Zumbusch, designer of the Beethoven memorial statue in 1880, and, later, in 1891, of the equestrian statue of Radetzky re-sited outside the War Ministry building on the Ringstrasse. In 1887, Maria Theresa surrounded by her generals and ministers was unveiled between the great museum blocks. Among the unsuccessful competitors was Johann Benk whose biggest work was to be the monument to Vienna's own Deutschmeister regiment, interesting mainly in that it is a memorial to the simple soldier, and not a prince or a general. Although completed in 1906, it is a retrogressive work. While a monument to Schiller by Johann Schilling had been erected in front of the Academy of Fine Arts in 1876, the nearest to the Ringstrasse that a statue to Joseph Haydn was allowed to get was on the Mariahilferstrasse, outside the church of that name. Sculptured by Heinrich Natter, and paid for by 'a group of citizens', it was completed in the same year as the Maria Theresa monument. When it was suggested that imperial bronze from cannons, such as was used for other monuments, might be made available, the answer came that there was none to be had. Franz Joseph nevertheless contributed to the statue.[1]

Mozart, in the pose of the Apollo Belvedere, surrounded by *putti* musicians, did rather better. His statue is by Viktor Tilgner who was born in 1844 in Pressburg (Bratislava) and died in Vienna in 1896, in the year that the Mozart monument was first placed near the Hotel Sacher. It is now in the Burggarten, formerly the imperial private garden in front of the Hofburg. Tilgner was much in demand and was one of the most prolific sculptors of the Ringstrasse and its style. His statues include the fancy dress Makart (1898) and the excellent bust to Bruckner (1899), both in the Stadtpark. He worked on the Burgtheater, the Neue Hofburg, and on both the museums on Maria-Theresia-Platz. He was rivalled only by the slightly older Anton Dominik Fernkorn (1813-78) director of the State foundry who died insane, and designer of the equestrian monuments to Prince Eugene (1865) and Archduke Carl (1859) on the Heldenplatz, the dolphin fountain in the Volksgarten and the fountain in the arcade of the Ferstelpalais on the Freyung (1860-1).

It was approximately in 1898 that hints of the *Jugendstil* began to be evident in sculpture, for example, the statue by Franz Vogl of the romantic dramatist Raimund, with the poet sitting below the muse of Poetry in white marble, which was erected outside the Volkstheater. In 1898 too, Carl Kundmann's

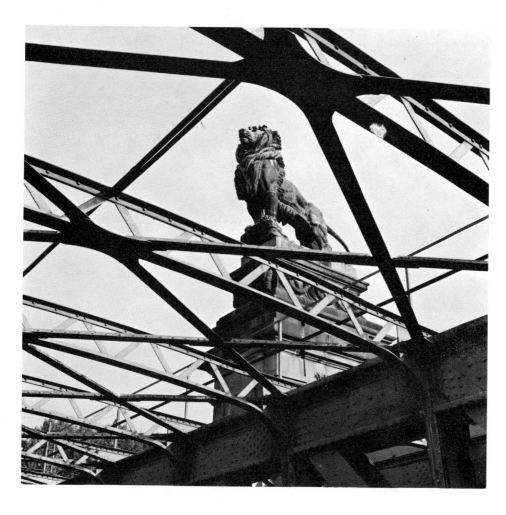

Rudolf Weyr
Bronze Lion 1898
Above bridge over Otto Wagner's
Nussdorfer dam
Photo Gert Rosenberg

colossal marble Pallas Athena was placed outside the parliament. The same subject as Klimt's painting of the same year, Klimt's professor, Laufberger, had already designed a Pallas Athena in mosaic outside the School of Applied Arts in 1873. In 1872, Kundmann's Schubert had been erected in the Stadtpark, and, in 1886, outside the distant Prater, his statue of Tegetthoff attended by horses, ship's prows and Victories, mounted on a rostral column. The monument to Grillparzer, which has the poet sitting in front of an architectural screen by Hasenauer and Weyr's six reliefs from Grillparzer plays, is fairly successful and by 1889 was placed in the Volksgarten. Kundmann was a professor at the Academy while Rudolf von Weyr (1847-1914) was a teacher at the School of Applied Art. Weyr did some massive reliefs on the walls of the baroque Peterskirche in 1906 and the two lions for Wagner's Nussdorf dam, beside the statues of Hans Canon in knickerbockers and wellington boots in the Stadtpark (1905) and of Brahms in front of the Technical University (1908). His most important work, the colossal *Austria's Power at Sea* of 1895, stands in front of the Hofburg's Michaelertor, and is flanked by the equally daunting *Austria's Power on Land* (1897) by Edmund Hellmer (1850-1935). Hellmer was often rector of the Academy. His huge monument to the Turkish wars in the Stephanskirche was unfortunately all but destroyed in 1945, but his *Franz Joseph giving the constitution to the seventeen Crown Lands* (1883) still stands in the

177

Edmund Hellmer
Austria's Power on Land 1897
Marble fountain in Michaelerplatz
(detail)
Photo Gert Rosenberg

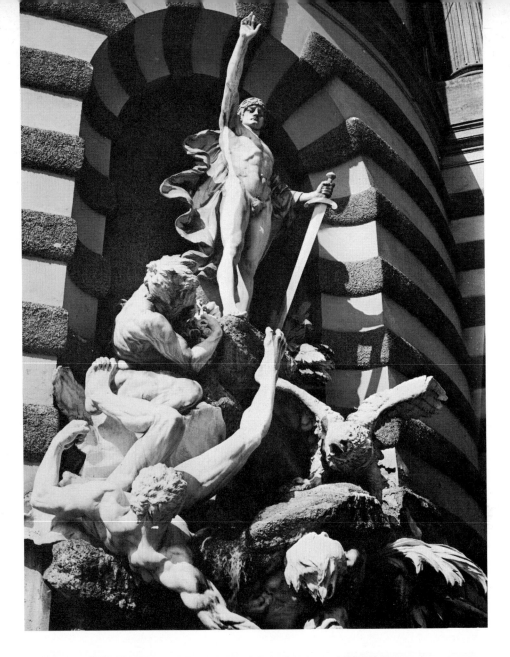

Josef Engelhart
Fireplace 1899
Carved wood and copper
Österreichisches Museum für
Angewandte Kunst, photo Museum

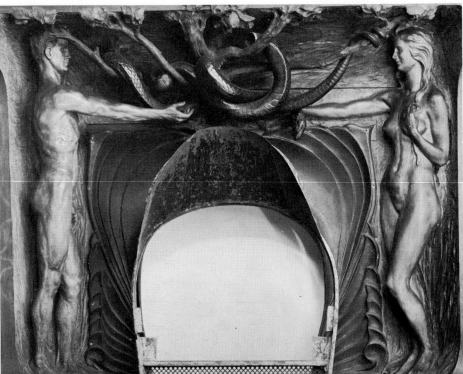

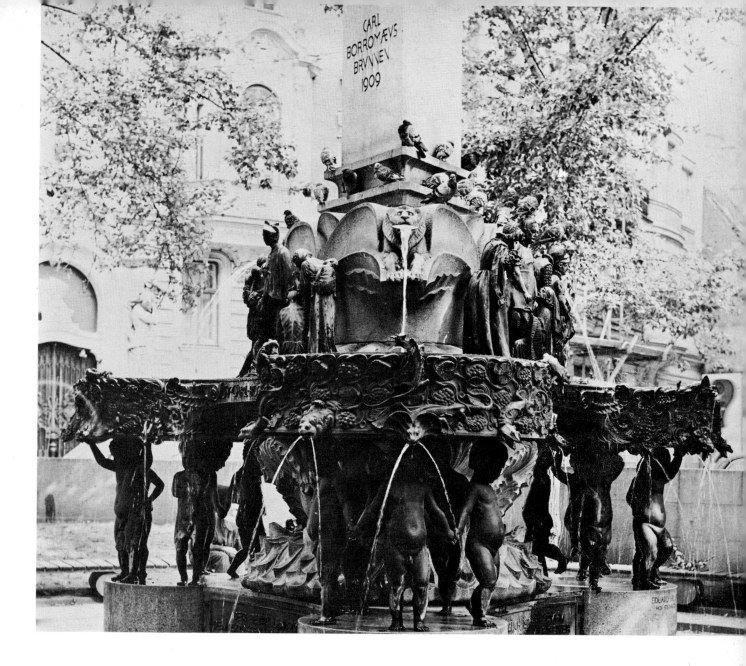

Josef Engelhart and Josef Plečnik
Borromäus Fountain 1909
(detail)
Photo Gert Rosenberg

pediment to the parliament building's portico. This group, showing the Emperor in a toga and wearing a garland above his bewhiskered face surrounded by figures representing the seventeen lands, was carved from one block of Lasa marble weighing thirty-eight tons. Hellmer was also responsible for the remarkable *Kastalia* fountain (1904) in the courtyard of the university, and a much less interesting *Goethe* (1900) on the Ringstrasse. He is best known by the Stadtpark's Johann Strauss monument, in which the composer plays his violin in a highly romantic pose surrounded by an arch of high relief marble nudes in the best spirit of the *Jugendstil*. The edges of the arch are picked out with a formal wreath of roses. It was finally erected in 1923, and the bronze figure of Strauss was originally gilded.

In his long career, Josef Engelhart also worked as a sculptor, and some of his work is faithful to the principles of the *Jugendstil*. For a remarkable fireplace dated 1899, he showed Eve reaching across to Adam, who is seen in profile. Above the opening for the fire the serpent twines in the tree of knowledge.

179

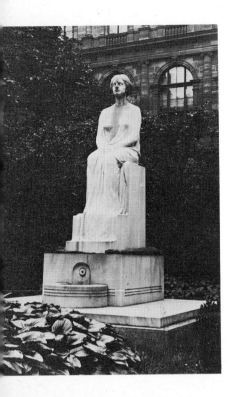

In 1903, he made a mourning youth in bronze, based on himself, for his family grave. Both works were shown in the Secession. In 1907, he did two heads, one of Alfonso Canciani, a sculptor, the other of Plečnik the architect. With the latter he was asked to make a monument to the Bürgermeister Lueger to celebrate the mayor's sixtieth birthday. The result was the highly satisfying *Borromäus* fountain in a small triangular square in the third district. An obelisk stands above a triple clover-leaf base. Putti support a basin covered with vines in relief, while exotic lizards crawl over the edge. Below the obelisk are grouped the poor, the plague-stricken and saint Charles Borromeo, quarter life-size. When it was finally unveiled in 1909, Engelhart was criticized for his naked children, and a local priest even collected signatures for a protest, but only made himself ridiculous. Engelhart's marble statue to the painter Waldmüller in the Rathauspark was completed in 1913 and erected in 1918, but the sacred spring had already turned into summer. However, the idea is good enough: a bare-footed Lower Austrian peasant girl, crouched at the painter's feet, looks at the drawing Waldmüller had done of her—a tactful reference to the romantic style of the artist. An art expert thought that Waldmüller would turn in his grave at being shown with only three waistcoat buttons.[2]

In addition to the *Borromäus* fountain there are five works in the true spirit of the *Jugendstil*. Arthur Strasser's *Marc Antony* (1899), which came to rest outside the Secession, has been mentioned in another context. However, his *Girl carrying a Pitcher* of 1896 is rather pedestrian. In 1900, Hans Bitterlich

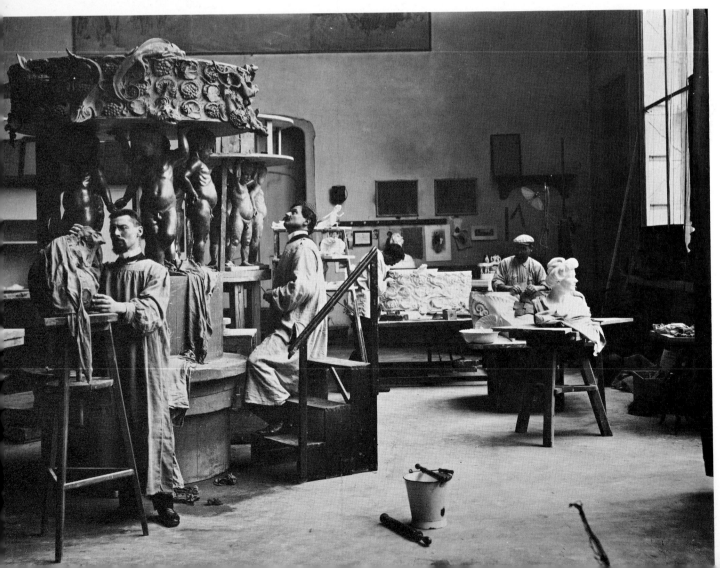

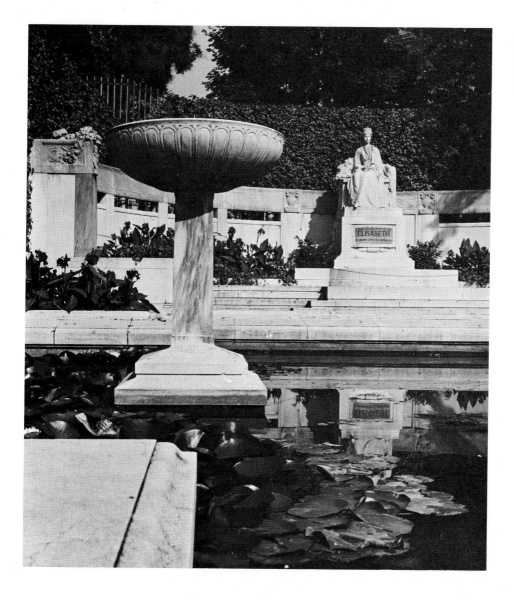

Sculpture by Hans Bitterlich and
architecture by Friedrich Ohmann
Monument to Empress Elisabeth 1905-7
In the Volksgarten
Photo Gert Rosenberg

(1860-1949) collaborated with the architect Fabiani in a monument to
Gutenberg. The seventh number of *Ver Sacrum* (1898) carried an article on the
alternative design by Schimkowitz and Plečnik which the magazine considered
to be much superior. In the photograph of the model, various figures encircle
a globe. Nevertheless, Bitterlich's design was carried out, and he also did the
marble monument to the Empress Elisabeth (1907) in the Volksgarten. The
sitting figure is unremarkable but the ensemble, the garden and the goldfish
pond by Ohmann is a delightful essay in the *fin-de-siècle*. Ohmann's pavilions
and terraces for the gardens surrounding the Stadtpark and the tunnel from
which the River Wien emerges have qualities that are more sculptural than
architectural. With their vases and creeper-clad balustrades they would make
an ideal for Maeterlinck, two of whose plays were translated in *Ver Sacrum*.
Finally, the strongly linear archangel Michael clinging to the front of the
Zacherlhaus was made out of beaten metal (1903-5) by Ferdinand Andri

Opposite top:
Edmund Hellmer
Kastalia Fountain 1910
Marble and bronze, Vienna
University, photo Austrian National
Library

Opposite below:
Josef Engelhart (left) and Josef
Plečnik (right) in Engelhart's studio
at work on the Borromäus fountain
(1908)
Photo Austrian National Library

Friedrich Ohmann
Design for Entrance to Tunnel over the
River Wien in the Stadtpark 1906
69 × 115 cm./27 × 45 in.
Historisches Museum der Stadt Wien,
photo Museum

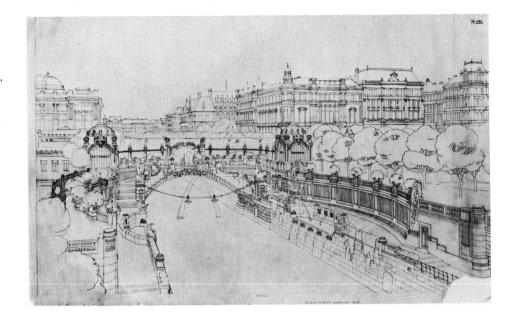

Friedrich Ohmann, with sculpture
by Franz Klug
Terraces and Tunnel over the River Wien
in the Stadtpark 1906
Photo Gert Rosenberg

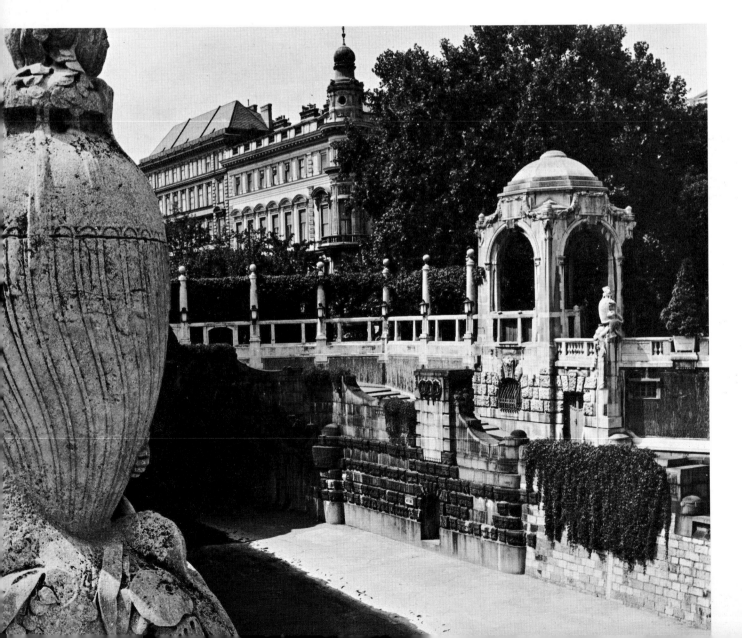

(1871-1956). Such an uncompromisingly *Jugendstil* figure is unexpected from an artist better known as the painter of scenes in rustic markets such as *The Butterwomen* of 1902.

Not every sculptural essay in *Jugendstil* got the support it deserved. In the Rathauspark there is Franz Seifert's (1866-1951) monument to Lanner and Strauss the elder, the two inventors of the waltz, who stand smiling life-size in bronze. Behind them runs a long, rounded, stone screen with waltzing couples in low relief while a few roses in high relief cascade down the steps at the feet of the composers. The architecture was by Robert Oerley. When it was put up in 1905, Otto Wagner wrote a bad-tempered letter to Bürgermeister Lueger complaining that the whole thing looked like a pissoir.[3] There is no more characteristic sculpture of the period except the bronze Mozart fountain of the same year by Karl Wollek (1862-1936). A long-haired Tamino in tights plays his magic flute to a Pre-Raphaelite Pamina who embraces him.

Josef Hoffmann employed a number of secessionist sculptors. He himself made a remarkably prophetic abstract over-door in the Beethoven exhibition of 1902, which has a falling motif possibly recalling some architectural rustication he had seen.[4] He only did one monument, that for Otto Wagner in 1930, and it is now hidden at the side of the Academy. It consists of a long thin square column, rather too severe for its subject. Franz Metzner's (1870-1921) collaboration on the tower of the Palais Stoclet has been mentioned already. His only works in Vienna are the caryatids high on Plečnik's Zacherl building. He was born in Bohemia, was self-taught and worked for a time as a designer for a Berlin porcelain manufacturer. He then taught in Vienna at the School of Applied Art between 1903 and 1907 before leaving finally for Germany where his rather teutonic style was probably better appreciated. A Nibelungen fountain intended to be placed in front of the Votiv Kirche was never carried out. To judge from the design, this was just as well.[5] In 1908, his bronze statue of Franz Stelzhammer, a dialect poet, was erected in Linz, and Metzner also worked on the Battle of Leipzig memorial from 1906-13. He was born in Bohemia near Pilsen and died in Berlin.

Richard Luksch was born in Vienna in 1872 and died in Hamburg in 1936, where, after 1907, he taught at the School of Applied Art. His wife, Elena Luksch-Makowskaja, was born in St Petersburg, the daughter of the well-known painter Makowsky. After studying under Repin, in 1899 she came to Munich with a scholarship. There, Luksch met her in the circles of Hölzel and Jawlensky and married her next year. Elena Makowskaja made three ceramic reliefs for the façade of the Bürgertheater (now destroyed), did sensitive woodcuts for *Ver Sacrum* and painted, in a charming combination of Russia and Klimt, her *Adolescentia* (1903). For the Beethoven Secession exhibition her husband did two life-size fountain figures in coloured cement, while she painted reliefs from Russian folk-lore with bronze inlay inserts. For an exhibition in Düsseldorf in the same year they carried out an indoor fountain to designs by Hoffmann. Luksch also worked as a sculptor in ceramics and did decorations for houses in Brno and Augsburg. The life-size figures in faience he did for the garden of the Palais Stoclet are similar in style to the small porcelain figures he was making at the same period. His two largest works are the colossal bronze saints, Leopold and Severin, who sit like pinnacles atop the twin towers of Wagner's Steinhof church (1906-7). Perhaps his most attractive works were the two figures of 1905 for the entrance of the Purkersdorf sanatorium, done in cement with inlays of coloured stone. Inside, a chequered border and a

Karl Wollek
Mozart Fountain 1905
Bronze, in Mozartplatz
Photo Gert Rosenberg

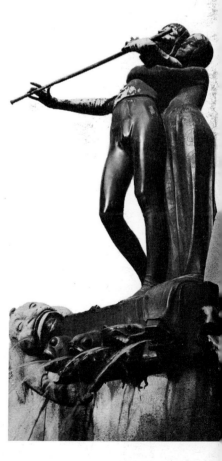

stylized leaf motif, two draped figures of a man and a woman face each other. Unfortunately, they have disappeared.[6]

Below the two monumental patron saints above the Steinhof church stand four angels in gilded bronze by Othmar Schimkowitz. Inside the church, to right and left of the tabernacle, two gilded copper angels kneel with their wings spread out behind them like two flags from an unknown country. There are also earlier works by Schimkowitz in Vienna. Two robust and rather angry-looking citizens in twelfth and fifteenth century costumes stand life-size in stone above the entrance to the Volksoper, built in 1898 as a people's theatre. In the same year he did the half-length bronzes for Wagner's Wienzeile no. 38 which are not unlike the later aluminium acroteria of the genii on Wagner's Post Office Savings Bank (1904-6). A Hungarian from Tarts, Schimkowitz was born in 1864 and studied under Hellmer and Kundmann. He also worked in the United States for Karl Bitter, an Austrian who emigrated in 1889, on Vanderbilt, Astor, Huntington and Child's commissions. He was a member of the Secession from its foundation until the closure in 1939, and president of the society in 1929. He was an ideal collaborator for Otto Wagner, the severe restraint of his figures being exactly what the architect needed.[7]

The young Kokoschka toyed with sculpture in 1908, and just before his death Schiele did a bronze self-portrait head. Two younger sculptors round off the cycle. Anton Hanak, who was born in 1875 in Brno and died in Vienna in 1934,

Sculpture by Franz Barwig and architecture by Josef Urban
Decoration for Imperial Stand at 60th Jubilee Procession June 1908
Photo Austrian National Library

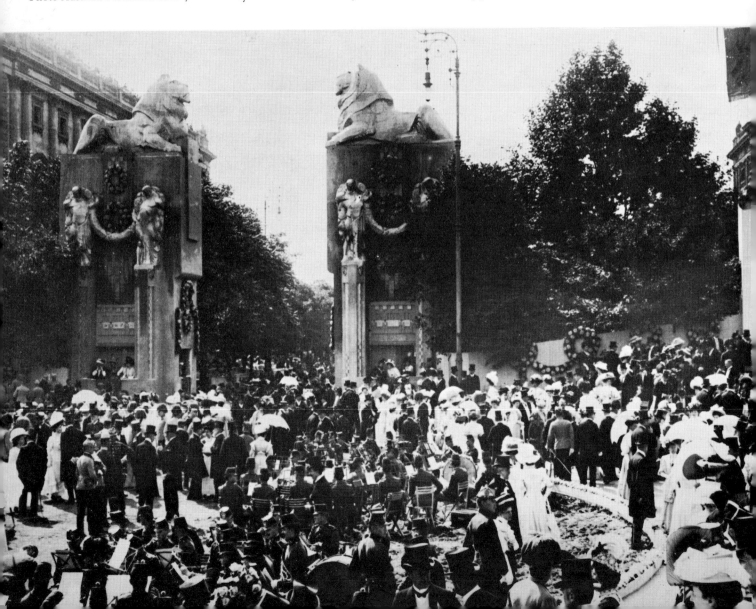

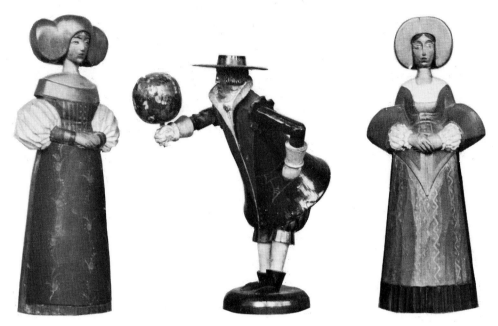

Franz Barwig
The Congratulator and Ladies 1908
Painted limewood, 20.8 × 23 cm./
8¼ × 9 in. high
Photo Bild-Archiv, Haus Barwig

studied with Hellmer at the Academy. One of his first works, signed by him in 1901, was the relief of Queen Victoria in Christchurch, Vienna. In 1904 he met his future patron Primavesi and travelled to Italy. From 1914 he taught at the School of Applied Art, and in that year he not only did the pediment sculptures on Hoffmann's Villa Primavesi in the Gloriettegasse, but collaborated with Hoffmann again on two standing figures for the façade of the Werkbund pavilion in Cologne, *The Creator* and *Transfigurement*. His standing figures seem to owe something to Rodin, for example *The Last Man II* (1917), but his other style is in the smoother mood of the late *Jugendstil*. His watercolour designs and sketches are carried out in purple washes in an individually knobbly brush-work. The head of Victor Adler on the Ringstrasse monument to the Republic (1928) is by him as is the city war memorial in the central cemetery (1920).[8]

Franz Barwig the elder was born in 1868. His most important work, the *Hercules and Hydra* fountain in Swiss stone-pine, painted and gilded, is over two metres high and was made for the Cologne exhibition of 1914 where it stood in a courtyard designed by Oskar Strnad. The cut-off heads of the Hydra have thin streams of water spurting in place of blood. He was best at figures of youths and animals and is remembered today as an animal sculptor because of his pelicans, monkeys and bears. For the Hagenbund exhibition of 1909 he made a series of painted wooden toys which exhibit the stylized charm of the period. He later spent two and a half years, from 1925 to 1927, working with a team of fourteen, including his eldest son Walter, on a Florida mansion on Palm Beach, Mar-a-Lago. This was designed by another Hagenbund member, Josef Urban, by this time working in America and later associated with designs for the Ziegfeld follies and the Metropolitan Opera. For the house, at first the residence of Mrs Marjorie Merriweather-Post, then that of Mrs Edward Hutton, the General Foods heiress, Barwig carved about ninety capitals and a series of animal reliefs. Once again one of the great Austrian *Gesamtkunstwerke* is on foreign soil. Built of Dorian stone, it has 36,000 antique

Franz Barwig
Swan Fountain 1927
Mar-a-Lago, Palm Beach, Florida
Photo Bild-Archiv, Haus Barwig

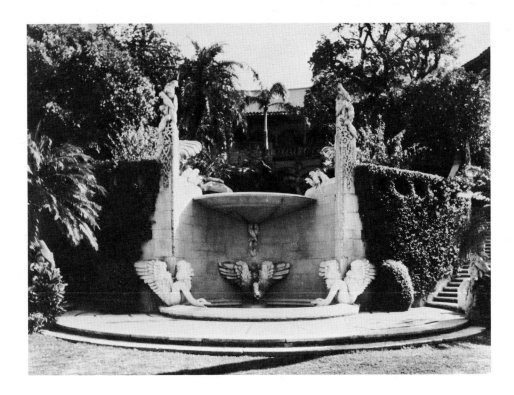

tiles from Spain and two shiploads of pink roof tiles from Cuba. The estate is large enough to have its own nine-hole golf course, and the property has now been offered as a residence for the President of the United States.

On his return to Vienna, Barwig carved animal figures for the Schönbrunn Zoo, but since it was no period for independent artists or for patronage, he began to feel more and more isolated and, in 1931, he shot himself.[9] Just before his death he executed a strange series of drawings of gloomy draped figures of death.

The Ring had its statues and decorative sculpture already. Sculptors still had opportunies for commissions at the beginning of the twentieth century. Without any outstanding names such statues as were executed showed that sculpture was not as exciting as the painting of the Secession.

GRAPHIC ART

'Ver Sacrum'

It hardly needs to be said that in a period of Austrian art where line was all important, the reproductive techniques of woodcut and engravings were bound to have a dominant role. *The Studio* was an influential source-book, and outline drawing, which had developed from Morris to Beardsley, with the attendant emphasis on plant and natural forms, was ideally suited to these techniques especially where, as in the case of woodcut, bold colour could be added. The growth of chromolithographic processes in the commercial printing of posters could be put to artistic and worthy purposes, as they had already been in France. Consequently, the artists of Vienna, still dependent on contours – and their two great exponents, Klimt and Schiele, certainly relied entirely on outline – were inevitably attracted to graphic art, and almost without exception involved in reproductions, in order to reach a wider public.

In 1879 the *Gesellschaft für graphische Kunst* was founded, so that subscribers could obtain prints as they already could for ceramics and even bronzes. The society continued until as late as 1935, but in the very first year of the Secession it started to issue annual portfolios (in 1899 there were two) besides a quarterly magazine, *Graphische Künste*. Original lithographs, engravings and woodcuts were issued with the magazine, but the portfolios, which were issued in an edition of about 1600 of between four to six prints each, continued until 1928. Many Secession artists contributed, and some of Moll's and Kurzweil's best work appeared in this way. Foreign artists also contributed and the only lithograph by Käthe Kollwitz was issued in 1906; in the year before there had been an engraving of Barnard Castle by Brangwyn.

The prints issued by the State Printing Office, the *Wandtafelwerk für Schule und Haus der k.u.k. Staatsdruckerei*, are not without importance. These large lithographs included a series of agricultural workers and harvesters by Andri in the rich autumnal reds, purples and oranges which he used so often, and there was a fine cottage and garden by Krenek. Danilowatz, Engelhart, Friedrich, Lenz, Kurzweil and Moll were amongst the other contributors, which anticipate the British School Prints of the period after the Second World War.

The most important graphic manifesto was *Ver Sacrum* from 1898 to 1903. In the six years of its life there were no less than fifty-five original lithographs and engravings, and 216 woodcuts; its last numbers consisted solely of graphics. The first two years were in a slightly larger format than the remainder, for in 1900 the whole appearance of the periodical changed, advertisements receded, and the artistic presentation under Roller transformed the individual numbers into beautiful examples of book production and typography. There were twelve issues per year on an average and the edition was between four to five hundred copies only.[1]

Adolf Loos's *Die Potemkinsche Stadt* first appeared in the seventh number in 1898, and the same year saw Bertha Zuckerkandl's important and equally aggressive article on 'Viennese Tastelessness'. In the earlier numbers, amongst the articles on artists and reproductions, there were artistic photographs, mostly of landscapes, by the Vienna Camera Club. The Jubilee exhibition of 1898 was commemorated with photographs of Otto Wagner's bizarre, tent-like vitrines of glass and silver for small objects of applied art. Two plays in translation by Maurice Maeterlinck appeared. Special articles were devoted to Rysselberghe, and two to Klimt, one in 1901 on his *Medicine* and in 1903 a brilliant series of reproductions from his drawings. In the last number of 1899, a series of poems by Stöhr and illustrated by him pointed the way to his own sad end, in 1917, when he hanged himself on his own printing-press in St Pölten. In one black and white illustration, a woman, unattainable and monumental, stands at the prow of a boat, while a man in modern dress sits at the stern. The rest of the poems and illustrations are full of such obvious symbols of Stöhr's inability to come to terms with women, including, one must suppose, his wife. The November of 1898, edited by Roller, was devoted to posters, and included two designs for calendars by Mucha. In 1960 Rilke wrote an article on Orlik. In 1902 an article on Beardsley by Arthur Symonds was illustrated with wonderful elongated decorations by Josef Hoffmann, anticipating Luksch's garden figures or Powolny pottery figures of 1905. Probably the most beautiful *Ver Sacrum* was number twenty-one in 1901 which contained abstract decorations in brick red by Moser, Roller and Auchenthaller to poems by Rilke.

In addition, the Secession issued its own portfolios. The founders' supplement and two further portfolios appeared in 1898 and 1899: the *Gründerbeilage* and *Gründermappen*. Portfolios for supporters were issued in 1906, 1907 and 1912 (*Förderermappen*) under the influence of Ferdinand Andri, who was president of the more conservative element after the split in 1905.

The catalogue to the famous fourteenth exhibition, that for Beethoven, in 1905 had a cover by Stolba that is a work of art in itself. Inside it contained twelve woodcuts by the best artists available in the medium: Andri, Jettmar, König, Kurzweil, Lenz, List, Luksch-Makowskaja (although as a woman, she could not be a member of the Secession), Moll, Moser, Myrbach, Orlik and Stöhr. This makes an impressive list, and some of it is so characteristic of their work that this small book, with its orange cover and woodcuts of about 131 × 131 mm, in either black and white or with lemon yellow, is the quintessence of the Secession and its ideals. This square format was much used in painting, as we have seen in the case of Moll's interiors and Klimt's landscapes of the Attersee. In 1908, a series of black and yellow woodcuts by Moll of 'Beethoven' houses was issued by the Werkstätte in the slightly larger format of 206 × 205 mm, contained in a handsome box covered with grey marbled paper.

Since from 1902 to 1906 Moll lived on the Hohe Warte in the house built for him by Hoffmann, at 19 Steinfeldgasse, he had only to walk a few steps to the subjects of his woodcuts, the Hohe Warte itself and the 'Beethoven' houses across the valley in Heiligenstadt. Max Kurzweil used themes from his stay in Brittany and was the only artist to do scenes by the sea. Oskar Laske specialized in the exotic scenes from Tunis, Scutari and the crowded markets there or in Bruges which suited his style flowered with figures like textile designs. In the same way Ferdinand Andri reverted again and again to the market women and peasants of Lower Austria. Living in a cottage in the village of Lassing near his birthplace, he identified himself completely with the countryside which he portrayed both in his paintings and in his graphic work.[2] Andri, who had been trained in Karlsruhe and was influenced by Hans Thoma, and Maximilian Liebenwein represent the more earthly type of Munich *Jugendstil*, while, in Vienna, the *Jugendstil* was usually more decorative and middle-class. The more conservative Ferdinand Schmutzer used his command of engraving technique to do portraits of Rudolf von Alt and Sigmund Freud, and the gifted Bohemian Emil Orlik did the well-known engravings of Hermann Bahr and Gustav Mahler. Having travelled to Holland and France in 1897 and to England in 1898, in 1900 he spent a period in Japan studying coloured woodcuts, in which he became a master. His coloured lithographs, such as *Sunday Morning in Brötzen* are stunningly attractive and clear, with a sparing use of figures.

Wilhelm List's fine lithographs, have a little of the sentimentality of *Art Nouveau* rather than *Jugendstil*, and Lenz shows this too in his three colour lithographs of the seasons, totally unlike his paintings of elegant street scenes in Vienna. Otto Friedrich was an extremely able colour lithographer, and his *Josefsplatz*, issued for the supporters of the Secession in 1906, is one of the most evocative prints of the era. Like Klimt at one time, he was certainly under the influence of Felicien Rops. He is probably underestimated and deserves a better placing in the artistic achievement at the turn of the century. Leopold Stolba's coloured woodcuts were as masterly as the work of Orlik. Slightly similar to this group is the painter, Ernst Stöhr, whose work has a melancholy quality seen in his engravings.

Rudolf Jettmar was a painter who worked for Wittgenstein, and the Thurn und Taxis family, at whose house in Duino he was a guest, like Rilke, but he is best known as an imaginative and sensitive engraver, lithographer and wood-cutter. He did a series of twelve *Hours of the Night* (1903-4) and *Labours of Hercules* in later life, his subjects being titans fighting with giants, or rocky castles and sensuous females in mythological swirls. From 1910 he taught at the Academy.

Ludwig Jungnickel was one of the leading animal artists in Europe. For the nursery at the Palais Stoclet, he made a frieze of parrots, foxes and panthers in a tight style of composition which is far from the pure naturalism before the *Jugendstil*. He enjoyed the patronage of the imperial house, and lithographs printed on a special paper are preserved in the Albertina. Another artist who benefited from imperial subvention, Franz Wacik, seems an equally unlikely candidate, as his inclination was more towards book illustrations. His dark but brightly coloured lithographs with their sharp outlines look like woodcuts. His slightly macabre subjects come from the world of fairy-tale and have something of the atmosphere of Arthur Rackham.

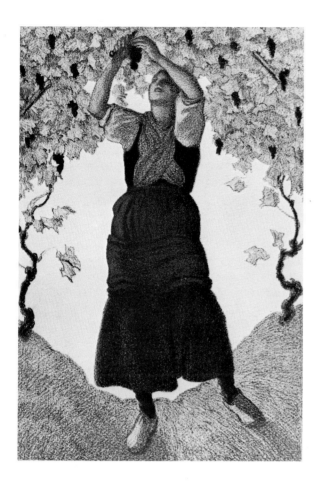

Ferdinand Andri
Grape Picker
Coloured lithograph for Gesellschaft
für v. Kunst, 34.5 × 23 cm./14 × 9 in.
Galerie Pabst, photo Galerie Pabst

Josef Engelhart
Young Layabout 1898
Lithograph, 23.5 × 19.1 cm./9½ × 7½ in.
Author's collection

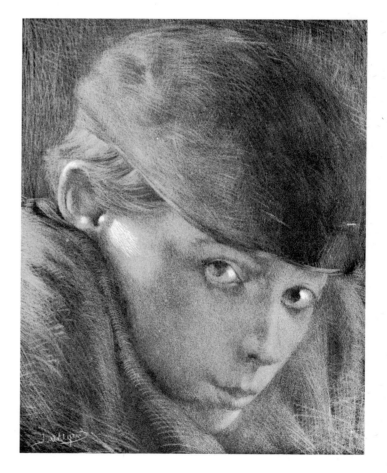

191

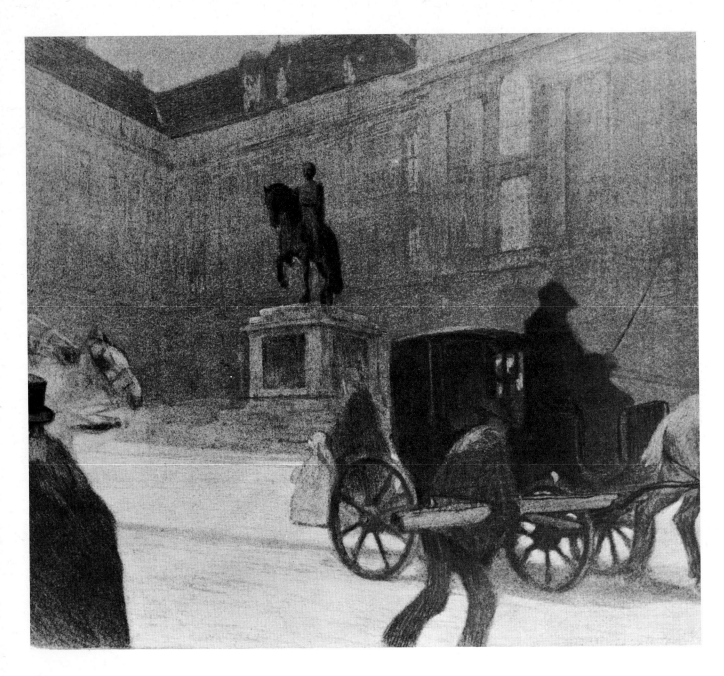

Otto Friedrich
Josefsplatz 1908
Coloured lithograph for Secession
portfolio, 28 × 32 cm./11 × 12½ in.
Author's collection, photo Gert
Rosenberg

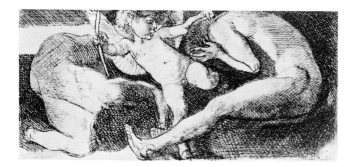

Rudolf Jettmar
Amor the Tyrant 1909
Etching, 4.2 × 5 cm./1¾ × 2 in.
Author's collection, photo Gert
Rosenberg

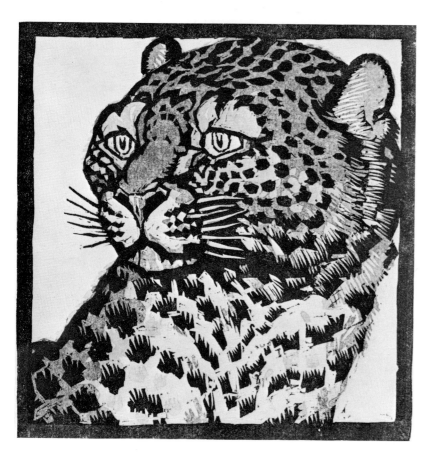

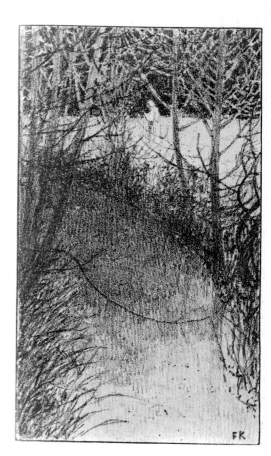

Ludwig Jungnickel
Panther c. 1910
Woodcut in black and orange,
15 × 14.5 cm./6 × 5¾ in.
Galerie Pabst, photo Galerie Pabst

Friedrich König
The Garden, Spring 1898
Coloured lithograph for *Ver Sacrum*,
18.5 × 11.2 cm./7½ × 4½ in.
Galerie Pabst, photo Galerie Pabst

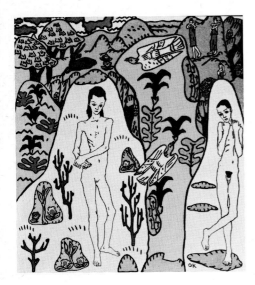

Oskar Kokoschka
Die Träumenden Knaben 1908
Lithograph, Wiener Werkstätte,
25 × 21 cm./9¾ × 8¼ in.
Photo Austrian National Library

Gustav Klimt
Music 1901
Woodcut? in red, pale yellow and
black, for *Ver Sacrum*, 17 × 8.5 cm./
6¾ × 3¼ in.
Galerie Pabst, photo Galerie Pabst

Opposite:
Oskar Laske
Tunis 1920
Signed, coloured lithograph, artist's
proof for *Graphische Künste*,
28 × 22 cm./11 × 8½ in.
Author's collection, photo Gert
Rosenberg

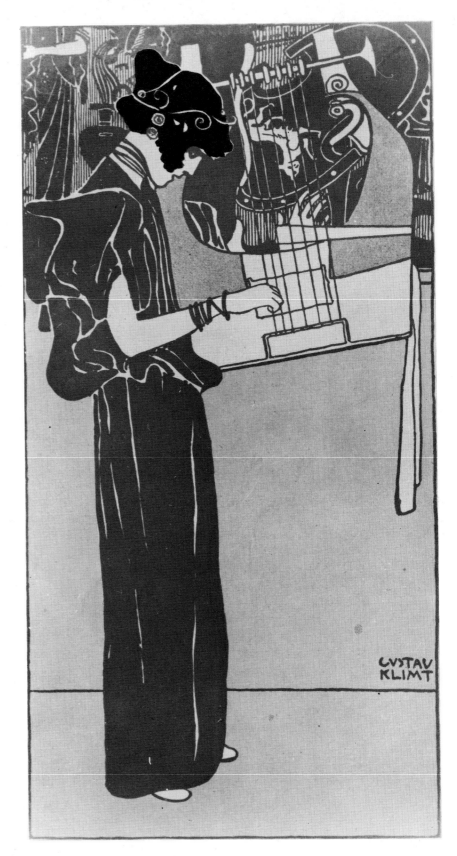

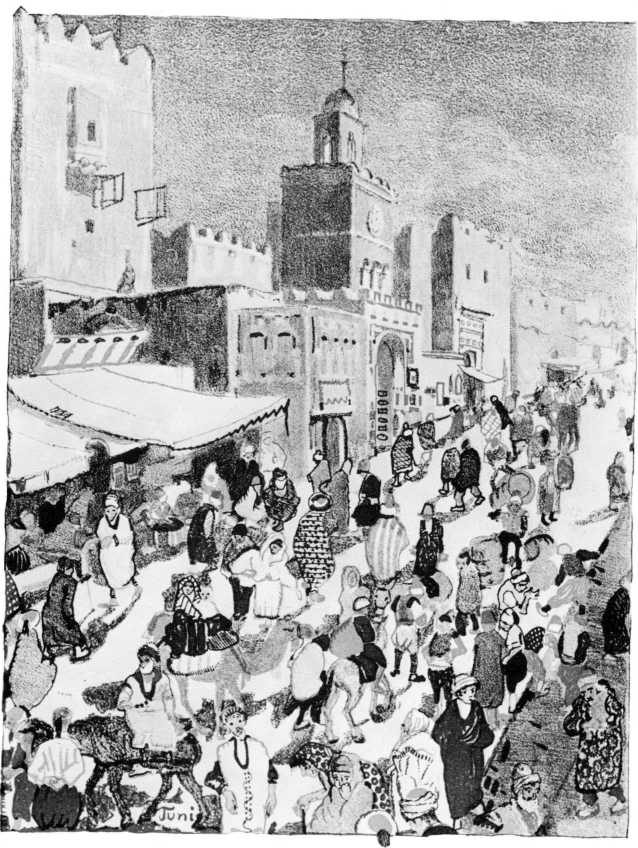

Tunis

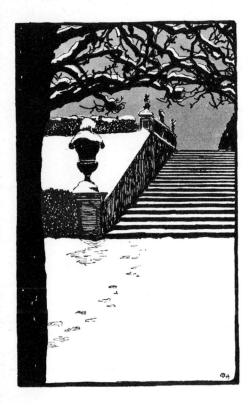

Wilhelm List
Belvedere Garden in Winter 1900
Woodcut in black and green for
Ver Sacrum, 14.5 × 9 cm./5¾ × 3½ in.
Photo Gert Rosenberg

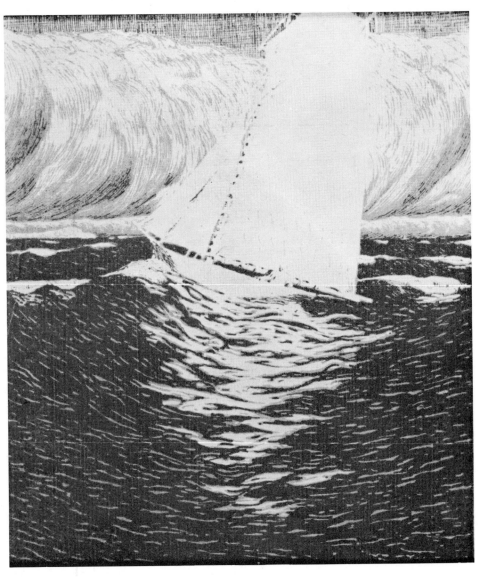

Max Kurzweil
Yacht c. 1900
Woodcut in blue and ochre,
unrecorded, 14.2 × 12.2 cm./
5½ × 4¾ in.
Author's collection, photo Gert
Rosenberg

Opposite:
Wilhelm List
Daphne
Coloured lithograph, 39.6 × 30.9 cm./
15 × 12 in.
Historisches Museum der Stadt Wien,
photo Museum

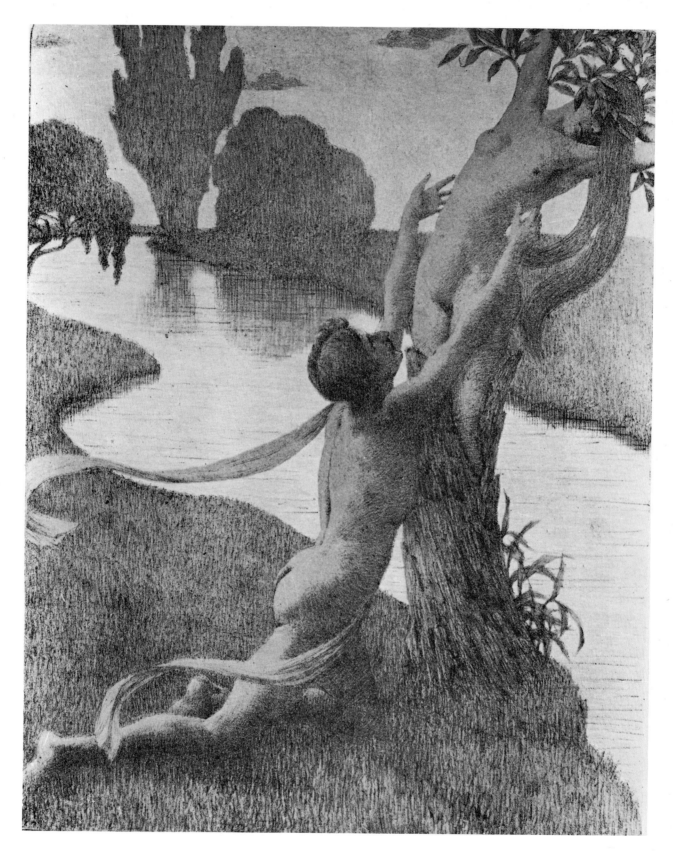

197

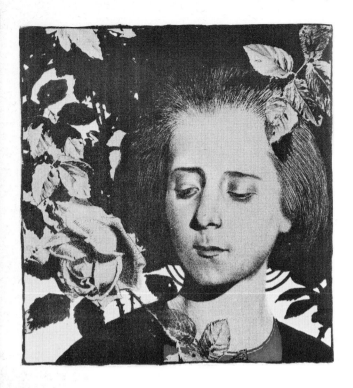

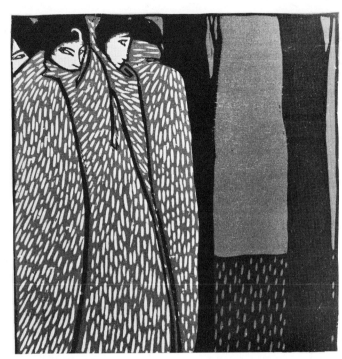

Kolo Moser
Girl 1898
Lithograph, 20 × 19.5 cm./8 × 7¾ in.
Author's collection

Kolo Moser
November 1902
Woodcut in brown and black for
Ver Sacrum, 15 × 14.5 cm./6 × 5¾ in.
Galerie Pabst, photo Galerie Pabst

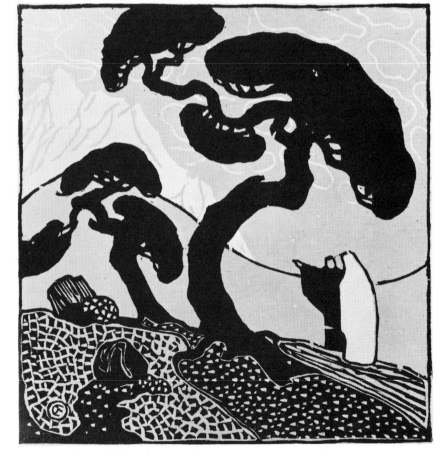

Emil Orlik
Two Figures Under a Tree 1902
Original woodcut in black and yellow
from Beethoven Exhibition Catalogue,
14 × 13.3 cm./5½ × 5¼ in.
Galerie Pabst, photo Galerie Pabst

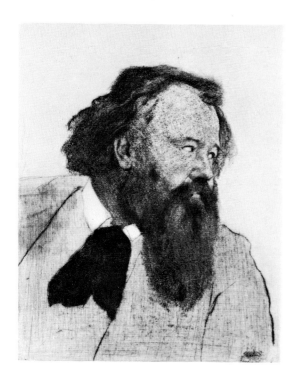

Emil Orlik
Hermann Bahr 1918
Etching, 29.5 × 19 cm./12 × 7½ in.
Galerie Pabst, photo Galerie Pabst

Kolo Moser
*Designs for the First Catalogue of the
Secession* 1898
Indian ink
Historisches Museum der Stadt Wien,
photo Museum

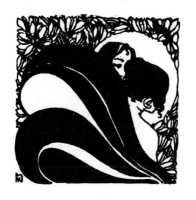
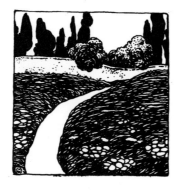
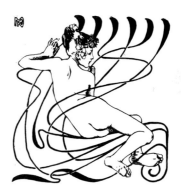
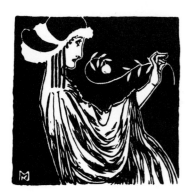
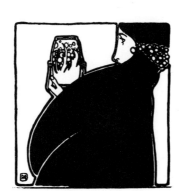
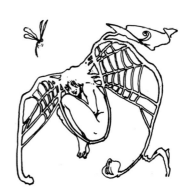

Maximilian Lenz
Spring 1898
Coloured lithograph for *Ver Sacrum*,
13.5 × 15 cm./5¼ × 6 in.
Galerie Pabst, photo Galerie Pabst

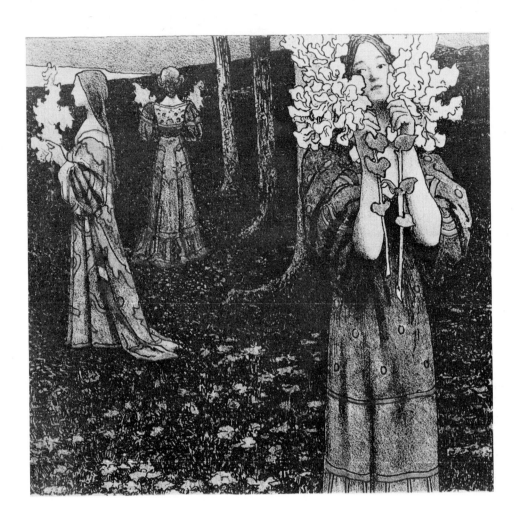

Oswald Roux
Winter 1905
Coloured lithograph, 28 × 47.5 cm./
11 × 18 in.
Galerie Pabst, photo Galerie Pabst

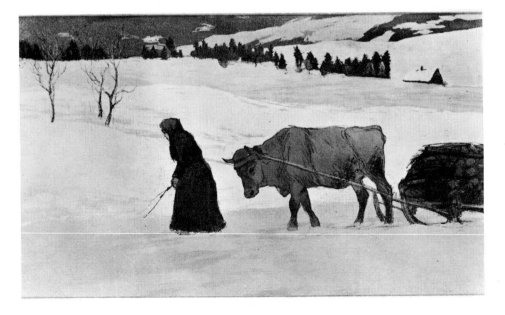

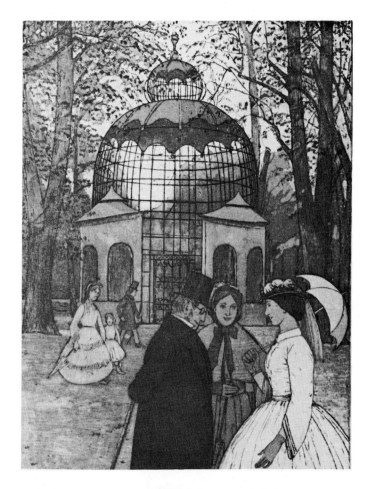

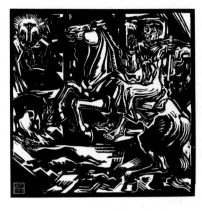

Robert Philippi
St Hubert c. 1918
Woodcut, 49 × 29 cm./19 × 12 in.
Galerie Pabst, photo Galerie Pabst

Leopold Stolba
Parrot House, Schönbrunn c. 1905
Acquatint, 19.5 × 13.5 cm./8 × 5¼ in.
Wiener Secession, photo Secession

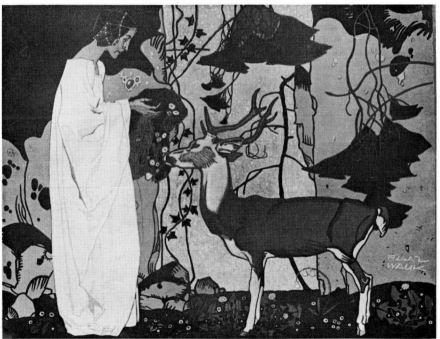

Franz Wacik
The Wood Nymph 1913
Coloured lithograph, 48.5 × 55.5 cm./
19 × 21 in.
Wiener Secession, photo Secession

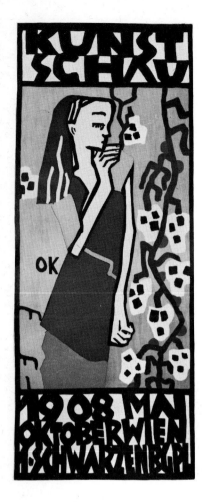

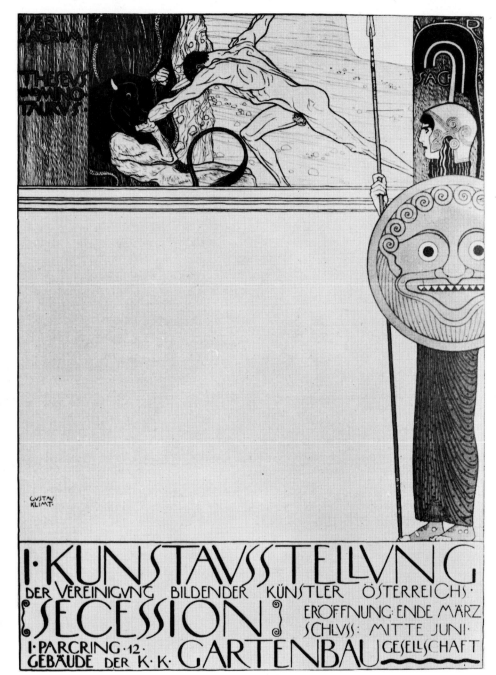

Oskar Kokoschka
Poster for Kunstschau 1908
Coloured lithograph, 96 × 65 cm./
38 × 26 in.
Galerie Pabst, photo Galerie Pabst

Gustav Klimt
Poster for First Secession Exhibition 1898
Coloured lithograph, version before
censorship, 63 × 47 cm./24 × 18 in.
Photo Austrian National Library

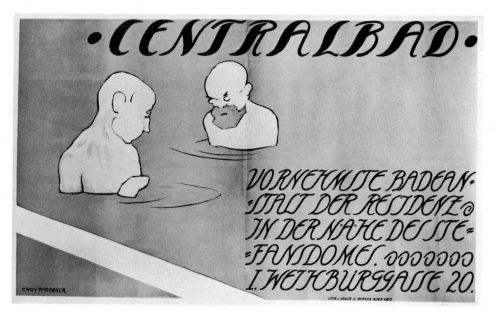

Hermann Grom-Rottmayer
Centralbad c. 1910
Coloured lithograph, 95 × 63 cm./
37 × 24 in.
Galerie Pabst, photo Galerie Pabst

Josef Auchentaller
Poster for Grado 1906
Coloured lithograph, 66 × 88.5 cm./
26 × 35 in.
Galerie Pabst, photo Galerie Pabst

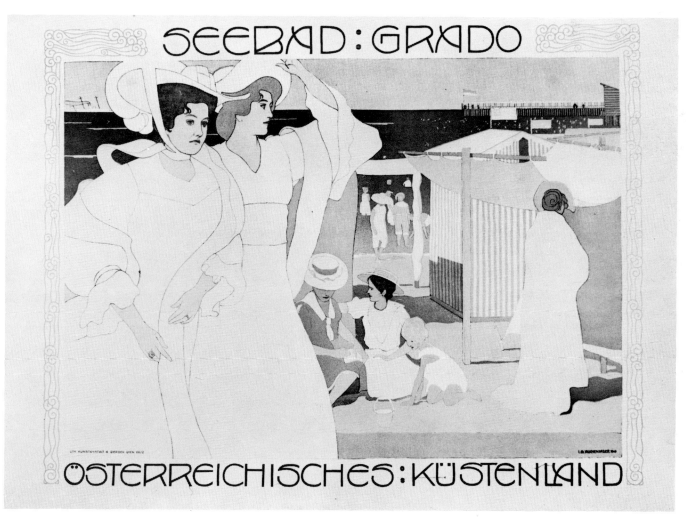

Berthold Löffler
Poster for Fledermaus Cabaret 1907
Coloured lithograph, 63 × 43.5 cm./
24 × 17 in.
Galerie Pabst, photo Galerie Pabst

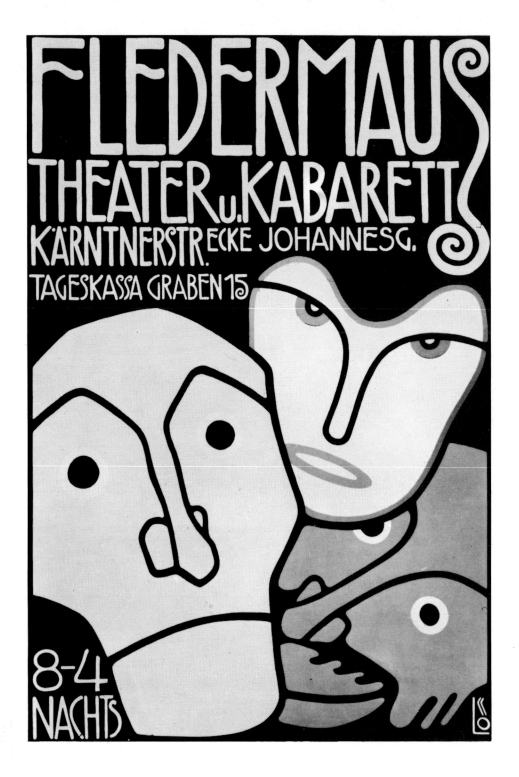

MUSIC

Mahler and the Vienna School

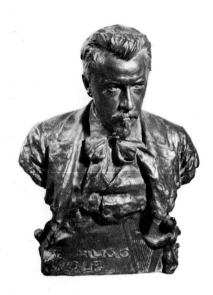

Franz Seifert
Hugo Wolf 1899
bronze, 43 cm./17 in. high
Historisches Museum der Stadt Wien,
photo Museum

In February of 1895, Anton Bruckner, short of breath and mortally ill, wrote a pathetic appeal to the Archduchess Maria Valerie, daughter of the Emperor, asking to be allowed to live in a lodge at the Belvedere, instead of his flat on the Schottenring. He was just well enough to move and died there on 11 October 1896.[1] He was buried as he wished under the organ in St Florian, where he had been the organist nearly fifty years before. Johannes Brahms attended the funeral with tears in his eyes, and died less than a year later on 2 April 1897, in his elective home, Vienna. On 22 February 1903 Hugo Wolf, the romantic *Lieder* writer, possibly the greatest of them all, died insane, disappointed by Mahler's production of his opera *Der Corregidor* and imagining that he himself had been appointed director of the opera house. The text was by Rosa Mayreder, his patron and friend, founder of the Austrian women's league who had married into the influential family of civil engineers associated with Otto Wagner. Mahler had been one of Wolf's closest friends and as a student had shared a room with him. In 1904, Wolf produced A *'Lieder' book with orchestral accompaniment.* In the words of Wolf's biographer, Frank Walker, 'It was an act of piety and at the same time marked the end of an era.'

The great tradition of Viennese light opera and operetta began with the younger Johann Strauss's opportunely timed *Fledermaus* of 1874, which helped the Viennese to forget the bank crash of the previous year, and continued with his *Zigeunderbaron* of 1885. In 1882 the conductor Carl Millöcker's *Der Bettelstudent* was produced. He died in 1899. *Der Vogelhändler* by Carl Zeller, a senior civil servant in the Ministry of Education responsible for the arts, was first performed in 1891. He was one of the many, who like Haydn, Schubert and Clemens Krauss, began as a choir boy with the Sängerknaben of the Hofkapelle. He died in 1898.

The tradition of operetta went on into the so-called silver age with the unexpected success of *The Merry Widow* by Franz Lehar at the Theater an der Wien in 1905, and continued with Leo Fall's *Dollar Princess*. There were many others including Robert Stolz, born in 1880, composer of some fifty operettas and musicals, whose first work was written in about 1910 and who emigrated in 1938 to Hollywood, where he wrote the music for more than a hundred films.

The opera house had opened on 25 May 1869 with a performance of *Don Juan* in German. The directorship of Wilhelm Jahn, from 1881 to 1897, was a brilliant period in which ten works were introduced into the repertory that are still performed today. The first performance of Massenet's *Manon* took place in 1890, and was given fifty-four times in four years. It was the period of *Tristan* conducted by Hans Richter, of *Othello*, of Cornelius's *Der Barbier von Bagdad*, but also of *Die Fledermaus* and *Hänsel und Gretel*. Then, in 1897, three years before Jahn's death in 1900, it was felt that a younger man must be appointed, as Jahn suffered from eye trouble and general fatigue. So, on 8 October 1897, the thirty-seven-year-old Gustav Mahler was appointed director by the Emperor. He held the post for ten years, which was, next to Jahn's, its longest tenure.

Mahler was born on 7 July 1860 in Kalist in Bohemia, the son of a Jewish merchant, and studied at the Vienna Conservatoire. His way to Vienna as a conductor led through the summer spa of Bad Hall, and conducting in the opera houses of Ljubljana, Olomoue and Kassel. After a spell as second conductor to Arthur Nikisch at Prague and Leipzig he was appointed in 1888 director at the Budapest opera house, where in 1890 he conducted a wonderful performance of *Don Juan*, to which, incidentally, Brahms had been more or less dragged as he was no admirer of previous performances of the work. In 1891, he resigned and went directly to Hamburg as first conductor under Bernhard Pollini with whom he had kept in touch since Leipzig. The Vienna appointment came about in the following way: Rosa Papier-Paumgartner had sung under Mahler at Kassel, when she had still been on the stage, and her favourite pupil Anna Mildenburg (who later married Hermann Bahr in 1909) reminded her teacher about him, and told her of his success in Hamburg, where Hans von Bülow admired his conducting. Rosa Papier was a personal friend of the manager of the opera house, and her influence with that of Brahms and the composer Karl Goldmark, among others, ensured the appointment of Mahler for a year as conductor in the first instance, once he had become a Roman Catholic, with the contract raised to the directorship within months. The greatest period of the Vienna opera then began, and Mahler's composing took second place. In 1902 he married Alma Schindler in the Karlskirche, and through her friend Klimt and her step-father Moll, he was close to the artists and painters of Vienna.

Eduard Hanslick (1825-1904), the doyen of Vienna's music critics, avowed enemy of Wagner and Bruckner, the original of Beckmesser in *Die Meistersinger von Nürnberg*, and by virtue of being professor of musical history at the university, the first fully professional music critic (of the *Neue Freie Presse*), is often thought of as a largely negative personality. Yet while Hanslick admitted to knowing the second symphony only by reputation, he wrote of Mahler's orchestral songs, of which he had heard five from the *Lieder eines fahrenden Gesellen* and from *Des Knaben Wunderhorn*:

'One cannot deny the contradiction between the idea of folksong and this artistic over-rich orchestration. But Mahler has executed this daring piece with exceptional sensitivity and masterly technique. Now, at the beginning of the new century, it is worthwhile repeating the novelties of the musical 'Secession' (Mahler, Richard Strauss, Hugo Wolf and so on); it is highly probable that the future belongs to them.'[2]

This extract from a long review is significant, not for the warmth of an old man of seventy-five, but in the linking of the ideas of the period under the shield of the Secession. The link was indeed close, because for the opening of the Beethoven exhibition at the Secession, in April 1902, the modest Klinger was surprised, on entering the halls, to hear an arrangement for brass by Mahler of the last phrase of Beethoven's Ninth Symphony, so that the tears ran down his cheeks.

Mahler was a different director to Jahn. Whereas Jahn had said to the company of the opera house, 'I love you all, as only a father can', Mahler told the chorus, 'What you theatre people call tradition is nothing but your slovenliness (*Schlamperei*).' Mahler was prepared to subordinate himself and

207

everyone else to the ideal of perfection, even if, as he said in his farewell letter to the opera, men are governed by the conspiracy of the inanimate object—a strange admission for the last of the great romantics. For example, the singers had to immerse themselves in their rôles. He brought Franz Schalk to conduct at the opera in 1900, and the young Berliner Bruno Walter in 1901. The innovations of this superb collaboration with the equally creative Alfred Roller with the *Tristan* and *Don Giovanni* productions have already been mentioned. Also the house lights were dimmed before the curtain went up (though the lights still go up immediately at the end of the performances). Latecomers were not admitted, although the Emperor, a great theatregoer, thought that people went to the opera to enjoy themselves. Mahler tried to quell the paid 'claque' system by forcing the singers to sign a statement that they would abandon this abuse, but he was not altogether successful as it still continues in one form or another to this day. Then, for Italian singers such as Caruso the performances were given in Italian.

Like many conductors since his time, Mahler never got on with the independent Vienna Philharmonic orchestra, whose members are formed from musicians of the opera pit. Although one of the Philharmonic leaders was Arnold Rosé, the husband of Mahler's sister, and, as leader of the quartet named after him, one of Schönberg's champions, this did not help. Mahler offered to resign over the refusal of the censors in 1905 to allow the performance of Strauss's *Salome* to coincide with the Dresden première. Instead, it was given in Graz in the presence of Mahler and Alban Berg in 1906. In spite of leading Viennese intellectuals trying to get him to stay he resigned in 1907. In December, he left Vienna for New York, and 200 friends came to the station to say goodbye. Private invitations had been sent out under the signatures of Anton Von Webern, Paul Stefan and two other friends. It was on the station platform that Alban Berg heard Mahler speaking for the first time, and it was Klimt who spoke the famous word *Vorbei*. An epoch was over.

From 1907 to 1911, Mahler conducted concerts in Berlin, St Petersburg, Helsinki and elsewhere. His daughter Maria Anna died in July 1907. In 1908 he was the conductor of the Metropolitan opera in New York. In the spring of 1909 he was in Paris, where Rodin was asked to do his head in bronze. In 1910 he acquired a piece of land on the Semmering and the house where Alma and Kokoschka were to be together. He conducted forty-eight concerts in America, and returned to Vienna worn out and died on 18 May 1911. The largest wreath was sent by the Vienna Philharmonic.

He is buried in the same place as his daughter, Grinzing, and the stone is by Josef Hoffmann. It has on it nothing but his name, for 'those who look for me will know who I was, and the others do not need to know'. The boy who wanted to be a martyr had grown up saying that his time would come. In this he had been justified. Nearby, Alma Mahler is buried with her daughter Manon Gropius who died in 1935, and to whom Berg dedicated his last work, the violin concerto 'To the Memory of an Angel' in the same year.

The Austrian lakes have often inspired composers. Brahms wrote his Second Symphony as the guest of friends at Pörtschach on the Wörthersee in 1877 and Bartok probably completed his Second Piano Concerto at a summer school on the Mondsee in 1931. The Schönbergs were to go to the Traunsee with Webern and Gerstl for the summer. Between 1893 and 1896, Mahler himself stayed at Steinbach on the Attersee with his sister Justine in an inn where there was a summer-house for his composing. After his marriage he spent the summer months at Maiernigg on the Wörthersee in a villa he had built, composing the Fourth to the Eighth Symphonies in a little summer-house, the *Komponierhäusl*. After the death of his daughter from diphtheria in 1907, of which the *Kindertotenlieder* of two years before had been a strange precognition, he never returned to Maiernigg. For the rest of the summer of 1907, Mahler fled to Schluderbach near Cortina in the South Tirol, and there sketched the *Lied von der Erde* which, again with some superstitious prescience, he called his Ninth Symphony. The actual Ninth Symphony was first performed after his death in Vienna in 1912 under Bruno Walter, but in his lifetime there were no first performances of his symphonies in Vienna. The Eight, the 'Symphony of a Thousand', had a carefully prepared first performance in Munich on 12 September 1910. There were eight soloists, 850 people in the choir, of which 250 came from the Gesellschaft der Musikfreunde in Vienna, 250 from Leipzig and 350 children from Munich, all carefully rehearsed, and an orchestra of 170, including a harmonium and an organist. Mahler conducted the work himself– his greatest, and an unqualified, personal triumph. Schönberg and the young Klemperer were at the rehearsals, Willem Mengelberg, one of his greatest supporters, came from Holland, and Stokowsky, who was to give the first performance of the Symphony in America, was present. Among the 3,000 in the audience, besides Reinhardt and Roller among others from Vienna, was Thomas Mann. The next year, Mahler, already very sick, died.

Just as Mahler had paid 50,000 kronen to finance the edition of Bruckner's works, so, at the very end of his life, he was anxious about Schönberg's future. 'When I go, he will have nobody else.' At his funeral there was a wreath from Schönberg and his pupils with a message indicating their devotion to his inspiration. Alma Mahler also recalls his discussing Schönberg with young musicians: 'If I do not often understand him, it is because I am old, he is young–so he must be right.'[3]

When, in 1949, two years before his death in 1951, Schönberg wrote from Los Angeles to the mayor of Vienna, General Körner (who became President of the Austrian Republic in 1951), thanking him for the citizenship of honour of Vienna awarded him on his seventy-fifth birthday, he said that Vienna and the music created there was his greatest pride. This gratitude may seem to contradict the fact that the performances of Schönberg's music and that of his friends were often the occasion of tremendous scandals. Yet despite those tempestuous scenes, the atmosphere existed in Vienna for this new music to be written and performed.

Schönberg was born in Vienna on 13 September 1874. He was self-taught and in 1900 began his *Gurre-Lieder*. The next year he married Mathilde, the sister of Alexander von Zemlinsky, who helped him in composition technique. He then went to Berlin for a time, and with Zemlinsky started the 'Society of creative musicians', *Vereinigung schaffender Tonkünstler*. His early pupils included Alban Berg, Anton von Webern and Erwin Stein.

The first performances in 1907 and 1908 of his first two string quartets, Op. 7 and 10, by the Rosé quartet caused a scandal, especially the second in the respectable Bösendorfer Saal. Marie Gutheil-Schroder from the State opera was in tears, and there were continuous shouts of 'Stop', 'Shut up', 'Quiet', 'Enough' and so on. Someone shouted 'Please air the hall before Beethoven is played.'[4]

Schönberg then taught at the Music Academy from 1910 to 1911 but when he learned that he was not likely to get a lectureship he moved to Berlin.

Next year he refused a call to the Academy and began to write *Pierrot Lunaire* which was then performed in many German and Austrian towns by an ensemble rehearsed by him. In it he used the spoken voice above an orchestra line for the first time. In February 1913 he had a success in Vienna with the first performance of the *Gurre-Lieder* under Franz Schreker, the conductor-composer and teacher of Krenek. But next month a concert of the Academic Society for Literature and Music created another and famous scandal. The highly important programme consisted of Webern's Piece for Orchestra Op. 6, Berg's Songs with Orchestra Op. 4, Zemlinsky's Songs with Orchestra, and Schönberg's own First Chamber Symphony Op. 9. Berg's setting of short postcard texts which he had received from Peter Altenberg, were completely unusual, and the large orchestral setting demanded particularly difficult effects and techniques. There was such an uproar that the police were called in and Mahler's *Kindertotenlieder* could not be performed.

In 1915 Schönberg returned to Vienna from Berlin, and in 1917 he began his oratorio *Die Jakobsleiter*. In 1918, he founded the 'Society for private musical performances', devoted to performing new music. The guests were

Franz Kopallik
The Bösendorfersaal 1913
Watercolour, 48 × 63.5 cm./19 × 25 in.
Historisches Museum der Stadt Wien, photo Museum

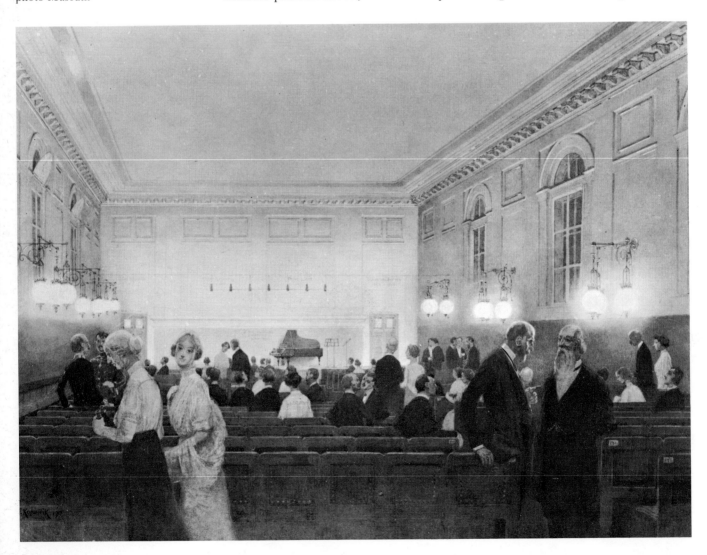

210

warned in the programme that neither applause nor disapproval nor press criticisms were permitted. For the first two years none of his music was done, but Stravinsky, Bartok and Ravel, besides Webern and Berg. Between 1918 and 1921, 154 new works were performed.

The account of Schönberg and his friends belongs in great part to a period beyond the terminus of this study, but mention should be made that the first theatrical performance of the first two acts of the opera *Moses and Aaron* under Hans Rosbaud in 1957 was one of the great events in recent musical history. Schönberg's life and intentions can best be summed up in the words of Moses at the end of the opera: 'I love my visions and I live for them.' Mahler lived and believed in the age of programme music, that is, he thought that music could often be explained in terms of images. The demystification of art in so far as it concerned music was centred on 'the theme shorn of its myth', to use Harald Kaufmann's phrase. In 1911 Schönberg, with his pupil and later hagiographer Josef Rufer, spoke for the first time about writing in twelve-tone rows. His book *Composition with twelve tones* appeared in 1923. Independently, Josef Matthias Hauer (1883-1959) had been working on a twelve-tone system, of universal application, and not limited only to composition. He wrote a number of books about his theories which he considered to have occurred to him before Schönberg's discovery, and composed many works, which have not had the success of the second Vienna School proper. The two rivals never met.

Alban Berg was born in Vienna on 9 February 1885. He was shaken by the death of Hugo Wolf, and after the first performance of Mahler's Fourth Symphony he took possession of Mahler's baton. In 1904 his brother showed some *Lieder* to Schönberg, who took him on as a pupil without payment, and two years later he gave up his job as a civil servant to compose. In 1908 he had an attack of bronchial asthma on the Ossiachersee, and his doctor was by chance Freud, who made a great impression on the younger man. In 1910 he first attended a reading by Karl Kraus. In 1919, he had the first performance of his Piano Sonata Op. 1 and of his String Quartet Op. 3 in the Ehrbar-Saal in the Viennese suburbs. In May, he married Helene Nahowski, and in the same year supported Schönberg with an appeal on account of his teacher's financial position.

Already in 1914 he had thought of an opera based on Büchner's *Wozzek* and began writing it soon after, publishing the score at his own expense in 1922. In 1925 Erich Kleiber conducted the first performance in Berlin, despite the attendant tumult and Pfitzner's intrigues to have a performance of his *Palestrina* instead.

In 1905, Berg had seen a performance arranged by Karl Kraus of Wedekind's *Pandora's Box*. Thirty-one years later, in the midst of the Spanish Civil War of 1936 and the threat of Nazi Germany, he wrote the last notes of his opera from the play, *Lulu*, but he died before seeing it performed (first done in Zürich in 1937). One of the last things he uttered was a quotation from the second act, when Dr Schön cries, 'This is the end of my life. There is plague in my house.' He did manage to hear the first performance of his 'Lulu Symphony', but on 24 December 1935 he died from blood poisoning. Anna Mahler, the composer's daughter, cast his death mask.

Humphrey Searle has described Anton von Webern as 'perhaps the purest exponent of the twelve-tone technique'. Webern was born on 2 December 1883 as the son of a mining engineer. He studied music in Vienna, obtaining a

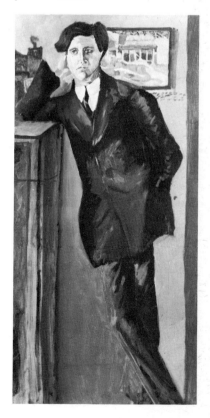

Arnold Schönberg
Alban Berg
175.5 × 85 cm./69 × 33 in.
Historisches Museum der Stadt Wien, photo Museum

doctorate in 1906. Having failed to become a pupil of Pfitzner in Berlin, he went to Schönberg in 1904 and remained with him until 1908. He conducted in the opera houses at Teplitz, Danzig and Szczettin, and in 1917 became the first conductor of the Prague opera house. From 1922 until 1934 he was conductor of the Viennese Workers' Symphony Concerts, until the Austrian political situation made this impossible, and he also conducted the excellent Vienna Workers' Choral Society. During the war he was helped by the Universal-Edition who employed him as an editor.

Webern was absolutely resolute in his pursuit of the twelve-tone technique. After 1930 he wrote hardly any more, and his brief oeuvre is made all the more exiguous by his almost telegraphic and minimal style. He became more and more isolated, keeping very few friends, among them the sculptor Josef Humplik (1888-1958) who had done his bust in 1928, a head of the dancer Grete Wiesenthal, and the death mask of Adolf Loos. He was married to an artist and poet, Hildegard Jone, who was born in 1891 in Sarajevo and died in Vienna in 1963. The couple were the owners of the remarkable self-portrait of Georg Trakl, to whose poems Webern wrote his *Lieder* Op. 14. He also put three of the wife's poems from *Viae Inviae* to music, Op. 23, and dedicated them to her.[5] At the end of the war he fled from his life-long home in Mödling to Mittersill near Salzburg where, on 15 September 1945, he was shot in error by an American soldier, when he failed to stop. His String Quartet Op. 28 was commissioned by Mrs Elisabeth Sprague Coolidge and played by the Kolisch Quartet in South Mountain, Mass. in 1938.[6]

The cultivation of Mahler and the second Vienna school in England and the United States, does not appear to be merely a phenomenon due to the political upheaval and spiritual emigration between 1934 and 1945. Neither Karl Böhm nor Karajan have recorded Mahler's symphonies, and most of the performances and recordings of the younger composers have been made outside Austria.

The linking thread of the cultural life of Vienna between 1898 and 1918 was the interplay of the arts in an astonishingly tight circle of imaginative effort. Furthermore, Vienna was no village where everyone knew everybody else, but an imperial capital. Long before 1918, *die erste Gesellschaft*, the ruling society of the aristocracy, the military caste and the imperial bureaucracy had resigned the initiative to the second estate of industrialists, bankers and intellectuals, yet the revolutionary forces of the spirit marched ahead of the self-destruction of the Empire, in a truly sacred spring of inspiration and creative activity.

Vienna, Whit Sunday 1973

Check List of Graphic Artists

B   Woodcut in Secession Beethoven Exhibition Catalogue 1902

G   Work issued by Gesellschaft für vervielfältigende Kunst between 1898 and 1919

H   Member of Hagenbund

HO   Illustrated and commented on in Hans H. Hofstätter *Jugendstil Druckkunst* Holle-Verlag, Baden-Baden 1968

M   Illustrated in Oskar Matulla *Wiener Secession Druckgraphik 1897-1972*

P   Executed posters

S   Member of Secession

V   Worked for *Ver Sacrum*

W   In exhibition *Wien um 1900* (1964)

WE   Worked for Wiener Werkstätte

ANDRI, FERDINAND 1871 Waidhofen/
Ybbs – 1956 Vienna
Pupil of Berger and Lichtenfels at
Academy
Woodcuts, lithographs, books
B, G, HO, M, P, S, V, W, ill.

AUCHENTALLER, JOSEF MARIA
1865 Vienna – 1940 Grado
Pupil of Franz Rumpler at Academy
Books
HO, P, S, V

BAYROS, FRANZ VON 1866 Zagreb–
1924 Vienna
Erotic books, illustrations, aquatints
W

BERNATZIK, WILHELM 1853 Mistelbach
– 1906 Hinterbrühl/Vienna
Pupil of Lichtenfels at Academy
Lithographs
M, S, V, W, ill.

BÖHM, ADOLF 1861 Vienna –
1927 Klosterneuburg

Pupil of Würzinger and Eisenmenger
at Academy
Books
HO, P, S, V, W, ill.

BRUSENBAUCH, ARTHUR 1881
Bratislava – 1972 Vienna
Pupil of Jettmar and Bacher at
Academy
Lithographs
M, S

CZESCHKA, CARL OTTO 1878 Vienna–
1960 Hamburg
Pupil of Greipenkerl at Academy
Taught at Kunstgewerbeschule,
1902-8
Books, woodcuts
HO, P, W, ill., WE

DANILOWATZ, JOSEF 1877 Vienna–
1945 Vienna
Pupil of L'Allemand and Unger at
Academy
Lithographs
G, W

DIVEKI (DIVECKY), JOSEF VON
1877 Farmos–1951 Sopron
Pupil of Lärisch and Löffler at
Kunstgewerbeschule
Books
G, HO, WE

ENGELHART, JOSEF 1864 Vienna–
1941 Vienna
Trained at Technical University
Lithographs, engravings
M, S, V, W

EXNER, NORA 1863 Vienna–
1920 Vienna
Pupil of Roller at Kunstgewerbeschule
Woodcuts
HO, V

FAISTAUER, ANTON 1887 St Martin bei

Lofer Salzburg–1930 Vienna
Academy
Lithographs
M

FISCHER, JOHANNES 1888 Feldsteig–
1955 Vienna
Lithographs
H, S

FRIEDRICH, OTTO 1862 Györ–
1937 Vienna
Pupil of Eisenmenger and Müller
at Academy
Lithographs, books
M, S, V, W

GROM-ROTTMAYER, HERMANN
1868 Vienna–1932 Vienna
Academy
Lithographs, books
H, M, P, S

GÜTERSLOH, ALBERT PARIS
1887 Vienna–1973 Baden
Books, etchings, engravings
M, S, WE

HÄNISCH, ALOIS 1886 Vienna–
1937 Vienna
Pupil of L'Allemand and
Griepenkerl at Academy
Aquatint, engravings
G, M, V, S

HARLFINGER, RICHARD 1873 Milan–
1948 Vienna
Engravings
M, S

HEGENBARTH, JOSEF 1884 Kamnitz,
Bohemia–1962 Dresden
Engravings
S

HELLER-OSTERSETZER, HERMINE
1874 Vienna–1909 Grimmenstein,

Upper Austria
Pupil of Myrbach and Karger at
    Kunstgewerbeschule
Aluminographs
W

HOFFMANN, JOSEF 1870 Pirnitz,
    Moravia–1956 Vienna
Studied architecture at the Academy
Books
HO, P, S, V, WE

JETTMAR, RUDOLF 1869 Zawodzie,
    Galicia–1939 Vienna
Pupil of Rumpler, Eisenmenger and
    Griepenkerl at Academy
Professor at Academy
Engravings, woodcuts
B, G, HO, M, S, V, W, ill.

JUNG, MORITZ 1885 Nikolsburg,
    Moravia–1915 Galician Front
Pupil of Roller, Czeschka and Löffler
    at Kunstgewerbeschule
Programmes for *Die Fledermaus*
Commercial art
HO, P, W, ill., WE

JUNGNICKEL, LUDWIG HEINRICH
    1881 Wunsiedel Franconia–
    1965 Vienna
Engravings, woodcuts, lithographs of
    animals and birds, books
G, M

JUNK, RUDOLF 1880 Vienna–
    1943 Vienna
Pupil of Löffler at Academy
Books, woodcuts
G, H, W

KALVACH, RUDOLF 1883 Vienna–
    1932 Kosmanos
Pupil of Löffler at Kunstgewerbeschule
Woodcuts
P, W, ill., WE

KEMPF-HARTENKAMPF, GOTTLIEB
    THEODOR 1871 Vienna–
    1964 Kitzbühel
Pupil of Berger at Academy
Aquatints, engravings
M

KLIMT, GUSTAV 1862 Vienna–
    1918 Vienna

Pupil of Laufberger and others at
    Kunstgewerbeschule
Books
HO, P, S, V, W, WE

KOKOSCHKA, OSKAR 1886 Pöchlarn
Pupil of Löffler at Kunstgewerbeschule
Lithographs, etchings, books
HO, P, S (since 1945), W, ill., WE

KOLLER, BRONCIA 1863 Sanok,
    Galicia–1934 Vienna
Woodcuts
W, ill.

KÖNIG, FRIEDRICH 1857 Vienna–
    1941 Vienna
Pupil of Kunstgewerbeschule and
    Academy
Woodcuts, lithographs, books
B, HO, V

KRENEK, KARL 1880 Vienna–
    1948 Vienna
Pupil of Kunstgewerbeschule, and of
    Lefler at Academy
Lithographs, woodcuts, linocuts
W, WE

KRUIS, FERDINAND 1882 Pisck,
    Bohemia–1944 Innsbruck
Pupil of Rumpler and others at
    Academy
Lithographs
G, P, W, ill.

KUBIN, ALFRED 1867 Leitmeritz–
    1959 Zwickledt
Lithographs, books
M, S

KURZWEIL, MAX 1867 Bisenz,
    Moravia–1916 Vienna
Pupil at Academy
Woodcuts, lithographs
B, G, HO, M, P, S, V, W, ill.

LANG, ERWIN 1886 Vienna–
    1962 Vienna
Pupil of Roller at Kunstgewerbeschule
Woodcuts (especially of Grete
    Wiesenthal, his wife)
H

LASKE, OSKAR 1874 Czernowitz–
    1951 Vienna

Studied architecture at Academy
    under Otto Wagner
Lithographs (especially of
    Mediterranean cities and Turkey)
G, H, M, P, S, W

LEFLER, HEINRICH 1863 Vienna–
    1919 Vienna
Pupil at Academy
Aquatints, books, commercial art
H, P, W, ill.

LENZ, MAXIMILLIAN 1860 Vienna–
    1948 Vienna
Pupil at Kunstgewerbeschule and of
    Eisenmenger at Academy
Lithographs, woodcuts
B, M, S, V, W, ill.

LIEBENWEIN, MAXIMILIAN 1869 Vienna
    –1926 Munich
Pupil of Berger and Trenkwald at
    Academy
Lithographs, commercial art
M, P, S, W

LIST, WILHELM 1864 Vienna–
    1918 Vienna
Pupil of Griepenkerl at Academy
Lithographs, woodcuts
B, M, S, V, W, ill.

LÖFFLER, BERTHOLD 1874 Nieder
    Rosenthal, Bohemia–1960 Vienna
Pupil of Kolo Moser and Matsch at
    Kunstgewerbeschule
Books, stamps
P, W, ill., WE

LUKSCH-MAKOWSKAJA (MAKOWSKY),
    ELENA 1878 St Petersburg–
    1967 Hamburg
Pupil of Repin at St Petersburg
    Academy
Woodcuts
B, V, W

MALLINA, ERICH 1873 Prerau,
    Bohemia–1930 Vienna
Pupil of Roller at Kunstgewerbeschule
Professor at Kunstgewerbeschule
Woodcuts, books
Never exhibited in his lifetime

MOLL, CARL 1861 Vienna–
    1945 Vienna

Pupil of Griepenkerl and Schindler
at Academy
Woodcuts
B, G, M, S, V, W, ill., WE

MOSER, KOLO(MAN) 1868 Vienna–
1918 Vienna
Pupil of Rumper and Griepenkerl at
Academy and of Matsch at
Kunstgewerbeschule
Lithographs, woodcuts, books
B, HO, M, P, S, V, W, ill., WE

MYRBACH, FELICIAN VON 1853
Zaleszczvki, Galicia–
1940 Klagenfurt
Pupil of Eisenmenger and Lichtenfels
at Academy
Lithographs, woodcuts, aluminographs
B, G, S, V, W

OPPENHEIMER, MAX (signed MOPP)
1885 Vienna–1954 New York
Engravings, books

ORLIK, EMIL 1870 Prague–
1932 Berlin
Aquatints, lithographs, woodcuts,
engravings, books
B, G, HO, P, M, S, V, W, ill., WE

PESCHKA, ANTON 1885 Vienna
Pupil at Academy
Lithographs
M

PHILIPPI, ROBERT 1877 Graz–
1959 Vienna
Lithographs, woodcuts
G

RANZONI, HANS, the elder 1868 Vienna–
1956 Krems
H, P, W, ill.

RIEDERER, ERNST 1868 Klagenfurt–
1950 Klagenfurt
Engravings
M

ROLLER, ALFRED 1864 Brno–
1935 Vienna
Pupil of Academy
Posters, books
HO, P, S, V, W, ill.

ROUX, OSWALD 1880 Vienna–
1961 Vienna
Pupil of Rumpler, Delug and Unger
at Academy
Engravings (mostly horses)
G, M, S

SCHIELE, EGON 1890 Tulln–
1918 Vienna
Learnt from Robert Philippi
Woodcuts, lithographs
M, WE

SCHMUTZER, FERDINAND 1870 Vienna–
1928 Vienna
Pupil of Unger for engraving at
Academy

Professor at Academy
Engravings
G, M, S, V, W

SEIBOLD, ALOIS, LEOPOLD
1879 Leibnitz
Pupil of Schmutzer at Academy
Engravings
M, S

STÖHR, ERNST 1860 St Pölten –
1917 St Pölten
Academy
Woodcuts, engravings
B, M, S, V, W

STOLBA, LEOPOLD 1863 Vienna–
1929 Vienna
Pupil of Academy
Aquatints, engravings, woodcuts
HO, M, P, S, V, W

WACIK, FRANZ 1883 Vienna–
1938 Vienna
Pupil of Roller at Kunstgewerbeschule
and Academy
Lithographs, books
G, HO, M, P, S, W

ZÜLOW, FRANZ VON 1883 Vienna –
1963 Vienna
Pupil of Griepenkerl at Academy and
of Czeschka at Kunstgewerbeschule
Lithographs, woodcuts, books
W, ill., WE

Footnotes

The Legacies of Dissolution

1 Stefan Zweig *Die Welt von Gestern* Bermann-Fischer Verlag, Vienna 1948.

2 'Kakania' is an indecent pun taken from the initials of *Kaiserlich und Königlich* (Imperial and Royal), first used by Robert Musil in *The Man Without Qualities*. 'Tarockania' appears in the plays of Herzmanovsky-Orlando and makes fun of bureaucrats who spend their days playing tarot. At the same time it suggests the card figures of the game.

3 Otto Basil, born in Vienna in 1901, one of the leading literary critics and historians in Austria, as well as being a poet and novelist. For long cultural editor of the Viennese newspaper *Neues Österreich*.

4 Basil, p. 93.

5 Franz Theodor Csokor, Prologue to *3 November 1918* in *Österreichische Dramatiker der Gegenwart*, OVA, Vienna 1969. F. Th. Csokor (1885-1969), dramatist, poet and novelist, leading exponent of Expressionism, especially in his play *Die rote Strasse* (1915-16). In exile 1938-45. For many years president of the Austrian PEN-Club. The play *3 November 1918* was translated into English by Gerald Sharp under the title *The Arms of No Return* (in manuscript form only).

6 A propos the Redl affair: 'This scoundrel has denounced every single Austrian spy. Redl betrayed our secrets to the Russians and prevented us from learning Russian secrets through our spys. This is why the existence of seventy-five Russian divisions remained unknown to us–hence our belligerence, and our defeat. If we had seen clearly, our generals would not have driven the Court dignitaries into war.' (Count Sternberg, Deputy. Quoted in the *Volkstheater* programme No. 12, 1969/70 on the occasion of a performance of John Osborne's *A Patriot For Me*.)

7 Albert Fuchs *Geistige Strömungen in Österreich 1867-1918* Globus Verlag, Vienna 1949, pp. vii-viii.

8 Bertha Zuckerkandl *Österreich intim, Erinnerungen 1892-1942* edited by R. Federmann, Verlag Ullstein, Frankfurt 1970, p. 22.

9 Basil, p. 63.

10 Zuckerkandl, p. 81.

11 Ilse Barea *Vienna – Legend and Reality* Secker and Warburg, London 1966.

12 A detailed treatment of the subject is given by Albert Fuchs.

13 Dr Karl Renner *Österreich von der ersten zur zweiten Republik* Vienna 1952.

14 Basil, p. 65.

15 Adolf Hitler *Mein Kampf* Munich 1925.

16 Wilfred Daim *Der Mann, der Hitler die Ideen gab* Isar-Verlag, Munich 1958.

17 A book by Hellmut Andics *Der ewige Jude. Ursachen und Geschichte des Antisemitismus* Molden Verlag, Vienna 1965, quotes a marriage proposal in verse, found in one of the *Ostara* booklets:
  'Ich suche ein arisches Mädchen zur Frau,
  Mit Haaren wie Gold und Augen rein blau,
  Von hoher Gestalt und kernigem Leib –
  Ein echtes, ein rechtes germanisches Weib. . . .'

18 Alfred Schick M.D., 'The Vienna Medical School, Glimpses of the Past' in *Pirquet Bulletin of Chemical Medicine* vol. 14, 1967.

19 Zuckerkandl, pp. 133-4.

20 Dr Max Neuburger *Die Entwicklung der Medizin in Österreich* Carl Fromme Verlag, Vienna 1918.

21 William Osler M.D., 'Vienna after 34 Years' in *The Journal of the American Medical Association* 1908.

22 Basil, p. 61.

23 Basil, p. 64.

24 Zuckerkandl, p. 44.

25 Basil, p. 60.

26 Zuckerkandl, p. 25.

27 Sigmund Freud *Briefe 1875-1939* S. Fischer, Frankfurt 1960.

28 *Der Reigen* was not performed in Vienna until 1921, one year after it had been performed in Berlin, and was the occasion of one of the rare, genuinely Viennese theatre scandals. The next was in 1965, during the visit of The Living Theatre.

29 For Hofmannsthal, see *Gesammelte Werke in Einzelausgaben* 15 vols., edited by Herbert Steiner, S. Fischer, Frankfurt 1945-59.

30 Lou Albert-Lasard *Wege mit Rilke* S. Fischer, Frankfurt 1952, p. 129.

31 Basil, p. 72.

32 Basil, pp. 72-3.

33 Gustav Janouch in a letter of 1 June 1963 which is in the author's possession.

34 Klaus Wagenbach *Franz Kafka* Rowohlt, Hamburg 1964.

35 Basil, p. 74.

36 Otto Basil *Georg Trakl* Rowohlt, Hamburg 1965.

37 Zuckerkandl, pp. 33-4.
38 Zuckerkandl, p. 74.
39 *Finale und Auftakt, Wien 1898-1914* edited by O. Breicha and G. Fritsch, Otto Müller Verlag, Salzburg 1964.
40 Breicha and Fritsch.
41 Robert Musil *Die Verwirrungen des Zöglings Törless* Wiener Verlag 1906 and New American Library.
42 Breicha and Fritsch.
43 Fuchs, p. 275.
44 Frank Field *The Last Days of Mankind, Karl Kraus and his Vienna* Macmillan, London 1967.
45 Quoted in *The Jews of Austria* edited by Josef Fraenkel, Vallentine, Mitchell, London 1967.
46 On the history of the film in Austria, see Rudolf Oertel *Macht und Magie des Films* Europa-Verlag, Vienna 1959.
47 On Max Reinhardt's films, see Dr Walter Fritz in *Action* Heft 5, August 1958. See also: Dr Walter Fritz *Der Wiener Spielfilm zu Beginn des 1 Weltkriegs* (thesis in manuscript form in Austria National Library).
48 Fritz Lang in a letter to the author (24 April, 1971).
49 On Erich von Stroheim, see Jon Barna *Erich von Stroheim* Verlag des Österreichischen Filmmuseum 1966.

The Ringstrasse and Otto Wagner

1 Robert Feuchtmüller and Wilhelm Mrazek *Kunst in Österreich 1860-1918* Forum, Vienna 1964, p. 107.
2 Werner Hofmann *Moderne Malerei in Österreich* Wolfrum, Vienna 1965, p. 98.
3 For the Ringstrasse, see Richard Groner *Wien wie es war* sixth edition, Fritz Molden, Vienna 1965. *Österreich Lexikon* Österreichischer Bundesverlag, Vienna 1966. *Dehio—Handbuch Wien* Anton Schroll, Vienna 1954.
4 Heinz Geretsegger and Max Peintner *Otto Wagner 1841-1918* English edition, Pall Mall, London; Praeger, New York 1970, p. 30. I have taken much of the information about Wagner from this detailed study.
5 Catalogue, Los Angeles County Museum 1967.

The Secession: Olbrich and Plečnik

1 Joseph M. Olbrich (1867-1908) *Das Werk des Architeken*. Catalogue with biography and list of works by Robert J. Clark, Hessisches Landesmuseum, Darmstadt 1967.
2 For Josef Plečnik, see Robert Waissenberger *Die Wiener Secession* Jugend und Volk, Vienna 1971, p. 170; *Kunstdenkmäler in Österreich, Wien* edited by Reinhardt Hootz, Deutscher Kunstverlag, Munich 1968; *Wiener Bauten 1900 bis Heute* edited by Karl Schwanzer, Österreichische Bauzentrum, Vienna 1964; Renate Wagner-Rieger *Wiens Architektur im 19. Jahrhundert* Österreichischer Bundesverlag, Vienna 1970, pp. 244, 251.
3 Otto Maria Graf *Die Vergessene Wagnerschule* Jugend und Volk, Vienna 1969, has a list of all Wagner's pupils with their dates of attendance at the Academy, and reproductions of sketches and designs.

Josef Hoffmann and the Palais Stoclet

1 Wilhelm Mrazek *Die Wiener Werkstätte* Catalogue Österreichisches Museum für Angewandte Kunst, Vienna 1967, p. 20. Translation of the foreword *W.W. Modern Industrial Art 1903 to 1932* Info. Austria, Vienna n.d., p. 24.
2 Renate Wagner-Rieger, pp. 228, 272, 274.
3 *Österreich-Lexikon*, pp. 119, 120
4 A strange building whose horizontal ribbing gave the general effect of an iced Viennese Torte. Hoffmann described it as follows: 'In Paris at the first World Exhibition of Applied Arts in 1925, I was permitted to build the Austrian pavilion and to win a great success for the Wiener Werkstätte and Austria, in addition to my other attempts in this direction.
For the first time I did not design a pavilion in the accepted manner, but a series of sections, which were planned by other architects in their own style, and joined together by connecting buildings. The main collaborators were Strnad and Behrens. On a terrace over the bar there was a Vienna coffee house. Behrens built a highly original greenhouse, which reflected his own special inclination for garden design.' (Josef Hoffmann *Selbstbiographie* c. 1950, for an intended book about his work, as yet unpublished, in *Ver Sacrum* Vienna 1972, p. 122. It contains other original information about the Wärndorfers, Primavesis etc.)
Oscar Strnad (1879-1935). Architect designer and stage designer. 1910: Villa Cobenzlgasse 21, Vienna XIX. Peter Behrens (1868-1940) taught at the Vienna Academy from 1921. With Hoffmann, Strnad and others built the Winarskyhof block of apartments in the twentieth district of Vienna. His most important buildings were in Berlin, and the German Embassy in St Petersburg (1911).
5 The best discussion of the Palais Stoclet is Eduard F. Sekler, 'The Stoclet House by J. Hoffmann' in *Essays in the History of Architecture Presented to Rudolf Wittkower* Phaidon, London 1967, richly illustrated and informative. This should be read together with Josef Hoffmann's *Selbstbiographie* (see note 4 above), but as the latter was written at the age of about eighty, it is not completely reliable.
6 Sekler, note 30, p. 257.
7 Many architects admired the Palais Stoclet; among them were Peter Behrens, Max Bill, Richard Neutra and Le Corbusier

(Sekler, note 33). It has been suggested that Le Corbusier was a pupil of Hoffmann's, but in fact he only spent two days with him in 1907. It is far more likely that Mies van der Rohe was a pupil. The Hoffmann entry in the *Österreich-Lexikon* is contradicted by Le Corbusier's own letter in the *Festschrift* commemorating Hoffmann's sixtieth birthday on 15 December 1930. See also Sekler, p. 243.

8 Fritz Novotny and Johannes Dobai *Gustav Klimt* Welz, Salzburg 1967, catalogue nos. 152, 153; Christian Nebehay *Gustav Klimt, Dokumentation* Christian M. Nebehay, Vienna 1969, pp. 381-88.

9 Josef Hoffmann, p. 118, Nebehay, pp. 388, 391-2.

Adolf Loos and Building Without Ornament

1 The best book on Loos is Ludwig Münz and Gustav Künstler *Der Architekt Adolf Loos* Anton Schroll, Vienna 1964. This production was financed by Kokoschka with money from the Copenhagen Erasmus prize. Most of the personal details in this chapter are from Elsie Altmann Loos *Adolf Loos der Mensch* Vienna 1968. Loos's own writings are reprinted in *Sämtliche Schriften* edited by Franz Glück, vol. I, Herold, Vienna 1962. See also *Adolf Loos* edited by Werner Hofmann, Austrian Ministry of Education 1962 (French text). It is worth mentioning that Loos was a great advocate of abandoning the use of capital letters in German nouns. All his essays were reprinted in lower case in various publications.

2 Presumably the excellent apricot and damson dumplings, and the yeast dumplings with poppy seed: *Marillenknödel, Zwetschkenknödel* and *Germknödel*.

3 N. Pevsner *Pioneers of the Modern Movement from William Morris to Walter Gropius* Faber, London 1936, p. 192. In *Pioneers of Modern Design* Penguin, London 1949, 1970; US edition 1964, Pevsner ranks him second after Wagner with Louis Sullivan, Frank Lloyd Wright and Henry van de Velde as admirers of the machine and its relation to design and ornament. Pevsner, *Pioneers of Modern Design*, p. 32 discusses at length the impossibility of translating *Sachlichkeit*. It has undertones of utility, fundamental down-to-earthness and so on.

The Wiener Werkstätte

1 Mrazek *Die Wiener Werkstätte*.

2 A check list of the British exhibits at the Secession from 1897-1914, including the eighth exhibition, is in *Vienna Secession Art Nouveau to 1970* Royal Academy Exhibition Catalogue, pp. 29-30.

3 600 kronen was worth about £30 or $145. 50,000 kr. was worth about £2500 or $12,100. All currencies then had more purchasing power than they have today.

4 For the Werkstätte, see Mrazek.

5 *Die Wiener Werkstätte, Modernes Kunsthandwerk von 1903-1932* Catalogue Österreichisches Museum für Angewandte Kunst, Vienna 1967, pp. 25-7.

6 Mrazek *Die Wiener Werkstätte*, p. 18.

7 Marcel Prawy *The Vienna Opera* Weidenfeld & Nicolson, London 1909, pp. 70 ff.

Künstlerhaus, Secession, Kunstschau and Hagenbund

1 For Makart, see *Hans Makart* Catalogue, Staatliche Kunsthalle Baden-Baden 1972, and for Romako, see Fritz Novotny *Der Maler Anton Romako* Anton Schroll, Vienna 1954.

2 Rudolf Schmidt *Das Wiener Künstlerhaus, eine Chronik 1861-1951* Vienna 1951, with an admirable year by year register of political and artistic events in Vienna.

3 Ludwig Hevesi *Acht Jahre Secession* Carl Koregen, Vienna 1906, p. 121.

4 Hevesi, p. 120.

5 Robert Waissenberger *Die Wiener Secession* Jugend und Volk, Vienna 1971, pp. 28-9.

6 Josef Engelhart *Ein Wiener Maler Erzählt* Wilhelm Andermann, Vienna 1943, p. 64. Commented on by Waissenberger, op. cit., p. 30.

7 Waissenberger, op. cit., p. 31.

8 For short biographies of Secession artists, see Waissenberger, pp. 253-277 and *Wien um 1900* Catalogue, Kulturamt der Stadt Wien 1904, pp. 115-27.

9 Quoted in Werner Hofmann *Moderne Malerei in Österreich* Wolfrum, Vienna 1965, p. 24.

10 For Kurzweil, see Fritz Novotny and Hubert Adolph *Max Kurzweil, ein Maler der Wiener Secession* Jugend und Volk, Vienna 1969.

11 Werner Hofmann, op. cit. pp. 68, 70. For biographical details on Moll see Alma Mahler-Werfel *Mein Leben* S. Fischer, Frankfurt 1960.

12 Josef Engelhart, pp. 87 ff., 91 ff.

13 Edith Hoffmann *Kokoschka, Life and Work* Faber, London, pp. 32-6.

14 Christian Nebehay, p. 423.

15 Werner Hofmann *Gustav Klimt* Studio Vista, London 1971, pp. 15-16.

16 Edith Hoffmann, p. 86 as happening in 1911 at a private view. Nebehay, p. 120 note 4 as on an earlier occasion.

17 Nebehay, op. cit. pp. 393-427.

18 Hofmann *Gustav Klimt* p. 15, Nebehay, p. 397.

19 Otto Kallier *Egon Schiele, Oevre-Katalog* Paul Zsolnay, Vienna 1966, p. 49, quoting Arthur Roessler, *Briefe und Prosa von Egon Schiele*, R. Lànyi, Vienna 1921, p. 97.

20 Robert Waissenberger, 'Hagenbund 1900-1935 Geschichte der Wiener Kunstvereinigung' in *Mitteilungen der Österreichischen Galerie* 1972, p. 70, pp. 54-130, a

comprehensive history with a list of members. Edith Hoffmann, pp. 86-99 and Oskar Matulla, 'Der Hagenbund und die Niederösterreicher' in *Kulturbericht aus Niederösterreich* 1964, p. 38.

Gustav Klimt, Leader of the Revolt

1 Munich *Music I* 1901; Dresden *The Birchwood I* 1912; Venice *Judith II* and *Salome* 1910; Rome *The Three Ages* 1912; Prague *Country Garden* and *Schloss Kammer* 1910 and *Die Jungfrau* 1914.
2 See Fritz Novotny and Johannes Dobai *Gustav Klimt* Welz, Salzburg 1967. Catalogue no. 12 is a lunette design (*c.* 1883). No. 19 *The Idyll* (1889) has strong associations with Makart apart from the obvious borrowing from the *Ignudi*.
3 Christian M. Nebehay, 'Alfons Mucha und Wien' in *Die Presse* 24 April 1972. Mucha was a commissioner for Austria at the World Exhibition in Paris 1900. In 1898 he did a cover for the November issue of *Ver Sacrum*.
4 Nebehay, p. 18, and Chapter XII including the quotation from Hans Tietze, 'Gustav Klimts Persönlichkeit. Nach Mitteilungen seiner Freunde' in *Die Bildenden Künste*, Vienna 1919, pp. 1-14.
5 Nebehay, p. 194. Reproduced in Waissenberger, p. 58.
6 Novotny and Dobai, catalogue no. 68.
7 Nebehay, p. 185 and pp. 340-1.
8 Nebehay, p. 289.
9 Jaroslav Leschko 'Klimt, Kokoschka und die Mykenischen Funde' in *Mitteilungen der Österreichischen Galerie*, vol. 57, 1969, pp. 16-40.
10 Nebehay, p. 233. See also Mario Amaya *Art Nouveau* Studio Vista, London; Dutton, New York 1966, p. 50.
11 Nebehay, pp. 422, 476.
12 Alma Mahler-Werfel.
13 Engelhart, pp. 100-101.
14 Alma Mahler-Werfel, p. 77.

15 Hofmann *Gustav Klimt* p. 25.
16 Hofmann *Klimt* p. 17.
17 Translation in full, Peter Vergo, 'Beethoven Frieze' in Burlington magazine, February 1973, p. 110.
18 Nebehay, p. 274 note 5.
19 Novotny and Dobai, pp. 385-6, Nebehay, pp. 248, 254. Hofmann *Klimt* p. 23.
20 Nebehay, p. 55.

Egon Schiele, the Self-seer

1 Quoted in Hofmann *Moderne Malerei* p. 120.
2 In full in Otto Breicha and Gerhard Fritsch *Finale und Auftakt Wien* 1898-1914. Otto Müller Salzburg 1964, pp. 234-7.
3 Breicha and Fritsch, p. 289.
4 For a full account with illustrations and extracts from the diaries, see Alessandra Comini, 'Egon Schiele in Prison' in *Albertina Studien* 1964, vol. 4, pp. 123-37. Her book *Schiele in Prison* (Thames and Hudson, and NYGS 1974) has just been published. See also Rudolf Leopold *Egon Schiele* Residenz, Salzburg 1972, p. 157.
5 In a letter to Adolf Opel.
6 The best biographical sketch of Schiele is in *Egon Schiele Leben und Werk* Catalogue by Hans Bisanz, Historisches Museum der Stadt Wien, 1968.
7 1 Leopold, p. 11. 2 Ottakar Maschka *Österreichische Plakathunst* J. Löwy, Vienna (n.d. 1916), p. 96. 3 and 4 Bisanz, pp. 22-32. But not for the Munich 1913 poster, O. Kallir *Das Graphische Werk Schieles* Paul Zsolnay, Vienna, 1970, pl. 12b.
8 Leopold, nos. 1 and 2.
9 Otto Kallir *Egon Schiele Oevre-Katalog der Gemälde* Paul Zsolnay, Vienna 1966.
10 Quoted in Leopold, p. 173.

Richard Gerstl, the Angry Young Painter

1 See Werner Hofmann *Schönberg-Webern-Berg-Bilder-Partituren-Dokumentation* Catalogue, Museum des 20. Jahrhunderts, Vienna 1969, p. 106 and Jan Meyerowitz *Arnold Schönberg* Colloquium, Berlin 1967, p. 16.
2 While awaiting Otto Breicha's monograph on Gerstl to be published, there is only his catalogue of the Secession exhibition *Richard Gerstl* 1966, and Hofmann *Moderne Malerei* pp. 104-10, who uses Breicha's dating for his illustrations. See also Otto Breicha, 'Gerstl der Zeichner' in *Albertina-Studien* vol. 2, 1965, on his drawings (all self-portrait heads) and *Finale und Auftakt*, pp. 181-2.

'The Tempest' and the Young Kokoschka

1 Edith Hoffmann *Kokoschka, Life and Work* Faber, London 1947, p. 26.
2 Fritz Novotny *Der Maler Anton Romako* p. 75 and note.
3 Jaroslav Leschko, pp. 24-8, with a reference to Georges Minne as an influence, p. 24.
4 The text is reprinted in Breicha and Fritsch, pp. 112-19. An excellent commentary in Edith Hoffmann, pp. 38-9 on both text and illustrations.
5 Hans Maria Wingler *Oskar Kokoschka — Schriften 1907-1955* Albert Langen/Georg Müller, Munich 1966, pp. 50-1. The whole episode and its implications is treated well in Hofmann *Gustav Klimt* p. 41. A conversation between the artist and Wolfgang Fischer, 'Kokoschka's early work', is in *Studio International* January 1971, pp. 4-5.
6 Hans Maria Wingler, *Oskar Kokoschka, Das Werk des Malers* oeuvre catalogue, Welz, Salzburg 1956, pp. 25, 27. I have taken most datings from this.
7 Reprinted in Adolf Loos *Sämtliche Schriften* vol. I, pp. 443-4.
8 Edith Hoffmann, pp. 61, 62.
9 Paul Stefan's monograph of 1912 dates it to 1907 as does Edith

Hoffmann. Wingler is undecided.

10 See Alma Mahler-Werfel's *Mein Leben* for all the episodes with herself. For Kokoschka's joining up see also Edith Hoffmann, p. 150.

Monuments and Fountains

1 Gerhardt Kapner *Die Denkmäler der Wiener Ringstrasse* Jugend und Volk, Vienna 1959, pp. 19, 20.
2 Engelhart, pp. 199-205.
3 Kapner, pls. 59-60.
4 Reproduced in Hofmann *Gustav Klimt* p. 39.
5 Reproduced in Hevesi, 'The Art Revival in Austria', *The Studio* 1906, pl. B12.
6 Joachim Heusinger von Waldegg, 'Richard Luksch und Elena Luksch- Makowsky – ein Künstlerpaar der Wiener Jahrhundertwende' in *Alte und Moderne Kunst* Hamburg 1972, on the centenary of Luksch's birth with portraits of him and his wife and further works.
7 For Schimkowitz and Wagner, see Geretsegger and Peinter, passim.

8 Wilhelm Mrazek *Anton Hanak* Österreichisches Museum für Angewandte Kunst, Vienna 1969, and Hanak Museum Catalogue Langenzersdorf, Vienna 1972.
9 *Franz Barwig 1908-1931* Catalogue Österreichische Galerie, Vienna 1909.

'Ver Sacrum'

1 See *Wien um 1900* p. 49 for bibliographical details. I am much indebted to valuable assistance by Professor Oskar Matulla on the graphic artists of the period.
2 Oskar Matulla, 'Ferdinand Andri und Lassing' in *Kulturbericht aus Niederösterreich* 1960, p. 84.

Mahler and the Vienna School

1 Gertrude Aurenhammer, 'Geschichte des Belvederes seit dem Tode von Prinzen Eugen' in *Mitteilungen der Österreichischen Galerie* 1969, p. 93 and letter text p. 138.
2 Eduard Hanslick *Aus neuer und*

neuester Zeit Allgemeiner verein für Deutsche Literatur, Berlin 1900, second edition, p. 77. I am most grateful to Professor Kurt Blaukopf for this important information.
3 Alma Mahler *Gustav Mahler, Memoirs and Letters* John Murray, London 1968. Kurt Blaukopf *Gustav Mahler* Allen Lane, London 1973, and Wolfgang Schreiber *Gustav Mahler in Selbstzeugnissen und Bilddokumenten* Rohwolt, Hamburg 1971 are the essential sources for Mahler.
4 See Bertha Zuckerkandl, pp. 87-90. For contemporary press accounts see *Schönberg Berg Webern: die Streichquartette eine Dokumentation* edited by Ursula von Rauchhaupt, Deutsche Gramophon, Hamburg 1971, pp. 147-154.
5 Oskar Matulla, 'Josef Humplik und Hildegard Jone-Humplik' in *Kulturberichte aus Niederösterreich*, Vienna 1965, October, p. 73.
6 For Schönberg, Berg and Webern, see W. Hofmann *Bilder-Dokumente-Partituren-Dokumentation*.

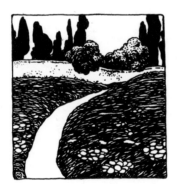

Index

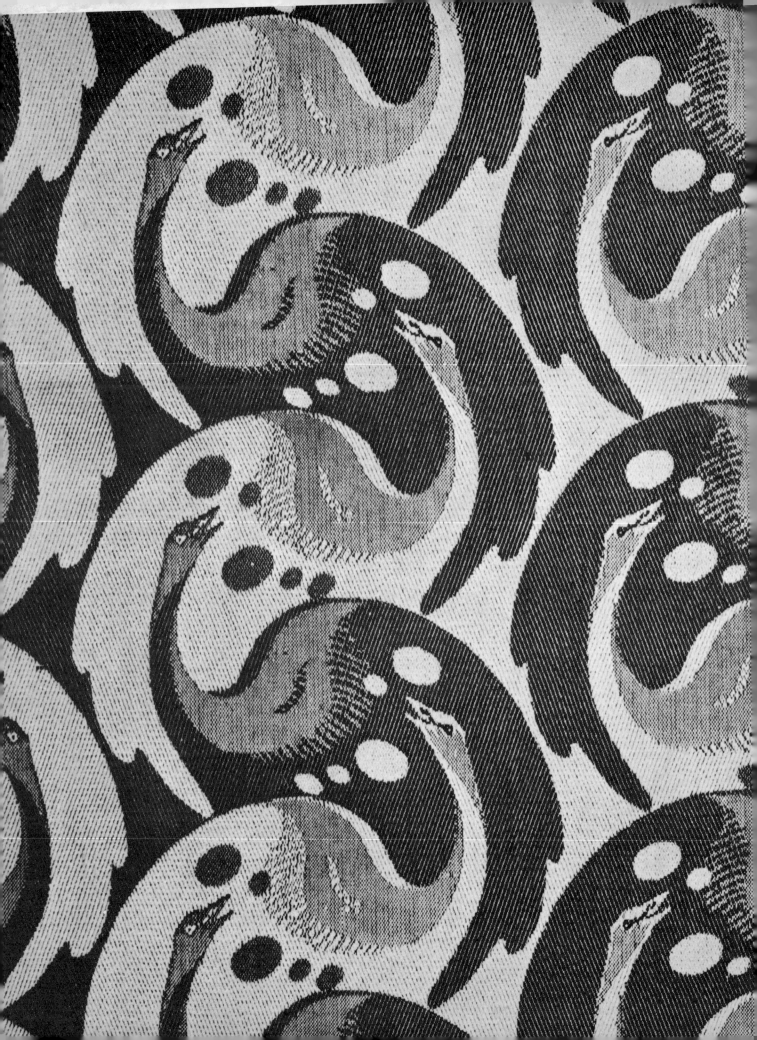